The Art of Grill & Smoker Cooking

By
J. E. Matthews

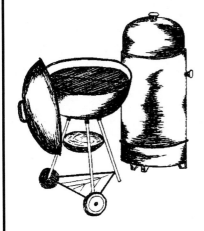

*A practical guide
to backyard cooking*

*Edited and Cover Design
by James Van Treese*

Northwest Publishing Inc.
5949 South 350 West
Salt Lake City, Utah 84107
801-266-5900

ISBN # 1-56901-052-8

Printed In the United States of America

Acknowledgments

I wish to acknowledge the people who provided their favorite recipes for this book, and those who have directed me to material on outdoor cooking to support research for the book. Alan Ballard and Linda Jenkins are acknowledged for reviewing the manuscript and providing valuable commentary. I wish to thank my mother, who gave me my first cookbook and Bill Buchanan, who introduced me to outdoor cooking. Finally, I wish to thank my wife Mary Lou, my sons John and David, and H.C. "Foots" and Elaine Hill for being the guinea pigs that tasted the recipes and especially for suffering through the recipes that did not turn out.

Many marinade, basting sauce, and table sauce recipes can be used with a variety of foods. The symbols above represent beef, poultry, seafood, pork, lamb, game, and vegetables, in that order. They are used in the recipe sections of this book to denote the additional types of food that a given recipe is especially suited to. For example, a barbecue sauce recipe under Barbecued Beef accompanied by the symbols for poultry, lamb, and pork, is also well suited to poultry, lamb, and pork barbecue in addition to beef.

Contents

Introduction

Outdoor cooking is *bourgeois cuisine* as opposed to *gourmet cuisine*. This does not imply that food cooked outdoors is of a lesser quality, merely that it is simply prepared and simply served. Most traditional recipes for outdoor cooking come from amateur cooks, not professional chefs. Almost three-fourths of the households in this country now have a grill or smoker for outdoor cooking, with the cooks almost equally divided between men and women (54% men and 46% women). Approximately 90% of these people state that they cook outdoors because of the flavor that results from cooking over an open fire, which cannot be reproduced in the kitchen. When the weather is nice, cooking outdoors is commonly the focus of a social gathering. In fact, the English word barbecue was long defined as the outdoor roasting of meat at large social gatherings. With the advent of brick barbecue "pits" and sheet metal grills during the twentieth century, barbecue moved to the backyard on a less grand scale.

The most popular foods cooked outdoors in this country are hamburgers, beef steaks, sausages (including hot dogs), chicken pieces, and fish in that order. Approximately 80% of the people who cook outdoors buy commercial basting sauces instead of making their own. These preferences for quickly cooked food and commercial sauces suggest that most people prefer a quick meal cooked outdoors for variety, rather than treating outdoor cooking as a specific style to be practiced and perfected. However, in certain parts of this country, outdoor cooking is a revered art form.

Cooking on a grill or smoker is distinctly different from cooking in a modern kitchen. The heat of outdoor cookers cannot be precisely controlled; hence, the cook must rely more on experience to judge the heat of a fire and when the food is done. Outdoors, food is cooked on a spit or a grate, rather than in a container. As a result, seasoning is prepared separately and is applied to the food as a marinate prior to cooking or by basting during cooking. Thus, an outdoor cookbook is primarily a collection of marinade and basting sauce recipes. The recipes in this book have been organized according to the type of food they were designed for, but many of them are suitable for a variety of foods. Just because a barbecue sauce recipe is suggested for beef does not mean it is not equally good with lamb, pork, game, or even poultry.

The objective of this book is to provide a variety of recipes as a starting point for experimentation. Certain combinations of seasonings are associated with certain foods; however, recipes should not be considered as exact formulas. Part of the joy of cooking is the experimenting with recipes and modifying them to suit your tastes. Peoples' tastes vary: for example, what one person considers to be spicy may be bland to another's taste. Recipes should be tailored to specific tastes. Discussion and footnotes are included to provide additional insight into the reasons, both scientific and historical, for certain cooking practices which have developed by trial and error over the years.

History

The Sinanthropus populations of China used fire approximately 360,000 years ago. Besides providing light, warmth, and protection from predators, at some point man learned to use fire for cooking. However, the art of cooking probably advanced little before 35,000 B.C. (end of the Upper Paleolithic period). Stone-lined hearths did not appear until 30,000-27,000 B.C. By 11,000 B.C. (end of the Lower Paleolithic period) Homo sapiens had replaced Neanderthal man, the ice age had drawn to a close, and man's technology was far advanced. From that time until the advent of recorded history in approximately 4,000 B.C., most basic culinary skills were probably developed.

During this early period, man like his nineteenth century tribal descendants, probably boiled his food. Boiling food significantly tenderizes it for chewing and allows the use of tough plants which would otherwise be inedible. One anthropologist has even suggested that the reduced chewing time resulting from eating cooked food significantly impacted man's technological development by freeing time for other tasks. Early cooking was probably done by placing water, food, and hot stones in shells, tightly woven baskets, or hide-lined holes in the ground. Pottery was not developed until approximately 7,000 B.C.

Agriculture not only impacted man's eating habits, but also significantly reduced the time required to provide food. There is some uncertainty concerning the domestication of animals, but sheep and goats were domesticated first in the Near East between 10,000 and 6,000 B.C. The pig was domesticated in China between 7,000 and 5,000 B.C., and cattle came next during the period 6,000 to 5,000 B.C. in Europe, and perhaps independently in Africa at about the same time. The first cultivation of plants occurred sometime between 8,000 and 6,000 B.C. This was possibly barley and first occurred in Anatolia (now Turkey), but cultivation with wooden implements leaves little trace for the archeologist. The shift from a hunting and gathering to an agricultural economy undoubtedly brought with it a dramatic increase in population density because of the ability of agriculture to feed more people.

FIRST U.S. COOKBOOK

The first cookbook written and published in the United States was *American Cookery* by Amelia Simmons, dated 1796. This book contained truly American dishes, such as corn pudding. Cookbooks in this country dated prior to this were of European origin and simply reprinted in the United States.

During the period 3,500 to 2,500 B.C., a variety of events led to a remarkable result: wild grass mutations in the Near East led to a fertile hybrid grain now known as wheat; irrigation was discovered; draft animals were domesticated; the plow was invented; the grinding wheel was developed; and, leavened bread was discovered. This combination of events led to the mass production of leavened bread, which allowed the Egyptians to produce more food than they could consume. Before, most of man's energy had been spent producing food; now time was available for other pursuits. However, the lack of wheat and leavened bread led inhabitants of the Tigris, Euphrates, and Indus valleys to remain dependent upon trade for food-stuffs. As a result, the spice trade was established. Grapes and wine making had been imported from the Caucasus, and the olive tree became widely distributed. Garlic, onions, lemons, sesame oil, mustard oil, ginger, and tumeric were popular. Three recently discovered Mesopotamian clay tablets, dated 1700 B.C. provide instructions for making stews, vegetable dishes, and meat pies. These tablets constitute the world's first known cookbooks. Many of these recipes are quite sophisticated, but interestingly called for very little salt.

Man shifted from bronze to iron implements, and the Babylonians developed tin-bearing glazes to waterproof pottery. However, man's increasing capability to feed himself brought dramatic increases in population and subsequent shortages in fuel, especially in arid regions around the Mediterranean Sea and throughout much of the Middle East. Cooking in these areas shifted from the use of wood fires to smaller, more efficient, charcoal fires. Population concentrations brought on by the silk industry in China, coupled with inadequate transportation, produced fuel shortages which resulted in most of the urban populations eating their food raw. Pork, and the fuel with which to cook it, became synonymous with wealth. These fuel shortages are believed to have led to the development of the stir fry method of cooking.

By the Roman Era, cooking had become highly sophisticated and exotic. Apicus wrote what was previously thought to be the world's first cookbook, describing the feasts of Emperor Claudius. Adequate food could be produced and preserved (by salting and smoking), and man now placed emphasis on making it more palatable. Common seasonings of the time included lavorge, coriander, rue, savory, cumin, pepper, cardamom, mint, caraway, parsley, juniper, and pennyroyal.

The Middle Ages, between the fall of Rome to the Huns (A.D. 476) and the fall of Constantinople to the Ottoman Turks (A.D. 1453), produced few advances in technology or the art of cooking. Probably the most significant development of this period was the chimney, during the twelfth century. The chimney led to the development of the fireplace, but early chimneys lacked a smoke shelf, which caused them to burn fuel rapidly. Queen Elizabeth I of England was forced to enact wood conservation laws to reduce fuel consumption in that country. The efficiency of fireplaces improved, and the fireplace continued in the Western world as the primary device for heating and cooking into the nineteenth centry. Only 11 years after the Gutenberg Bible was printed, DeAguila published the first cookbook printed with movable type *Dehonesta Voluptate* (1475).

During the next four centuries cooking was greatly influenced by exploration, which brought about the exchange of foodstuffs and cooking styles. The Age of Exploration brought the tradition of barbecue. It was the custom of many American Indians to slowly roast meat over a smokey fire. The word for this cooking style was *bocan*, which became the French word *boucan*. By 1661 the French word *boucanier* denoted one who smoked meat. During the eighteenth century, the word was also used to describe the collection of French and English renegades and runaway bond servants who lived in St. Domingo (now Hispaniola), hunted wild cattle, and plundered Spanish treasure ships. The English variation of the word is buccaneer. The Indian word for the green wooden grate on which they cooked was barbacoa. By 1697 the Indian word *barbacoa* had been incorporated into the Spanish language of the Caribbean and North American regions. The most widely accepted origin of the English word "barbecue" (also spelled "barbacue") is the Spanish, or Indian, word *barbacoa*. The first documented use of the word barbecue in the English language was not until 1809. It was defined as a social function where whole animals were roasted.

A second, less widely accepted theory, states that the word barbecue originated with the Acadian (Cajun) French of Louisiana. This theory purports that the word came from large outdoor gatherings where a whole animal was literally spitted from whisker to tail *barbe à la queue*. Given the choice, I prefer to think that barbecue is Native American in origin; the French already have their share of culinary glory. However, many nineteenth century cookbooks in the United States have barbecued beef recipes where the meat is cooked in a pot with water. This simply adds to the confusion over the origin of the word.

PRESERVING MEAT

Sun drying is the oldest means of preserving food. The reduced moisture content limits the variety of bacteria that will grow on the food. Smoke drying meat appears to have originated with the Sumerians (approximately 3000 B.C.). The pyroligneous acid of smoke not only further reduces the variety of bacteria that can grow on the meat, but also tends to mask the objectionable flavor of putrefaction from improperly dried meat. By the 5th century B.C. the process of dry salting and brine pickling had been discovered. Salt further reduced the varieties of bacteria that can live on meat. Romanized Gaul became famous throughout the Empire for its cured hams. The curing process not only preserved the meat but made it quite flavorful. Saltpeter (potassium nitrate) was probably an early impurity in salt, and it was eventually discovered that when saltpeter was used in conjunction with salt (sodium chloride) an even more effective perservative was formed. The use of a salt and saltpeter combination to preserve meat also led to the process of corning. The word comes from corn, meaning grain or grain-like. In the manufacture of gunpowder, the powder was spread out to dry the individual grains, or corned. The word later became associated with the curing of meat because of the grain-like appearance of the coarse salt on the meat. Corning beef, mutton, and pork became the standard process for meat that became too rank to be sold fresh. Corning meat was a common practice in butcher shops well into the 20th century. Corned beef has now become an expensive delicacy rather than a cheap staple for poor immigrants who could not afford fresh meat.

The buccaneers were taught by the Indians to season their smoke-roasted meat with locally available seasonings, such as salt and allspice. Dry-rub seasonings are still common with Mexican barbecue, such as Cabrito Asado, and Texas barbecue aficionados rely primarily on salt, pepper, and wood smoke for seasoning. Dry-rubs are also traditional throughout much of the southeastern United States.

The origin of tomato-based barbecue sauces in this country is not clear. When the Conquistadors arrived in Mexico, they found that the Aztecs served sauces made of tomatoes and chili peppers with their meat. However, many people in this country believed tomatoes were poisonous, even until the late nineteenth and early twentieth century. This suggests that tomato sauces have only recently become popular. In North Carolina, the eastern part of the state uses dry-rub seasonings or vinegar-based barbecue sauces, while the western part uses tomato-based barbecue sauces. The eastern part of the state was settled long before the western part, possibly supporting the theory that tomato barbecue sauces came later. No matter what their origin, tomato-based barbecue sauces now dominate restaurant barbecue and supermarket shelves.

In 1744 cooking technology changed significantly when Benjamin Franklin published a pamphlet on his Pennsylvania Fireplace. It was designed as a heating device that was more efficient than the conventional fireplace, but it evolved into the wood-burning iron stove that served for both heating and cooking. While the iron stove was gaining popularity, the northeastern United States was running short of firewood. By approximately 1870, wood consumption for fuel had peaked in the United States. Coal, coal oil, and kerosene became the principal cooking fuels of urban America. However, wood-burning stoves remained common on farms until the Rural Electrification Administration brought them electricity after World War II.

Although the stove replaced the fireplace as the primary means of cooking indoors, cooking outdoors over wood embers remained popular in much of this country, especially in the rural South and West. Outdoor cooking was done on an iron spit or a grate over a fire pit dug in the ground. By the beginning of the twentieth centry, stone or brick "barbecue pits" had come into backyard use. These devices were permanent above-ground structures that contained the fire, had an iron grate for cooking, and a chimney to direct smoke away from the cook and the guests. These wood-fueled devices remained popular for backyard cookouts until the 1950's. Brick and stone pits are no longer common, but the fire pit in the ground is still used in many areas for large picnics, especially when a whole hog or side of beef is barbecued. However, the brick barbecue pit did develop into a commercial version in the South. These came to be associated with the smell of hickory smoke and the familiar roadside sign, PIT BAR-B-Q.

Braziers, fueled by wood embers from the hearth or charcoal, have existed for thousands of years. It was common in this country during the late nineteenth and early twentieth centuries to take a charcoal fueled brazier on picnics to broil meat. Charcoal was readily available at coal yards, since it was required by blacksmiths. As the number of blacksmiths declined, so did the availability of raw charcoal, but the nation wide use of charcoal did not escape Henry Ford's notice. A man named Stafford had devised a way to press powdered charcoal and starch (as a bonding agent) into the now-familiar pillow-shaped briquets. Model-T Ford automobiles had many wooden parts, and their manufacture produced huge piles of scrap wood. In 1923 Ford used his scrap wood to produce charcoal and manufactured charcoal briquets. Although the briquet did not burn as hot as raw charcoal, it could be easily packaged in small quantities and distributed. These were first marketed under the name "Ford Charcoal Briquets," and were sold through Ford automobile agencies. This new endeavor was managed by Henry Ford's brother-in-law, E.G. Kingsford. The brand name was later changed to "Kingsford," and the Kingsford Products Company is now one of the country's major charcoal briquet producers.

Prior to World War II, raw charcoal, charcoal briquets, and wood were used for outdoor cooking. Wood was used to barbecue over pits in the ground and stone or brick above-ground pits. Charcoal, both raw and briquet, was used in sheet metal braziers. After World War II outdoor entertaining increased dramatically in this country, with the spread of the suburban concrete slab house and patio. Soon the now-familiar three-legged, sheet metal brazier was added to the inventories of supermarkets. By the 1960's, covered grills and smokers made from sheet metal were also in common use. By 1965, over 300 million tons of charcoal briquets were sold annually in this country. This figure has now more than doubled, but gas-fueled grills are rapidly replacing charcoal-fueled grills, because of their convenience.

Chemistry

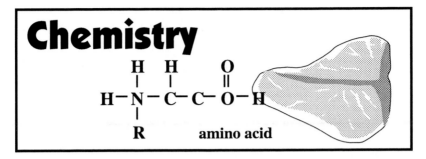

$$H-\overset{\displaystyle \overset{H}{|}}{N}-\overset{\displaystyle \overset{H}{|}}{\underset{\displaystyle \underset{R}{|}}{C}}-\overset{\displaystyle \overset{O}{\|}}{C}-O-H$$

amino acid

Meat contains protein and fat, both of which are important to the nutrition of man. **Protein** molecules, some of the longest in nature, are formed by linking a group of smaller molecules from end to end. The smaller molecules are known as **amino acids**. All of the proteins in living cells are made from only 21 different amino acids; however, the average protein molecule is constructed by linking 200 individual amino acid molecules. Man, and most other animals, can synthesize 12 of these amino acids from other molecules, but they cannot produce the remaining nine. These nine "essential amino acids" are synthesized only by plants; man must acquire these nine amino acids either from plants (mainly seeds) or from the meat of other animals.

In the **muscle** of animals, thousands of long, elastic protein molecules bond together to form a muscle cell. These muscle cells bond together to form muscle fiber bundles. The muscle fiber bundles are then bound together by connective tissue, termed **collagen**. Collagen is formed from inelastic protein molecules. In addition to forming connective tissue in muscle, collagen is the major constituent of hide and tendon.

Fats, both animal and plant, belong primarily to a group of chemicals called triglycerides, which are formed by bonding one molecule of **glycerol** to three molecules of **fatty acid**. Fat also consists of long chains of molecules. The **oxidation** (burning) of these fatty acids is what produces the energy required by animals. All animal cells contain small amounts of fat, which they constantly burn in order to function. However, for animals to function without constantly eating they must be able to store fat for use between meals. This is the function of specialized cells called **adipose** cells, which are sometimes concentrated to form layers of "fat," or disbursed through other tissue including muscle. The former type is the distributed fat that produces the "marbling" of a "well-fattened" beef steak. Carbohydrates, primarily from grains, can also be oxidized by the body for energy, but fats have over twice the fuel value of carbohydrates. This "fuel" value of food is measured in units of heat, the **calorie**.

The meat we eat is composed of muscle and collagen cells, both of which are built from protein, and adipose cells, which store fat. It is the relative proportion of these three types of cells that control food value, tenderness, flavor, and cooking requirements of meat. The relative tenderness of meat of different individuals within a single specie of animal depends upon several factors, primarily their diet and the general health of the animal. Age is considered by some to have only a secondary influence upon tenderness. The factors that control the tenderness of a specific cut of meat are the relative quantities of collagen, distributed fat, and the size of muscle fiber bundles. Large muscle fiber bundles and large amounts of collagen produce tough meat. Large quantities of adipose cells distributed throughout the meat and small muscle fiber bundles produce tender meat. This is why a well marbled loin with its small muscle bundles, low collagen content, and high distributed fat content is the most tender cut. The large muscle bundles, the increased amount of collagen, and the reduced amount of distributed fat make the rump tougher.

Lamb is similar to beef in the relative tenderness of its cuts. Pork, however, is always tender because of its generally low collagen content and high distributed fat content. Wild game is generally tougher than domesticated animals because of its lower fat and higher collagen content. Fish has almost no collagen and is quite tender.

If meat is allowed to sit for a period of time after slaughter, natural **enzymes** (primarily proteolytic acid) will slowly begin breaking down (hydrolyzing) its collagen. This natural **tenderizing** is known as **aging**. Upon slaughter, the enzymes immediately begin to hydrolyze protein. Artificial tenderizing can be achieved by using plant enzymes that produce a similar effect. **Papain**, an enzyme present in papaya fruit, is a common ingredient of commercially available tenderizers. The **bromelin** of pineapple will also tenderize meat. However, tests suggest that these externally applied enzymes do not penetrate quickly into meat. Puncturing the meat with a fork or ice pick will speed enzyme penetration. To achieve tenderizing in this manner, several days of marinating are generally required to achieve anything more than a superficial effect. Meat cut thin across the grain, such as steaks, can be tenderized by overnight treatment.

Putrefaction is the result of bacteria. Commercial meat packers age whole carcasses using the outer layer of fat as a covering to protect the meat from bacteria. They also use ultraviolet light in their coolers to retard bacterial growth. The first bacteria that multiply on the meat surface require oxygen. After the bacteria invade the meat, a second type of bacteria, which do not need oxygen begin to multiply. These anaerobic bacteria produce foul-smelling incompletely oxidized byproducts (mercaptans and alkaloids). The decision when to stop aging meat is a tradeoff between the tenderizing effect of enzymes and the adverse effects of bacteria.

Fats are divided into two basic chemical groups. **Saturated fats** contain all the hydrogen atoms chemically possible. **Unsaturated fats** contain less than the maximum amount of hydrogen. If two or more hydrogen atoms are missing from each fat molecule, the fat is termed **polyunsaturated**. The unsaturated and polyunsaturated fats acquire oxygen atoms when exposed to the air, filling the spaces left by missing hydrogen atoms. This process is known in chemical terms as oxidation, and, in layman's terms, as going **rancid**. Rancid food does not endanger your health, but significantly alters the flavor of food. Seafood is high in polyunsaturated fat and will quickly go rancid if not properly cared for. The "fishy" taste sometimes associated with seafood is the result of rancid fat from improper handling or storage. Beef is high in saturated fat and is not readily susceptible to rancidity. This is why beef and some game, including certain fowl, are aged or "hung," while pork and seafood are not.

Freezer burn is not a chemical action, but is the loss of moisture from meat. The loss is caused by a process known as **sublimation**, where water converts directly from a solid (ice) to a gas (water vapor) without ever going through a liquid stage. Freezer burn is not dangerous, but destroys the flavor of food.

When meat is placed in marinades containing acids (e.g., acetic acid of vinegar or citric acid of citrus juice) the muscle fibers are chemically broken down, tenderizing the meat. Marinades are also absorbed by collagen and muscle. Collagen and muscle are **gels** (this is a specific molecular structure), and gels absorb large quantities of fluid. When collagen is heated in the presence of ample fluid it turns to gelatin. Thus, if marinating has caused collagen to absorb fluid, cooking will transform the tough inelastic collagen into soft gelatin, tenderizing the meat. However, deep penetration by a marinade does not take place in a matter of hours, but requires days for a large cut of meat. Pot roast which has been slowly cooked in fluid has thin veins of translucent gray gelatin in it. This gelatin is collagen that has been completely gelatinized.

Heat causes the proteins in muscle to **coagulate**, which toughens it. For example, eggs are almost entirely protein, so they become coagulated and toughened by the heat of cooking. Therefore, the effect of cooking upon the tenderness of meat is a tradeoff between gelatinizing collagen and coagulating muscle. Heat will also cause the fat in adipose cells to liquefy, expand, and burst the cell walls. When this happens to adipose cells that are dispersed throughout muscle tissue, it disrupts the muscle fiber bundles and connective tissue to further tenderize the meat.

The relative quantities of collagen, muscle, and fat determine how a given piece of meat is best cooked. Some meats require marinating to tenderize and add fluid to collagen prior to cooking. Cuts with large muscle fiber bundles, such as eye of the round, should be thinly sliced perpendicular to the grain for serving. Cutting the muscle fibers into short lengths produces a more easily chewed slice of meat. Pork, with its high fat and low collagen, is generally tender. The low fat and collagen of most seafood make it most tender when raw, cooking only toughens it by coagulating its protein.

FATS AND OILS

The term fat has a specific chemical definition, but in common usage the terms fat and oil are used to indicate the solid and liquid forms of the chemical group called fats. A fat is solid at room temperature and an oil is liquid. Shortening, lard, butter, and margarine are fats. Lard and butter come from animals and are high in saturated fat. Margarine, shortening, and oils come from plants and are generally low in saturated fat. However, certain oils, such as palm and coconut oil, are very high in saturated fat. Many vegetable oils have hydrogen added to them (hydrogenated) to keep them from becoming rancid. Hydrogenation converts unsaturated fat into saturated fat.

The temperature at which fats and oils smoke and burn varies. Margarine is used in this book for basting sauces instead of butter because it withstands higher temperature. Corn and soybean oils are both good for basting because both have high smoke and burning temperatures. Olive oil is called for in many recipes primarily because of its mild flavor and moderate burning temperature.

Fire & Smoke

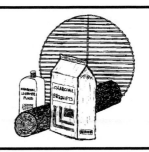

Heat

Conductive heat results when each molecule passes heat on to its neighbor. This is what causes one end of a metal rod to get hot when the other end is placed in a fire. **Convective heat** is the result of hot air rising because it is lighter than cold air. This is what makes the upstairs of a house warmer than the downstairs. However, the major difference between stove or oven cooking and cooking over coals is radiant heat. **Radiant heat** is electromagnetic radiation similar to radio waves or light. Radiant heat makes the sunshine feel warm on a cold day, or singes one side of your body while the other side remains cold when you stand in front of a hot fire.

The heat sources of modern grills and smokers are burning charcoal, burning gas, or the electrical resistance of a heating element. **Charcoal** heats by conduction, convection, and radiant heat. **Burning gas** heats by conduction and convection. However, gas grills also have a layer of porous lava rock above the gas burners. When heated, the lava produces radiant heat similar to burning charcoal. **Electric** broilers and roasters are essentially the same as an electric oven. These are not specifically dealt with in this book, but the recipes can be used with them. Electric moist smokers function the same as charcoal-fueled smokers.

Direct heat cooking is accomplished by placing food directly over the burning charcoal or the heated lava of a gas grill. Cooking is accomplished primarily by radiant and conductive heat. **Indirect heat** cooking is accomplished by placing food to the side of the charcoal or heated lava. This reduces the effect of radiant heat and food is cooked primarily by conductive heat. **Smoking** is accomplished by totally eliminating radiant heat and cooking with only conductive and convective heat. This style of cooking also utilizes wood smoke for flavoring, which gives the process its name.

Grills & Smokers

Three basic types of grills and smokers are used in this country: open grills, covered grills, and moist smokers. **Open grills** have been popular for millen-

12 **The Art of Grill & Smoker Cooking**

nia. In this country Mexican ceramic *braceros* and the heavy metal *hibachis* from Japan are relatively common, but the American-style, sheet-metal brazier is by far the most common. Braziers consist of a shallow bowl that holds charcoal and has a grate above for cooking. They cook with radiant and conductive heat, but their open top significantly reduces the effect of conduction. Some models have a wind shield, or hood, on one side to increase the effect of conduction. Hooded models may also have an electric-driven spit, or rotisserie. Most sheet metal braziers also have adjustable cooking grates to allow the distance between the charcoal and food to be varied to control heat. Some versions come with short legs for table-top use; others are long-legged and free-standing.

Covered grills cook by conductive and radiant heat. Their lids contain heated air, which increases the effectiveness of conductive heating. The three primary types of covered grills are kettles, cylinders, and wagons. Kettle grills are almost spherical in shape and have a removable lid. They generally have three dampers in the bottom and one in the lid, to control ventilation. Cylinders consist of a horizontal cylinder with an attached lid that is hinged, or rotates back, to open. Cylinders generally have a damper on each end of the bottom half, and a loosely fitted lid, or a chimney for ventilation. Wagons consist of rectangular boxes, the upper half being a hinged lid. Wagons are usually of heavy construction, and derive their name from the fact that most of them have wheels on at least one end to facilitate moving them. Wagons usually have a damper at each end of the base half, and a single damper in the lid. Rotisseries are usually available for wagons. Both cylinders and wagons commonly have a thermometer built into their lid. However, grill thermometers are subject to many influences and should not be relied upon. Covered grills usually have a lower grate to hold charcoal and an upper grate for cooking.

Gas grills are available in kettle and wagon models, with either bottled or natural gas hookups. It should be noted that bottled gas (propane) grills use different burners than natural gas (methane) ones. Gas grills are constructed with a burner beneath a grate that holds a layer of small pieces of porous lava rock. The burning gas conductivity heats the lava and air in the cooker. The heated lava further heats the air by conduction, but also produces radiant heat to simulate burning charcoal. Some kettle grills have an adjustable shield above the gas burner, which can prevent the lava from being heated, simulating indirect heat. Large gas wagon grills often have two independent burners to allow lighting the burner on one end and placing the food on the other, for indirect cooking. However, many gas grills, either kettle or wagon, are single burner without deflector shields and allow only direct cooking, but at adjustable heat levels.

Moist smokers cook by convective and conductive heat, and are available in charcoal or electric models. Radiant heat is completely eliminated by placing a pan of water between the charcoal fire or electric heating element and the cooking grates. These smokers are available in one or two cooking-grate models.

Building a Fire

To start gas grills and electric smokers, follow the manufacturer's instructions. Charcoal briquets require slightly more effort, but produce a better flavored final result. Several types of briquet are available, with a wide range in their quality. Poor-quality briquets have sawdust or coal added as cheap filler and do not burn well. Some higher-priced brands have hickory or mesquite sawdust added to produce smoke flavoring. Other briquets come saturated with starting fluid, are sealed in air-tight bags, and are ready to light. These are convenient for picnics. For home use buy good quality "plain" briquets without wood chips or lighting fluid, and keep bags tightly closed and stored in a dry location.

Three methods of lighting charcoal briquets are recommended: electric starters, chimney starters, and starting fluid. For **electric starters,** place the electric starter in the middle of a pile of briquets and plug it in until white ash begins to form on the briquets (10-15 minutes). Unplug the starter and remove it from the pile of briquets; take care because it will still be hot. It is a good practice to have a specific place (such as a cement block) available to place the still-hot starter. Arrange the briquets as desired for cooking and wait for them to become fully ignited. If some have not started to ignite, place them on top of ones that have. If an extension cord is used with the electric starter, be sure to use one of heavy-duty construction. If the cord becomes warm during use, the wire gauge is too small. Get a heaver extension cord.

For **chimney starters**, follow the manufacturer's instructions. After the briquets ignite (approximately 30 minutes) remove them from the chimney, with a mitten and tongs, and arrange them in position for cooking. If necessary, add more briquets on top of the ignited ones. Chimneys can also be constructed from a 3-pound coffee can, or a 1-gallon canned-food can, by punching dime sized holes around its sealed base or by cutting out the base. Place two crumpled sheets of newspaper in the bottom. Place several small pieces of dry wood (no more than 1/2 inch in two of their three dimensions) on top of the paper. Fill the can with charcoal briquets and light the paper through one of the holes. If the bottom is cut out, place the chimney on the grills charcoal grate for starting.

Electric starters and chimney starters are quite good for small fires, but the best method of starting a large charcoal fire is with charcoal-starting fluid. Charcoal

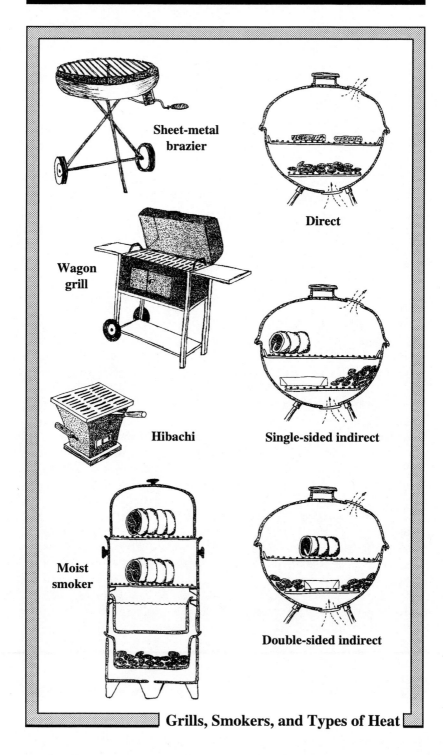

Sheet-metal brazier

Direct

Wagon grill

Hibachi

Single-sided indirect

Moist smoker

Double-sided indirect

Grills, Smokers, and Types of Heat

starting fluid is a mixture of flammable hydrocarbons that are less volatile than gasoline or kerosene, making it much safer to handle. *NEVER* **use gasoline or kerosene for starting fluid, and** *NEVER* **add starting fluid once a fire is lit.** To light, place charcoal briquets in a pyramid and thoroughly soak them (be sure to include the ones on the edges) with starting fluid. Use approximately 1/2 cup of fluid for each 25 briquets. Let the briquets sit for one minute, then light them in several places around the edge of the pyramid. The coals will be ready for cooking in approximately 30 minutes. There is no flavor difference between starting fluids. Once the charcoal is ready for cooking, all of the fluid has been burned. However, some people maintain that they can detect a hydrocarbon flavor on food cooked over a fire ignited with starting fluid.

One safe method of **accelerating** the lighting process, or assisting a **"struggling"** fire, is to fan the briquets vigorously. Use a small piece of plywood or stiff cardboard, fan the fire with long powerful strokes. This provides forced air ventilation, which will accelerate ignition, is very efficient, and safe. Another safe method is to thoroughly soak briquets with starting fluid (in a tin can). Allow the fluid to soak in, then place the briquets (with tongs) in critical areas, lighting them with a long fireplace match. Briquets are ready for cooking when they are completely covered with a layer of white ash. At night they will have a cherry-red glow. Do not put the lid on a covered grill or smoker until the coals are completely ignited.

The "heat" of a charcoal fire depends upon the number of briquets, the size of the grill, the weather, and a variety of other factors. The heat of a charcoal grill cannot be precisely controlled. Therefore, its heat must be judged. An approximate method for estimating the temperature of a fire, is by the time that you can hold the palm of your hand at cooking grate level.

200°F - 300°F	**low fire**	**6 seconds**
300°F - 350°F	**moderate fire**	**4 seconds**
375°F or higher	**hot fire**	**2 seconds**

For **direct heat** cooking, a **hot fire** consists of a double layer of briquets. A **moderate fire** is a single layer of briquets. A **low fire** is a single layer of briquets, with space between briquets. In all cases, the briquets should extend beyond the edges of the food being cooked, or the outer pieces will not cook at the same rate as the ones in the center.

Indirect heat is more difficult to quantify because it is much more dependent upon the grill. In general, an indirect fire requires approximately twice as many briquets as the diameter of the grill in inches (width of a cylinder or wagon

---

BRAZIER

Man has cooked on braizers for thousands of years. The shallow clay *eschara* of the Greeks was fueled by embers from the hearth, and used to broil the Greek equivalent of the shish kebab (*souvlakia*). By Roman times wood was becoming scarce around the Mediterranean Sea and the charcoal-fueled *craticula* came into use. In Asia, food cooked on a charcoal-fueled brazier is commonly available from street vendors and in restaurants. The English word brazier comes from the French word *braise* , meaning hot charcoal.

---

grill). Double-sided indirect cooking is accomplished by placing one-half of the briquets on each side of the grill and the food in the center. This produces a more even heat than single-sided indirect. For recipes where the food is first seared with direct heat, then roasted on indirect heat, use single-sided indirect with slightly more briquets than normal (**moderately hot indirect**).

When using a charcoal-fired covered grill, close the dampers and lid after cooking. This extinguishes the coals for reuse. To reuse, simply stir or shake briquets to remove loose ash. Place unused briquets on top of the used ones, and light with starting fluid or an electric starter. If using a chimney starter, ignite new briquets and place them for cooking. Place used (but unlit) briquets on top them.

For moist smoker cooking, follow the recommendations of the manufacturer. The quantity of briquets will depend upon the size of the item being cooked and the cooking time that will be required. A 5-pound bag of charcoal contains approximately 70-80 briquets, which is enough fuel to cook approximately 3 to 4 pounds of meat.

Cooking

Broiling, roasting, and smoking are the three styles of cooking dealt with in this book. **Broiling** is the rapid cooking of food placed directly over a hot fire (direct heat). Broiling uses conductive and radiant heat. **Roasting** is the slow cooking of food that is placed directly over a very low fire (direct heat), or off to the side of the fire (indirect heat). Roasting also utilizes conductive and radiant heat, but with much less radiant heat than broiling. The **smoking** dealt with here is very slow roasting with wood smoke. It uses only conductive and convective heat. This is not the process used for curing meats such as ham (where temperatures are too low to cook).

It is the judgment required to balance the effects of radiant and conductive heat, to cook food until done without burning, that makes outdoor cooking an art. Broiling is done quickly on direct heat. It is used for small, or thin, cuts of meat whose interior will cook before the outside can burn. Many people broil steaks, hamburgers, hot dogs, or fish fillets because they are quick and relatively foolproof. Cooking larger cuts of meat requires more caution. Radiant heat is deceptive; it can char the outside of food while the interior remains uncooked. Thick cuts of meat should be roasted by placing them back from the heat (indirect) to reduce the effect of radiant heat allowing it to cook by conduction. The best procedure is to use a meat thermometer, and watch the meat so the outside does not burn. Most meat thermometers have a meat doneness scale on them, but Table 1 presents the temperatures of various degrees of doneness for reference.

Meat	Doneness	°F	°C
Beef	Rare	140°	60°
	Medium	150°	66°
	Well	160°	71°
Pork	Fresh	170°	77°
	Precooked	130°	54°
Lamb	Rare	140°	60°
	Medium	150°	66°
	Well	160°	71°
Poultry	–	185°	85°
Seafood	–	120°	49°

TABLE 1: Meat Temperatures The temperatures listed are for judging the doneness of beef and lamb. The temperatures for pork, poultry, and seafood represent the minimum to which their interior should be heated before eating

Moist smokers eliminate radiant heat, which makes them safe for inexperienced cooks, but more time is required for cooking than on a covered grill with indirect heat. **The major mistake made with moist smokers is not allowing sufficient time for cooking.** This is not a major problem because undercooked food can be finished in an oven. The slow cooking of meat increases enzyme activity, which tenderizes it, and liquefies the fat, which allows it to disperse throughout the meat. This helps to keep the meat moist. Moist smokers also have the advantage of moist air which helps prevent meat from drying out. These factors all combine to yield a tender, juicy piece of meat.

During the course of a year, the outside temperature can vary by 100°F. Because of this temperature variation, the cooking times of grills, and especially smokers, can vary significantly with season. Wind can significantly increase cooking time by reducing the amounts of convective and conductive heat available. The size of the cooker, the size of the fire, and the proximity of the food to the fire also cause variations in cooking times. The combination of these factors results in the fact that cooking times cannot be precisely stated.

Experience and a good thermometer are the best means of determining when the food is done, but Tables 2, 3, & 4 provide approximate cooking times for meal planning.

TABLE 2: Cooking times (broiling)
Cooking times are given in minutes for a covered grill (lid on) using direct heat. Thin cuts cooked to medium or less will cook in the same time on an uncovered grill. Thicker and more well done items will require longer on an uncovered grill.

| | | | | Cooking Time (Minutes) Each Side | | | | |
| | | | Thickness | | Med. | | Med. | |
Meat	Cut	Fire	(Inches)	Rare	Rare	Med.	Well	Well
Beef	Steak	Hot	3/4	2	3	4	5	6
			1	5	6	7	8	9
			1-1/2	8	9	10	11	12
			2	10	11	12	14	16
	Hamburger	Hot	3/4	2	3	4	5	6
			1	5	6	7	8	9
Pork	Chops/Steaks	Medium	1/2	–	–	–	–	6
	Ham (Cured)	Medium	1/2	–	–	–	–	6
Lamb	Chops/Steaks	Hot	3/4	2	3	4	5	6
			1	5	6	7	8	9
Fish	Fillet/Steak	Med-Hot	1/2	–	–	–	–	4
			1	–	–	–	–	5
	Scale on Fillet or Split Fish	Med-Hot	1	–	–	–	–	20 to 30

TABLE 3: Cooking times (roasting)
Cooking times are in hours for a covered grill (lid on) using indirect heat. Fire temperatures are indicated. Items under 5 pounds can be cooked on a rotissarie with higher heat and longer cooking times. Large items (over 5 pounds) should not be attempted on the average open grill.

| | | | | Cooking Time (Hours) | | |
Meat	Cut	Lbs.	Fire	Rare	Med.	Well
Beef	Roast	3 to 5	Med.	1-1/2 to 2	2 to 3	3 to 4
		5 to 7	Med.	2 to 3	3 to 4	4 to 5
	Standing Rib	3 to 5	Med.	1-1/2 to 2	2 to 3	3 to 4
Poultry	Chicken (Pieces)		Med.	–	–	1
	Chicken (Split)		Med.	–	–	1
	Whole Fowl	1 to 2	Med.	–	–	1
		2 to 4	Low	–	–	1-1/2 to 2
		4 to 6	Low	–	–	2 to 3
Seafood	Fish (Whole)	2 to 3	Med.	–	–	1/2
Pork	Roast	3 to 5	Med.	–	–	3 to 4
	Ham (Processed)	3 to 5	Med.	–	–	2 to 3
	Spareribs		Med.	–	–	1 to 2
Lamb	Leg (Butterflied)	4 to 6	Hot	–	1 to 1-1/2	2 to 3
	Leg (Bone In)	5 to 7	Med.	–	1-1/2 to 2	3 to 4

TABLE 4. Cooking times (moist smoker)

Cooking times are given in hours for the top grill of a two-grill charcoal fueled moist smoker. The lower heat of a moist smoker allows the cooking of larger pieces of meat, but considerably more time is needed and planning is required.

Meat	Cut	Weight Lbs.	Charcoal Lbs.	Cooking Time Hrs.
Beef	Roast	3 to 5	5	3 to 5
		5 to 7	7	5 to 7
		7 to 10	9	7 to 10
Poultry	Whole Birds	1 to 3	4	3 to 4
		3 to 5	6	4 to 5
		5 to 10	8	6 to 10
		10 to 15	10	10 to 12
Pork	Roast	3 to 5	5	4 to 6
		5 to 7	7	6 to 8
		7 to 10	9	7 to 9
	Ham (Precooked)	3 to 5	5	3 to 4
		5 to 10	7	4 to 5
	Ribs	10	8	4 to 5
	Chops	1" Thick	6	3 to 4
Lamb	Leg/Roast	4 to 6	6	4 to 6
Game	Roast	3 to 5	5	4 to 6
		5 to 7	7	6 to 8

NOTE: When using moist smokers never use less than 5 pounds of charcoal, and never lift the lid for the first 2 hours of cooking. Briquets will burn at a rate of approximately one pound per hour, and most foods will require approximately 1 hour of cooking time per pound of weight.

NOTE: The objective of moist smoker cooking is long slow cooking with wood smoke. The cooking times are for medium well to well done. If beef, lamb, or game are to be cooked to a lesser degree there will be less smoke flavoring. If you like rare or medium-rare meat, a covered grill is recommended.

Char & Smoke Flavoring

The distinctive flavor of grill- and smoker-cooked food comes from three sources: the seared or charred exterior of the food, smoke from rendered fat or the oil of basting sauces, and wood smoke. When meat is exposed to the intense heat of direct cooking it begins to burn or char on the edges, corners, and where it touches the cooking grate. The flat surfaces begin to acquire a rich brown color. This process is often referred to as **charbroiling**. The exact chemistry of the charbroiled flavor has not been determined, but is related to the coagulation and carbonization of muscle protein, and the caramelizing of meat sugars.

If **oil** or **rendered fat** are heated, they first reach what is known as the smoke temperature, and then the combustion temperature. At the smoke temperature, oil begins to vaporize and form smoke. Oil bursts into flame at the combustion temperature. If oil or fat drips onto burning charcoal, or heated lava rock of a gas grill, it is quickly heated well above its combustion temperature. At that temperature fat and oil will burn if sufficient air is available; if not, they will simply produce smoke. When the lid of a covered grill is raised, the sudden supply of air causes the smoking oils to burst into flame. If direct cooking is desired, but not the fat smoke flavor, cook on an open grill, or covered grill with lid removed. Rendered fat can produce considerable flame, so keep water handy in a plastic squeeze bottle or a water pistol to control the flames. Squirt the charcoal or lava directly, not the flames. When cooking on indirect heat neither rendered fat or oil drop on the charcoal or heated lava; therefore, neither flame nor smoke is produced. A foil pan placed under food cooked on indirect heat is recommended to collect rendered fat and excess sauce as it drips.

When **wood** is heated to its ignition temperature, a complex mixture of water vapor, gases, and liquid distillates are given off. If sufficient air is available, much of this mixture will burn producing flames. If the air supply is limited these distillation products form a dense white smoke. Pyroligneous acid is the substance responsible for the bulk of wood smoke flavor, and is the principal ingredient of most artificial smoke flavorings. Charcoal is the solid carbon residue left after the gases and distillates are driven from wood heated in the absence of air. When charcoal burns it produces no flame or smoke. Black smoke is a sign of incomplete combustion, and has an undesirable flavor.

To produce wood smoke, place chunks of wood directly on a charcoal fire, or the lava of a gas grill. Chunks of approximately 1 inch dimension are recommended. Let the wood begin to flame before closing the lid to cook. If an open grill is used, the wood chunks must be very green or well saturated with water (soaked for several days). Wood chips, thoroughly saturated with water, can also be used for smoke production. However, chips will quickly dry out and burn, requiring replenishment during cooking. Since replenishment while cooking is not always easy, a method of wood smoke production with chips is to place them in a small metal pan. Place the pan on the charcoal or hot lava. This prevents the wood from igniting, but also prevents the charcoal beneath from burning properly. This technique is best on the lava of gas grills. It should be noted that gas grills with deflector shields cannot produce wood smoke when used in the indirect mode, because the lava is not heated.

Most **hardwoods** are acceptable for smoke flavoring food, but softwoods (conifers) are not recommended. Different woods produce different flavors, but only a few are truly distinctive. **Hickory** produces the most pungent and distinctive smoke flavor and is commercially available. **Mesquite** and **apple** wood are also commercially available. Apple has a mild flavor, while mesquite has a rather sharp flavor, or "bite." **Oak** is readily available in the form of firewood, has an acid flavor, and is a good choice. **Alder** is mild flavored and is commonly used in the Pacific Northwest. **Wild cherry** has a sweet flavor which is well suited to game. **Sassafras** has a mild flavor with a pleasing and distinctive aroma. If you have a garden, fresh herbs can also be used. They will burn rapidly, but provide a pleasant and subtle flavor to mild foods. For example, fennel is commonly used by the French with fish. On the Gulf Coast, **bay (laurel)** wood produces a mild flavor well suited to seafood, and its leaves are also excellent for more subtle flavoring.

The best hardwood for smoke flavoring is that from **nut** or **fruit trees**. For those with access to forests or orchards, Table 5 provides a list of common woods and vegetable matter used for smoke flavoring. Some of these have become popular in certain regions out of necessity. For example, coconut shell is a by-product of copra production and is the most readily available wood product in much of the tropics.

TABLE 5. Woods for Smoke Flavorings
Listed are the varieties of wood, and other vegetable products, which are commonly used for smoke flavoring food. The recommended varieties are indicated by an asterisk. Both the wood and leaves of the laurel (bay) tree can be used.

Common Name	Genus/ Family	Common Name	Genus/ Family
Alder*	Alnus	Hickory*	Caray
Apple*	Malus	Laurel (Bay)*	Lauraceae
Ash	Fraxinus	Maple	Acer
Bayberry	Myrica	Mesquite*	Prosposis
Beech*	Fagus	Oak*	Quercus
Birch	Betula	Peach	Prunus
Cherry*	Prunus	Pear	Pyrus
Chinaberry	Melia	Pecan*	Carya
Coconut (Shell)	Cocos	Persimmon*	Diospyros
Corn (Cob)	Zea	Plum	Prunus
Fennel*	Foeniculum	Sassafras*	Sassafras
Grape (Vine)	Vitis	Willow	Salix

Grill & Smoker Maintenance

• Keep grills and smokers covered or under a roof. Rust is the principal cause of their deterioration with age.

• Remove ash from the base of charcoal cookers, especially around the dampers of covered grills. This allows proper ventilation for the charcoal to burn.

• Line the base of open grills with heavy duty aluminum foil. This facilitates emptying ash, and makes cleaning easier.

• Periodically replace the lava rock of gas grills, as sauce and fat residues build up on them. Between replacements, periodically operate the grill on maximum direct heat for 30 minutes to 1 hour, without cooking. This process burns off some of the buildup, much the same as the cleaning cycle of electric ovens.

• Empty and wash the water pan of moist smokers after every use. Failure to do this will result in the growth of mold and slime in the pan. After washing, lightly coat the pan with vegetable oil to prevent rust (non-stick cooking sprays are good).

• Do not clean cooking grates too thoroughly, or food will stick to them. Before each use, brush or scrape them while over a hot direct fire. If cooking on indirect heat, clean the portion over the fire and then rotate or shift the grate to clean the remainder.

Accessories

Many catalogues are filled with accessories for grill and smoker cooking, but your kitchen probably already contains most of what you will need. Only a few specialized items are essential - the rest depends upon how much you like gadgets. You will need a **padded mitten** to protect your hand, a long-handled **spatula** (at least 15"), and a long pair of **tongs** (at least 15") that can be operated with the padded mitten. The mitten should be the cheap supermarket variety, which can be thrown away when soiled, but the spatula and tongs should be stainless steel. These can be found in kitchen supply houses. **Do not use a meat fork, because every time you puncture meat it leaves a hole for juice to run out.** A wide variety of **brushes** are available for basting, but a pastry brush (the type with a plastic cap that slides off the base of the bristles) is the easiest to clean. You do not want leftover basting sauce from one meal to spoil the next. A good strong **flashlight** which can be held under your arm (leaving both hands free) is invaluable, because there is seldom enough light to carefully inspect the food while cooking after dark. The rechargeable ones are well suited. A **meat thermometer** is also advisable, one that is easy to read and which can be easily wiped off while in use. Heavy smoke will form a deposit while cooking, making it difficult to read. Although you probably have all of the necessary **sauce pans** for making sauces, two-cup and four-cup sizes are especially useful.

For skewer-cooked foods, both disposable wooden and reusable metal **skewers** are available. Metal skewers should have metal handles for use on a covered grill. Otherwise, the handles will burn. It is quite difficult to remove meat from a hot skewer at the dinner table. A simple solution is to use large skewers (15-17 inches) for cooking, and remove the food to a platter for serving. The small wooden skewers are best for appetizers and are disposable, but care must be taken not to burn them. They should be soaked in water before use, and the food cooked slowly on indirect or low direct heat.

Every kitchen has knives, but very few have sharp knives. Since most of the recipes in this book are for meat, it is useful to have **sharp knives** to cut it. A variety of knives are useful, but only a few are really necessary. The most useful all-purpose kitchen knife is a good quality boning knife. This knife has a relatively straight blade and is about 10 to 11 inches long. The only way to keep it sharp is honing it on an oil stone. Check with your local sporting goods store for a medium stone, honing oil, and instructions on how to use them. A sharpening steel (they are also now made of ceramic) is only of value if you have good, well-maintained knives. Unless you enjoy owning and maintaining good knives, an electric knife is the best choice for slicing roasts and carving turkeys. If you are a fisherman, you probably already have a fillet knife. If you buy your fish, have it filleted and skinned if necessary.

For cooking whole fish, a **fish holder** is a necessity. These devices are made from metal rods and are hinged so they can be opened. The fish can be basted while in the holder. Without these devices it is very difficult to turn or remove a whole fish from the grill without falling apart. Before you buy a fish holder, be sure to measure your grill to ensure that the holder will fit under the lid. However, they can be used, leaving the handle sticking out from under the lid. The partially open lid causes some heat loss and a slightly longer cooking time may be required.

The only useful accessory I have not found commercially available are **hooks** for hanging meat in a moist smoker. Spareribs and oriental roast pork are best cooked while hung by a hook in a moist smoker. Hanging (or standing ribs on edge) allows the rendered fat to drip free of the meat. This can be accomplished by making small s-shaped hooks from heavy wire or small round-stock. One end should be sharpened and hooked into the meat while the other is hooked on the upper cooking grate (double grate smoker). If you have a shop, you can even make an attachment which extends into the domed lid to replace the grate of the smoker, allowing more room for hanging meat.

Drip pans are useful when roasting meat on indirect heat. They will eliminate the mess of rendered fat and excess sauce. A ball of pure **cotton string** is handy for tying roasts and poultry. Metal **poultry skewers** may be used for trussing; heavy, double pointed **toothpicks** are also useful. Old herb **bottles** (with shaker tops) are useful for storing and applying dry seasoning blends, and barbecue sauce or salad dressing bottles are useful for storing unused basting sauces.

FORK

The fork dates back to 6,000 B.C. in Turkey, but appears to have been forgotten until it reappeared in an inventory of King Edward I of England (1272-1307). At that time, forks had only two prongs and were not commonly used. This novel "new" implement was even mentioned in the *Canterbury Tales*.

NEVER use a fork for turning meat on a grill. Forks puncture meat allowing juice to run out. Always use tongs or a spatula.

Seasonings

Food cooked on a grate or spit requires a different means of applying seasoning than that cooked in pans, skillets, or roasters. Grill- and smoker-cooked foods are seasoned by marinating prior to cooking and by basting during cooking. A wide variety of ingredients are used in these seasonings: herbs, spices, aromatic seeds, vegetables, fruits, plant extracts, alcohols, acids, oils, and even minerals are used in these marinades and sauces.

Herbs are the leaves of low-growing annual or perennial plants, such as thyme, oregano, or rosemary. **Spices** usually come from the roots, bark, berries, or fruit of perennial plants or trees. Most spices are native to, and are still grown primarily in, tropical Asia. **Aromatic seeds** usually come from delicate, lacy plants such as caraway and anise. Coriander is an aromatic seed from a plant whose leaves are used as an herb, cilantro. Several widely used **generic seasoning blends** such as curry powder, chili powder, Worcestershire sauce, mustard, and tomato catsup are often used in sauces.

Ingredient	Equivalent
Bacon, 1 slice	1 TBS drippings
Bell Pepper, 1 medium	1/4 Cup dehydrated
Garlic, 1 med. clove	1/8 tsp. dry powder
Ginger, 1 tsp. grated	1/4 tsp. dry powder
Herbs, 1 unit fresh	1/3 Unit dried
Lemon, 1 medium	3 TBS juice
Onion, 1 medium	1 TBS dry powder
Tomato, 1 medium	2 TBS tomato paste

TABLE 6: Seasoning Equivalents Fresh ingredients called for in the recipes are listed with their processed equivalents. There are distinct differences in flavor between these equivalents, but they can be used interchangeably.

Many cookbooks call for fresh herbs, but with the exception of parsley most of them are not readily available. For that reason, all of the recipes of this book call for dried herbs in the form of whole or crumbled leaves. If fresh herbs are substituted, larger quantities must be used (see Table 6). Spice quantities are stated for dry ground or powdered. Liquid measures are normally used for measuring sauce and marinade ingredients. Table 7 gives liquid measures and their common equivalents. A nonstandard abbreviation (using all capital letters) is used for **tablespoon (TBS)** to more clearly distinguish it from the abbreviation for **teaspoon (tsp)**. Dry measures are used for such items as flour, corn meal, or bread crumbs. However, there is only a small difference in volume between liquid and dry measures, and the difference is not critical.

Selected **fresh vegetables** such as onions, garlic, carrots, celery, and bell peppers are called for because they are readily available and keep well in a refrigerator, although **dehydrated-powdered** garlic and onion are also used. **Fruit juices** can be bought in small cans or squeeze bottles. Small quantities of canned **pureed fruit** are most easily obtained as baby food. Fresh tomatoes are available year-round, but often lack adequate flavor for cooking. **Canned tomatoes** are usually preferable to store-bought fresh ones.

U.S. Measures			Metric (ml)
6 Drops	=	1 Dash	
15 Drops	=	1/4 tsp	= 1.25
1 Dram	=	3/4 tsp	
		1 tsp	= 5
3 tsp	=	1 TBS	= 15
2 TBS	=	1 oz.	= 30
1/2 Cup	=	1 Gill	= 120
8 Oz.	=	1 Cup	= 240
2 Cups	=	1 Pint	= 480
2 Pints	=	1 Quart	= 970

TABLE 7: Liquid Measures
Measures and their approximate metric (rounded off) equivalents. Liquid measures are used for dry herbs and ground spices, as well as liquids.

NOTE: A common, but imprecisely defined, dry measure also used for herbs and spices is the **pinch**. A pinch is the amount of material held between the thumb and first finger (approximately 1/8 tsp). It is the dry measure equivalent of a dash.

NOTE: Butter is sold by the pound, but is commonly packaged in quarter-pound "sticks." A quarter pound of butter (margarine) is 8 TBS, or 1/2 cup liquid measure.

The use of commercially available sauces has been minimized; however, generic sauces such as catsup, mustard, soy, and Worcestershire are used. The thin, vinegary American style hot sauce has come to be known by the brand name **Tabasco**. One generic sauce available in most oriental grocery stores, is **oriental chili sauce**. Several other commonly available generic oriental sauces or spice blends are also called for, namely **hoisin** , **oyster sauce**, and **5-fragrances powder**, all of which are available in oriental grocery stores and many supermarkets. When using wines or liquors for cooking, use only those of good enough quality to drink, **cooking wines** are not recommended.

The word **marinade** comes from the same root as the word marine, and originally meant to pickle in salt brine. Brines are still used for marinating, but since the advent of refrigeration, marinades are now used primarily for flavoring and may not even contain salt. Marinating for a few hours will thoroughly coat food with seasoning, but it will not penetrate to season the interior. Marinating for only a few hours is usually done in a sauce which will also be used for basting while cooking. Marinating for 2-3 days is required to deeply flavor large cuts of meat, such as roasts.

The **dry rub** was developed for cooking over embers, and they are seldom used in the kitchen. They consist of blends of salt, herbs, and spices, which are rubbed onto the surface of the meat. The meat is then left to marinate for a few hours to a day. Historically, dry rubs are commonly associated with barbecue.

Another technique unique to grill cooking is the marinating and broiling of vegetables. This can be done for whole or sliced vegetables, or as skewered pieces on shish kebabs. The vegetables can be marinated raw, or blanched (or partially cooked in a microwave) and marinated. The decision of which technique to use is purely a matter of taste and convenience. Tables 8 & 9 provide blanching and microwave cooking times.

Dictionaries generally define a **sauce** as a condiment to be served with food. This type of sauce is referred to in this book as a **table sauce**, while the principal type of sauce recipe presented is termed a **basting sauce**. There are numerous classifications for table sauces, but not for basting sauces. A simple functional classification for basting sauces is used in this book: thin sauces, thick sauces, and glazes. **Thin sauces** are often used for marinating, as well as basting, and can usually be applied throughout the cooking process without fear of burning. **Thick sauces** usually have a high sugar content and burn easily. They include

TABLE 8: Blanching Times
Add vegetables to lightly salted boiling water. The cooking times indicated are from when the water reboils after adding the vegetables.

Vegetable	Size	Cooking Time After Boiling
Artichoke Hearts	Whole or halves	1-2 Minutes
Bell Peppers	Cleaned quarters	1-2 Minutes
Eggplant	1 to 1-1/2 inch cubes	1-2 Minutes
Mushrooms	Medium whole	Remove from heat
Onions	Small whole or halves	4-5 Minutes
Potatoes	Small whole or halves	6-10 Minutes
Squash, Summer	Split	2 Minutes
	1 inch slices	1-2 Minutes

most commercial barbecue sauces, and should be applied only toward the end of cooking. Many barbecue cooks refer to thick sauces as **finishing sauces** because they are applied only after the meat is fully cooked. Thick sauces are often used in combination with thin sauces or marinades. For example, equal portions of brine, vinegar, and oil make an excellent thin basting sauce for poultry to precede the application of a thick sauce, such as a tomato-base barbecue sauce.

Smokers do not have the radiant heat of a grill; thus there is less chance of burning a thick sauce while smoking. However, thick sauces should not be applied until the fat is rendered and removed, especially with pork or poultry. Some recipes also start with a thin basting sauce, which after the food is almost cooked, are thickened by the addition of more ingredients such as tomato sauce to produce a thick sauce for finishing the meat.

Glazes are a special basting sauce used to form a seal over food. Glazes usually contain sugar, syrup, or fruit other than tomato. Glazes have a very high sugar content and should be applied only after food is cooked to form a sweet coating, or glaze, over the food. They are especially good with pork and fowl, but will burn very easily if not applied with caution. Use glazes only after the food is fully cooked. Table sauces require little discussion here because they are dealt with in most cookbooks for indoor use.

TABLE 9: Microwave Cooking Times

Cooking vegetables in a microwave serves the same purpose as blanching. Most microwave cookbooks have extensive tables of cooking times for fresh vegetables. Those times can be generally reduced by 1/2 to approximate blanching or precooking.

Item	Quantity	Cooking Requirement High Power Setting
Artichoke Hearts, Fresh	4 whole or 8 halves	Place in covered dish with 1/2 cup water and 1/4 tsp salt, cook for 5 minutes.
Bacon	4 slices	Cover with a paper towel. Cook for 2 minutes, rotate once.
Bell Pepper	2, cleaned and quartered	1 Minute, rotate once
Eggplant	1 medium, cut in 1-1/2" cubes	Place in covered dish with 2 TBS water and 1/4 tsp salt, cook 4 minutes.
Onions	2 small or 1 medium, halved	Place in covered dish with 1/2 cup water and 1/4 tsp salt, cook for 5 minutes.
Potatoes	2 medium, cut for French fries	6 Minutes, rotate once
Squash, Summer	2 split in halves, or 1" slices	6 Minutes, rotate once

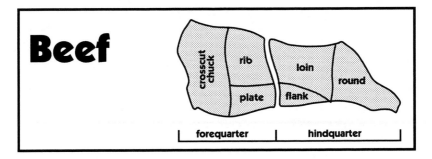

Beef

crosscut chuck | rib | loin | round | plate | flank

forequarter | hindquarter

A beef is butchered by cutting the carcass lengthwise down the backbone to produce two **sides of beef**. Each side is then cut between the 12th and 13th rib to divide the side into a forequarter and a hindquarter. The hindquarter is further subdivided into three primal cuts; the round, the loin, and the flank. The forequarter is subdivided into three primal cuts; the crosscut chuck, the rib, and the plate. Further subdivision of these primal cuts by your butcher produces the retail cuts found in grocery stores and meat markets.

The **loin** and **rib** sections are the juiciest and most tender portions of the beef carcass. The section of the loin toward the round is called the **sirloin**, and the section toward the rib is called the **short loin**. Any steak sliced from the sirloin is known as a sirloin steak. The "flat bone" sirloin, which is cut from the end nearest the short loin, is generally considered to be the choicest sirloin steak. A sirloin steak is sometimes divided to yield a **top sirloin, filet,** and **culotte steaks.** Next to the flat-bone sirloin, but in the short loin, is the **porterhouse** steak. Proceeding forward through the short loin are the **T-bone steak** and finally the **club steak**. On one side of the bone of a porterhouse is the **tenderloin steak**, or **filet mignon**; on the other side is the **New York** or **strip steak**. A T-bone steak has a longer bone than a porterhouse, which divides a small tenderloin from a sizable strip steak. The final cut is the **club steak**, which has no tenderloin and only a short strip steak. The only steak cut from the rib section is the **rib steak**. When the bone is removed a rib steak becomes a **Delmonico steak**. When a Delmonico steak is trimmed of fat it becomes a **rib-eye steak**.

The choicest beef roasts are also from the loin and the rib. When the loin is used for roasts, the tenderloin, or filet, is first "pulled," leaving the strip loin and sirloin. The tenderloin can be left whole, subdivided into smaller tenderloin roasts, or sliced into filet mignon steaks. The strip loin, the top sirloin, and the bottom sirloin are then separated. The **strip loin** is sold either bone-in or boned. The **bottom sirloin** is subdivided into **flap, ball,** or **triangle tip** roasts. The **top sirloin**, also referred to as a **coquille** or **sirloin butt**, is normally boned before retailing. The manner in which the top sirloin is further subdivided into smaller roasts or steaks varies from region to region.

The term **"prime" rib** is not used in the meat-cutting industry, but is a marketing term designed to get a premium price. The premium portion of the rib cut is the center one-third, but it has no specific name. First, the tip of the ribs are cut off in a strip. This piece is known as the **short ribs**, which are fat but rich and tasty. The remainder is then subdivided into "oven-size" **rib roasts**. Trimming the fat and feathering the bones to expose the rib bones yields a **nude rib roast**, which if boned becomes a **Spencer roast**. If the Spencer is trimmed of all fat, a **rib-eye roast** is produced.

Less tender roasts and steaks come from the round and chuck. The central one-third of the round is sometimes left whole and marketed as a **cafe round, ship round, steamship round**, or **buffet round**. These cuts are too large for most grill or smoker cooking, but are commonly used for grander-scale outdoor cooking. The round is generally cut into the **top round** (inside), the **bottom round** (outside), and several less desirable cuts. The top round, or smaller pieces of it, are lean, mild-flavored roasts. However, they should be tenderized or marinated before cooking. When the entire bottom round is cut from the round, it includes the **eye of round**. Both the bottom round and eye of round are lean and flavorful, but are somewhat tough. The eye of round is a modest sized roast without much peripheral fat. Both top and bottom round can be sliced into steaks. These are best cut thick to serve several people.

The crosscut chuck is subdivided into three cuts: the chuck, the foreshank, and the brisket. The foreshank is the front leg, and is not a good cut for grill or smoker cooking. The **chuck** is normally boned and subdivided into several roasts: **boneless inside chuck, boneless neck, chuck rib** or **pot-roast, chuck tender**, and **triangle**. The chuck is also commonly ground into the most flavorful of all "**hamburger**" meat. If the chuck is to be sliced for steaks, the bone is usually left in and a variety of different steaks can be cut, for example, the **blade bone chuck** or **7-bone chuck** steaks (there are not seven bones, but the single bone looks like the number 7). All contain bone and internal veins of fat and are the least desirable of beef steaks for grilling. However, if you take care to choose chuck that is next to the rib section (they are separated only by a knife cut), you essentially get a rib cut at one-half the price.

The **brisket** is sold either whole or divided into several pieces. Brisket flavor is excellent, but may have a lot of fat. Brisket is the number one choice for commercial barbecued beef, primarily because of its size and flavor, and the fact that it used to be a cheap cut of meat. **Beef ribs** come from the short plate. They are bony, but tasty and easy to separate and eat, making them a good choice for barbecue. The **flank steak** and **skirt** come from the flank. Flank steak is tough, but has excellent flavor and can be thinly sliced for serving. The **skirt** is also tough, but is commonly grilled and thinly sliced for Mexican dishes, such as Fajitas. Most other cuts of beef are not well suited for grill or smoker cooking, except for ground beef and sausage, both of which are excellent choices.

Also in the beef category are veal and baby beef. **Veal** is specifically defined by law, and is raised in a very special manner. Its carcass is butchered similar to lamb. Because of its delicate flavor, it is best to broil steaks or chops without heavy wood smoke. Rib and loin chops or cutlets from the leg are good choices. **Baby beef** is a recent development, and has no legal definition. It is essentially a calf of 7 to 10 months in age, which has not been fattened on grain. Baby beef cuts are smaller in size than comparable cuts of beef and have much less fat. Because of their lower fat content, baby beef and veal should not be overcooked or they will tend to be dry.

MARINATING

To marinate food in a liquid marinade, mix the marinade ingredients in a heavy-duty plastic bag that zips closed. Add the food to be marinated, zip the bag three-fourths closed, and squeeze out as much air as possible before closing the bag. Plastic bags require only a third as much marinade as using a bowl, are more effective, and work equally well for room temperature or refrigerated marinating. Frozen meat can even be defrosted in a plastic bag of marinade.

When using a dry rub or paste (e.g. mustard) as a marinade, apply the seasoning and wrap the food to be marinated in plastic wrap to seal it from the air.

Beef Steaks & Burgers

Broiling, or grilling, is the rapid cooking of meat over high direct heat. It is used for thin cuts and the objective is to sear, or cauterize, the meat to seal in juice. Do not use a fork for handling meat; use tongs that will not cause punctures that release juice. Raw meat should not be salted and left to stand, for this will also extract juice. **Salt just before or after cooking.** Steaks are usually seasoned by marinating or by serving with a table sauce. Table sauces allow individual choice at the table. If you prefer the simple taste of beef, sprinkle the meat liberally with coarse-ground black pepper and pound it with the back of a large spoon. The spoon drives the pepper into the meat and helps to keep it from falling off during cooking. Another subtle flavor is added by rubbing the meat with a crushed fresh garlic clove. Garlic powder can produce a bitter taste if used just prior to cooking on high heat. Some cooks like to lightly butter (margarine) or brush meat with olive oil before grilling. Brushing with any type of fat or oil will cause the meat to brown more easily and help seal in juice.

Broiling on an open grill, often referred to as char-broiling, will produce flames that singe, or char, the meat. Broiling on a covered grill will produce abundant smoke from rendered fat, which also flavors the meat. When broiling, meat is not usually on the grill long enough for basting unless it is quite thick, nor is the meat on long enough to use wood smoke for flavoring.

The **porterhouse, filet mignon, strip, T-bone, club,** and **rib steaks** are the choicest cuts. Whole filets, whole tenderloins, and thick cut (1-1/2 to 3 inch thick) **sirloin steaks** can be broiled and carved to serve several people. **Blade chuck** and **7-bone chuck** steaks are less tender but tasty. **Top, bottom, and full round** steaks are generally best when marinated or tenderized. **Flank steaks** are tough, but have excellent flavor and are good if thinly sliced across the grain for serving.

Ground chuck usually has a relatively high fat content, but is the most flavorful of all ground beef. As with steaks, a simple charcoal-broiled **hamburger**, without salt or pepper, is delicious. There are a number of ways to season ground beef prior to cooking to produce a wide variety of flavors. Some additives tend to make a burger dry, which can be counteracted by adding vegetable or olive oil. To keep hamburgers from falling apart when handled, add a beaten raw egg or egg yolk. Chopped onions are also commonly added. The meat itself can even be blended, but be sure it is cooked well done if raw pork is added. Ground precooked ham or bacon are safe to add.

Herb Steak

Use strip or sirloin steaks sliced about one-quarter inch thick and carefully trim excess fat. Veal and baby beef are also very good with this recipe. Brush the meat with the following mixture and marinate for 1/2 hour at room temperature. Lightly sprinkle both sides of the meat with crumbled **rosemary** leaves. Broil directly over very hot coals.

1/4 cup olive oil Blend ingredients thoroughly.
1 TBS lemon juice
1 clove garlic, minced

Steak Teriyaki

Serves 4

Trim a 2 to 2-1/2 pound, 1-1/2 inch thick steak (sirloin, tenderloin, or round) of excess fat, and slice it into 1/4-inch-thick strips. Marinate the meat for 30 minutes in the marinade-baste below. Broil the meat directly over a hot fire. If you are cooking the meat only to rare, there will not be time to baste while on the grill. Even for the rare meat, some of the remaining marinade can be heated and poured over the cooked meat just prior to serving. An alternative is to serve the spiced sauce below with the meat at the table.

MARINADE-BASTING SAUCE
1/3 cup soy sauce Blend ingredients thoroughly.
1/3 cup sherry
1/3 cup chicken bouillon

SPICED SAUCE
1/4 cup marinade sauce (above) Blend ingredients
1 TBS sugar thoroughly over low heat.
1-1/2 tsp dry mustard

2 TBS cornstarch Blend thoroughly and add to the above
2 TBS cold water ingredients. Heat and blend thoroughly.

Judy's Flank Steak

Serves 4 to 8

Marinate 2 to 4 pounds of flank steak refrigerated in the marinade below for 24 hours. Broil the steak directly over hot coals to medium rare (3 to 5 minutes on each side). Remove meat and slice it thinly on a diagonal across the grain of the meat (the thinner the slices the better). Place on a heated platter and pour the remaining marinade (heated) over the meat.

1/2 cup soy sauce	Blend ingredients thoroughly.
1/4 cup dry red wine	
1 TBS brown sugar	
1/2 tsp ground ginger	
1 clove garlic, minced	

Romanian Flank Steak

Cover both sides of steak with fresh coarse-ground black pepper. Pound with a large spoon to help the pepper to stick. Brush the steak with the below mixture. Broil over direct heat on a covered grill. If necessary baste the meat when it is turned. If desired, any remaining baste can be poured over the sliced meat. Slice the meat thinly across the grain (the thinner the better).

2 TBS olive oil	Saute for 2 to 3 minutes.
1 clove garlic, minced	

London Broil

Serves 4 to 8

A London Broil is another term for flank steak. Marinate 2 to 4 pounds of flank steak for 12 to 24 hours, depending upon how strong a flavor you want. Broil the meat directly over hot coals to medium rare (3 to 5 minutes per side). Slice the meat thinly across the grain for serving. The marinade can be heated and served as a table sauce.

2 TBS vegetable oil	Saute until tender.
1 medium onion, chopped	
1 clove garlic, minced	
1/4 tsp black pepper	
1 bay leaf	
1 cup beef broth	Add and simmer for 15 minutes.
1/4 cup vinegar	
1 TBS tomato paste	

CHATEAUBRIAND

Chateaubriand is a thick-cut tenderloin steak named after Francois de Chateaubriand (1768-1848). It is cut from the center of the filet mignon and is usually grilled and topped with béarnaise sauce.

Steak with Green Pepper Corns

Serves 4

Trim four 3/4-inch thick strip-steaks of peripheral fat and bone. Save two strips of fat (without bone). Place each steak between two pieces of waxed paper and pound it to a thickness of approximately 3/8 inch (about 1/2 their original thickness, but not too thin, or they will be difficult to handle with tongs while cooking). Brush the steaks with the marinade below and stack them on a plate for 2 to 3 hours at room temperature. Broil the steaks directly over a hot fire, approximately 2 minutes per side for medium rare.

MARINADE

2 TBS green peppercorns, crushed	Blend ingredients thoroughly
2 TBS olive oil	
1 TBS soy sauce	

TABLE SAUCE

2 strips of fat (from steaks)	Brown in a sauce pan until 1 tsp of fat is rendered, then discard the strips of fat.
1-1/2 TBS flour	Add to rendered fat and blend thoroughly.
1 TBS Dijon mustard	
1 TBS dried parsley	
1 green onion, sliced	
1 cup beef broth	Add broth slowly while blending to produce a smooth sauce. Once the sauce is thinned, add the remaining ingredients and simmer for 10 minutes.
1/4 cup dry red wine	
1 tsp lemon juice	
1/2 tsp Cognac	
1/4 tsp Worcestershire sauce	

Stuffed Steak

Serves 4 to 6

Prepare the mixture below and spread it on a 3/4-inch-thick boneless steak, such as sirloin. Place a similar steak on top, and sew the two steaks together with cotton string or heavy thread. Broil over hot direct heat. Use a cooking time of 1-1/2 times that required for a 3/4-inch-thick broiled steak.

1/4 lb margarine   Saute ingredients until translucent.
1 clove garlic, minced
1 medium onion, thinly sliced

1 cup fresh sliced mushrooms   Add and saute until tender.

This basic recipe can be modified by adding a variety of ingredients to the stuffing. Optional ingredients are listed below, but if added in quantity they may require the addition of more butter.

green pepper, chopped
chili peppers, minced
tomatoes, chopped (skinned and seeds removed)
semi-hot peppers, chopped (seeds removed)
assorted herbs (parsley, thyme, rosemary, oregano)

Cube Steak

Serves 4

This cut of meat is not a common choice for grill cooking. However, it has good flavor and is well suited to marinating and broiling. Marinate 2 pounds of cube steak for one hour at room temperature in the below marinade and broil directly over a hot fire. Retain the marinade, add **1 can (8 oz.) tomato sauce**, and blend thoroughly. After you turn the steaks, baste the top liberally with sauce. When the steaks are done, turn and baste the remaining side before removing them from the grill. Cube steaks are also delicious without marinating. Simply brush with **margarine** or **olive oil**, sprinkle with **coarse ground black pepper**, and broil. Cook for approximately 2 minutes on each side for medium rare.

1/2 cup white wine   Blend ingredients thoroughly.
1/4 cup vegetable oil
2 cloves garlic, minced
2 TBS lemon juice
1 TBS sherry
1 TBS soy sauce
1 TBS Worcestershire sauce
1/2 tsp black pepper

SALISBURY STEAK

A Salisbury steak is simply a hamburger without a bun. It is named for the nineteenth century British physician, James Salisbury, who included broiled ground beef patties as part of his famous health diet. The term is most often used on restaurant menus in the belief that it sounds more elegant than the term hamburger, or hamburger steak.

Anthony Burgers

Serves 5

This is an excellent all around burger recipe. It is full of juice and produces considerable smoke when broiled on a covered grill, giving it a very distinctive flavor. Cook it only on a covered grill, or it will burn, because of the olive oil in addition to the normal amount of beef fat.

2-1/2 lbs ground beef   Blend ingredients thoroughly.
1 large onion, chopped
1 egg yolk
2 TBS tomato-based barbecue sauce
1 TBS dried parsley leaves
1-1/2 TBS olive oil
1/2 tsp dried thyme
1/4 tsp black pepper
1/4 tsp salt

Bacon-Cheese Burgers

Serves 4

The key to this burger is pre-fried bacon. If raw ground bacon is added to ground beef, the result tastes like sausage. Fry bacon crisp and drain it on a paper towel to remove excess grease. The second important factor in this recipe is sharp cheddar cheese. A mild cheese will be overpowered by the other flavors.

2 lbs ground beef   Blend ingredients thoroughly.
5 slices bacon, fried and crumbled
3/4 cup sharp cheddar cheese, grated
2 tsp Worcestershire sauce
1 tsp oriental chili sauce
1/2 tsp salt
1/4 tsp black pepper

Pakistani Burgers

Serves 4

The meat patties can be served on buns or pita bread, if sandwiches are desired. They may also be formed into meatballs and cooked on skewers for those who prefer kebabs.

2 lbs ground beef   Blend ingredients thoroughly.
1/2 small onion, chopped
1 clove garlic, minced
1 TBS olive oil
1/4 tsp ginger
1/4 tsp ground cinnamon
1/4 tsp ground cloves
1/4 tsp ground turmeric
1/4 tsp salt
1/4 tsp black pepper

Blue-Cheese Burgers

Serves 6

Divide 3 pounds of ground beef into 12 portions. Form each portion into a thin patty. Form six patties with raised edges like a bird's nest. Prepare the filling below. Place a scoop (approximately 2 to 3 tsp) of filling on the meat patties with a raised edge, and place the remaining patties on top. Crimp the edges, press and mold the patties to keep them from falling apart while cooking. Cook the burgers as desired directly over hot coals on a covered or uncovered grill. When the burgers are almost ready to come off the grill, additional filling can be spread on top of the burgers if desired. Leave the burgers on long enough for the topping to melt.

1/4 lb blue cheese, crumbled   Blend ingredients thoroughly.
2 green onions, finely chopped
1/2 cup mayonnaise
2 TBS Parmesan cheese

Herb and Onion Burgers

Serves 3

This is a simple, but tasty recipe. The oil will cause considerable smoke when cooked on a covered grill, or flame if cooked on an open grill. If you prefer less smoke, but a somewhat drier burger, reduce the amount of oil. This is a good recipe for "hamburger steaks," a larger burger that is served without a bun.

1-1/2 lbs ground beef	Blend ingredients thoroughly.
4 green onions, chopped	
2 TBS olive oil	
1 TBS dried parsley	
1 tsp dried basil	
1/2 tsp dried oregano	
1/2 tsp black pepper	
1/4 tsp salt	
1/4 tsp cayenne	

CHAR-BROILING STEAKS

For rare and medium rare steaks, take them directly from the refrigerator to the grill. By the time their interior is hot, the outside will be charred on the edges and where it touches the grill. For medium well to well done meat, let the steaks come to room temperature before cooking. This will raise their temperature by 30° F, or more, before cooking. Warming the meat before cooking allows its interior to cook before the outside becomes too badly burned.

Marinades

Marinate steaks for 1 to 4 hours at room temperature, or 2 to 8 hours refrigerated. The recipes below are adequate for approximately one large or two moderately sized steaks.

Wine Marinade

Makes 3/4 cup

1/2 cup dry red wine
1/4 cup olive oil
1 clove garlic, crushed
1 bay leaf
1 tsp dried parsley
1/2 tsp dried thyme
1/2 tsp black pepper
1/2 tsp salt

Blend ingredients thoroughly.

Mustard Marinade

Makes 3/4 cup

Thoroughly coat steaks with **American** or **Creole mustard** and marinate for 2 hours at room temperature. Do not remove the mustard; it will burn off as the meat cooks. This provides a hint of mustard to the meat, but not a strong flavor.

A second method is to prepare the marinade-basting sauce below. This is good for marinating steaks and kebabs, or as a basting sauce for roasts. It is also a good dressing for spinach salad.

1/2 cup olive oil
1/4 cup wine vinegar
5 tsp Creole mustard
1 tsp salt
1/2 tsp white pepper
1/2 tsp Dijon mustard

Blend ingredients thoroughly.

Worcestershire-Soy Marinade

Makes 3/4 cup

1/4 cup olive oil
1/4 cup soy sauce
1/4 cup Worcestershire sauce

Blend ingredients thoroughly.

Lemon-Oregano Marinade

Makes 3/4 cup

1 lemon, sliced
2 TBS lemon juice
1 bay leaf
1 tsp black pepper
3/4 tsp dried oregano
1/2 tsp garlic powder
1/2 tsp salt

Blend ingredients thoroughly and let stand at room temperature for 30 minutes.

1/2 cup olive oil

Add and blend thoroughly.

Bourbon Marinade

Makes 3/4 cup

1/2 cup bourbon whisky
1/4 cup soy sauce
2 TBS Worcestershire sauce
1/2 tsp black pepper
1/2 tsp curry powder
1/4 tsp dry mustard

Blend ingredients thoroughly.

Table Sauces

These table sauces are designed for broiled steaks which are mildly seasoned. Season the steaks only with salt and black pepper, or rub lightly with a crushed garlic clove. If desired, the steaks can also be lightly brushed with margarine or olive oil.

Lemon Butter

Makes 2/3 cup

1/4 lb butter, room temperature	Blend ingredients into a paste.
1 TBS lemon juice	Let stand for 2 to 3 hours.
1 TBS white wine	
2 tsp Worcestershire Sauce	
1/4 tsp garlic powder	
1/4 tsp white pepper	
1/4 tsp salt	

Blue-Cheese Sauce

Makes 1 cup

1/4 lb butter	Saute for 3 minutes over
2 TBS dried chives	medium heat.
1/4 lb blue cheese, crumbled	Reduce heat, add and blend. Simmer for 15 minutes stirring frequently with a whip until smooth.

Brown Sauce with Mushrooms

Makes 1-1/2 cups

2 TBS butter	Blend and cook a light brown roux.
2 tsp bacon drippings	
2 TBS flour	
1 tsp dried parsley	Add to roux and blend ingredients
1/8 tsp black pepper	thoroughly.
1/8 tsp garlic powder	
1 cup beef stock	Add to roux, bring to a boil while stirring constantly. Reduce heat and simmer for 10 minutes.
1 TBS butter	Add to the sauce above, blend
1/4 cup red wine	thoroughly, and continue to simmer
1/2 lb fresh mushrooms, sliced	on low heat for 30 to 60 minutes.

Maitre d'Hotel Butter

Makes 1/2 cup

1/4 lb butter, room temperature	Blend ingredients into a paste.
1 TBS dried parsley	Let stand for 2 to 3 hours.
1/2 tsp salt	
1/8 tsp white pepper	
1/8 tsp lemon juice	

Béarnaise Sauce

Makes 1 cup

3 egg yolks 3 TBS lemon juice 1 tsp dried parsley 1/2 tsp dried tarragon 1/2 tsp dried chives 1/4 tsp white pepper	Blend ingredients thoroughly in a food processor or blender.
1/4 lb butter, melted and still bubbling	Slowly add to processor while it is running.

Green Onion Sauce

Makes 1/2 cup

1/4 lb butter 2 green onions, chopped 2 TBS dried parsley 1 tsp dried chervil	Blend ingredients and simmer over low heat for 5 minutes.
1/4 tsp black pepper 1/8 tsp salt	Remove from heat, add, and blend.

Roasted Beef

Roasts are large cuts of meat that cannot withstand the intense radiant heat of direct cooking without burning before their inside is cooked. A covered grill or moist smoker is recommended. Roasts are an excellent choice for rotisserie or spit cooking. When cooked on a grate the meat must be periodically turned. Spit cooking provides continual rotation which causes rendered fat and excess basting sauce to flow around the meat, which causes self basting. Spit cooking requires less tending, but cooking on a grate produces equally good results.

A sprinkle of tenderizer or a couple hours of marinating will not produce a noticeable tenderizing or flavoring effect. If you want marinade flavoring and more tender meat, marinate a roast for 2 to 3 days. Just salt, pepper, and wood smoke are adequate for flavoring; but a combination of marinades, basting sauces, dry rubs, and table sauces can be used with beef roasts.

The loin and rib sections provide the choicest roasts. The **standing rib**, **rolled rib**, **rib eye (Spencer)**, **tenderloin (filet)**, and **sirloin tip** are all excellent choices, as are thick (2 to 3 inch) **sirloin steaks**. Flavorful, but less tender, cuts for roasting come from the chuck, the round, and the rump. With these roasts, prime grades are recommended because of their increased tenderness. The eye of round is a tasty, lean, flavorful roast, but is tough and should be sliced thin. **Chuck** or **round** cut into 2 to 3 inch thick slices and **boneless rolled rump** are also good. The **brisket** is flavorful, but has considerable fat. The less tender roasts are best marinated, brushed with oil (or high oil basting sauce) seared on all sides, and slowly cooked until done.

A roast retains heat longer than thinner cuts of meat. After it has been removed from the cooker a roast will continue to cook. Only slicing will prevent further cooking. In general, if a roast is removed from the cooker and covered with aluminum foil it will cook to one additional degree of doneness; e.g. if removed while medium rare it will cook to medium when allowed to stand. Therefore, they must be either removed early or the rest of the meal should be planned around the timing of the roast. The safest procedure is to prepare other dishes to coincide with the timing of the roast.

SPIT DOGS

At the beginning of the 19th century, dogs (spit dogs) were used on treadmills in English taverns to provide the mechanical power for turning spitted roasts of meat while they cooked. There is one incident on record of drunken sailors hiding all of the spit dogs in Portsmouth, preventing the town from having their traditional Sunday roast .

Creole Roast Beef

Repeatedly puncture a 3 to 5 pound eye of round with an ice pick. Other cuts of beef, trimmed of peripheral fat, can also be used. Marinate the roast in the refrigerator for 3 days in the marinade below. Remove the roast from the marinade, let it drain for 15 minutes, brush it thoroughly with vegetable oil, and cover it with a liberal amount of black pepper. Roast the meat with indirect heat on a covered grill until done. Baste with additional vegetable oil if necessary. Moderate amounts of mild wood smoke can be used with this recipe. This is an excellent recipe for rotisserie cooking.

1 can (10-1/2 oz) concentrated   Blend ingredients thoroughly.
   French Onion soup
1/2 cup dry red wine
1/4 cup chili sauce
2 tsp Worcestershire sauce
1 tsp horseradish

Cajun Roast Beef

Blend the marinade below and inject it into a 3 to 5 pound beef roast with a hypodermic needle and a 3-cc syringe (available at drug stores). A smaller needle and syringe will become clogged by particles in the marinade. Keep filling the syringe and injecting the meat until all of the marinade has been used, and the marinade is evenly distributed throughout the meat. Let the meat marinate in the refrigerator for at least 3 days. Any cut from the round, or other lean cuts of meat, are a good choice for this recipe. With these tougher cuts, be sure to thinly slice the meat across the grain for serving. After marinating, brush the meat with vegetable oil and cook on indirect heat in a covered grill. Cuts such as the eye of round are excellent for rotisserie cooking.

1 bottle (2 oz) onion juice   Blend ingredients thoroughly.
1 bottle (2 oz) garlic juice
1 TBS Worcestershire sauce
1 tsp liquid Crab Boil
1 tsp Tabasco

Mexican Roast Beef

Rub a 3 to 5 pound beef roast, trimmed of fat, with **2 TBS Worcestershire sauce**. Then, rub the roast with the dry-rub below and wrap it in plastic wrap. Refrigerate the meat for 24 hours. Remove the plastic wrap and brush the meat with vegetable oil. Roast with medium indirect heat on a covered grill until done. If the roast is boneless, this makes a good choice for rotisserie cooking. Moderate to heavy wood smoke of almost any variety is suggested.

1 TBS chili powder
1/2 tsp salt
1/2 tsp cumin
1/2 tsp onion powder
1/2 tsp oregano
1/4 tsp garlic powder
1/4 tsp cayenne

Blend ingredients thoroughly.

TOUGH MEAT

Tough cuts of meat, such as flank steak or skirt meat, should be thinly sliced perpendicular to the grain for serving. This cuts the meat fibers into short segments, which makes the meat much easier to chew.

Precooked Roast Beef

Serves 4 to 6

Precooking meat before it goes on the grill is not normally recommended, because water-soluble proteins are lost, which removes part of the meat's flavor. However, if the cooking liquid is saved for use in a gravy or table sauce the flavor is eventually returned to the meat. The recipe that follows is suggested for tougher cuts of beef. Use a 2 to 3 pound piece of brisket, or round steak, trimmed of excess fat. For precooking, rub the meat with the dry rub (below), or one of your choice. Place the brisket in a small roasting pan, and add the simmering ingredients (below). Cover the pan tightly with aluminum foil and cook in a 250° F oven for 3 hours. Many beef marinades can also be used for simmering. After simmering, let the meat drain for 15 minutes. Cook the meat on the indirect heat of a covered grill or, preferably, a moist smoker with heavy wood smoke. Slice the meat thinly across the grain for serving, and accompany with the table sauce below.

DRY RUB

3/4 tsp salt   Blend ingredients thoroughly.
1/2 tsp black pepper
1/2 tsp onion powder
1/4 tsp cayenne
1/4 tsp garlic powder

SIMMERING INGREDIENTS

1 carrot, sliced
1 stalk celery, sliced
1 onion, sliced
1/2 cup water
1/4 cup dry red wine
1 tsp Worcestershire sauce

TABLE SAUCE

1/2 cup broth (from brisket)   Blend ingredients thoroughly
1/2 cup sour cream   and simmer until hot.
1/4 cup dry red wine
2 TBS Dijon mustard

Marinades, Basting Sauces & Dry Rubs

There are several ways to season beef roasts. Marinating for several days adds fluid, which will help tenderize the meat, and give it a deep flavoring. After marinating drain the meat for 15 minutes and brush it with vegetable oil before cooking, or baste with other basting sauces that contain oil. Whether or not the meat is marinated, its surface can be seasoned with dry rubs or basting sauces. If only a dry rub is used, rubbing the roast with oil before applying the dry rub is recommended. Finally, beef roasts can be served with a table sauce. The **All Purpose Marinade** below is mildly flavored and can be used with most any dry rub, basting sauce, or table sauce.

All Purpose Marinade

Makes 2-1/2 cups

1 cup water
1/2 cup dry red wine
1/4 cup vegetable oil
1 carrot, sliced
1 stalk celery sliced
1 medium onion, sliced
2 cloves garlic, crushed
3 TBS vinegar
2 TBS Worcestershire sauce
1 bay leaf
1/2 tsp black pepper
1/2 tsp beef bouillon powder
1/4 tsp chili powder
1/4 tsp salt
1/4 tsp cayenne

Blend ingredients thoroughly.

Seasoned Marinade

Makes 2 cups

1/4 cup vegetable oil   Saute until onion is translucent.
2 TBS bacon drippings
1 medium onion, chopped

1 bay leaf   Add and saute for 5
1 tsp chili powder   additional minutes.
1/2 tsp black pepper
1/2 tsp cayenne
1/4 tsp celery seed, crushed

1/2 cup vinegar   Remove from heat, add ingredients,
1/2 cup water   and blend thoroughly.
2 TBS Worcestershire sauce
1 TBS lemon juice
1 tsp salt

Burgundy Baste

Makes 1 cup

1/4 cup vinegar   Simmer for 20 minutes.
2 TBS brown sugar
1 TBS Dijon mustard
1-1/2 tsp salt
1 tsp dried tarragon
1/4 tsp black pepper
1 medium onion, sliced

1/4 cup margarine, melted   Add remaining ingredients
1/2 cup burgundy wine   and blend thoroughly.
2 TBS Worcestershire sauce

Spice Baste

Makes 1-1/2 cups

1/2 cup water
1/2 cup vegetable oil
1/4 cup brown sugar
1 TBS vinegar
1 TBS soy sauce
1 TBS Worcestershire sauce
1/2 tsp onion powder
1/4 tsp dry mustard
1/4 tsp Angostura bitters
1/4 tsp garlic powder
1/4 tsp chili powder
1/4 tsp cayenne
1/4 tsp white pepper
1/4 tsp black pepper

Blend ingredients thoroughly.

Herb and Sherry Baste

Makes 1-1/4 cups

1/4 lb margarine
2 TBS sherry
1-1/2 tsp dried rosemary
1 tsp dried thyme
1 tsp dried parsley
1 clove garlic, minced
1/4 tsp cayenne

Melt margarine, blend ingredients thoroughly, and saute for 5 minutes.

1/2 cup dry white wine
1 tsp lemon juice

Remove from heat. Add and blend.

Whiskey Baste

Makes 3/4 cup

1/4 cup vegetable oil 1 clove garlic, minced 2 slices onion, chopped	Saute until translucent.
1/4 cup bourbon whiskey 2 TBS soy sauce 1 tsp Worcestershire sauce 1/2 tsp black pepper	Remove from heat, add ingredients, and blend thoroughly.

Foots'
Seasoning Salt

Makes 1-1/4 cups

This is an excellent all-round seasoning, which can be used instead of salt in most recipes. For that reason it is here referred to as a seasoning salt instead of a dry rub. Rub this mixture on a roast a little more heavily than you would plain salt in most recipes. The recipe makes a large quantity, but is hard to reduce and still maintain the proper proportions.

1 cup salt 2 TBS cayenne 1 TBS black pepper 2 tsp garlic powder 2 tsp chili powder 2 tsp white pepper 2 tsp onion powder	Blend ingredients thoroughly.

Fennel Dry Rub

Makes 1/2 cup

The following recipe makes a sizable quantity, but is hard to reduce and still maintain reasonable spice proportions. Rub this mixture on a roast a little more heavily than you would plain salt in most recipes.

1/3 cup salt
1 tsp chili powder
1 tsp cayenne
1 tsp paprika
1/2 tsp black pepper
1/2 tsp white pepper
1/2 tsp onion powder
1/2 tsp garlic powder
1/2 tsp fennel seed, crushed
1/2 tsp celery seed
1/4 tsp dried oregano

Blend ingredients thoroughly.

Table Sauces

Many roasts need no special flavoring. The richness of a rib roast demands nothing except a good beverage to go with it. However, the sauces below can be offered at the table with a beef roast (they can also be used on broiled steak). The **Table Sauces** listed under **Steak & Burgers** can also be served with roast beef.

Horseradish Sauce

                                                    Makes 3/4 cup

1/3 cup prepared horseradish, drained   Blend ingredients
1 TBS white wine vinegar   thoroughly
1 tsp sugar
1/2 tsp dry mustard
1/2 tsp salt
1/2 tsp white pepper

1/2 cup cream, chilled   Fold in and let stand for 30 minutes,
                                                    then blend again.

Oyster Sauce

Makes 1 quart

This mild, delicately flavored sauce is not well suited to highly seasoned meat. It goes well with lightly seasoned beef, baby beef, and veal cooked with light amounts of mild wood smoke. Fish stock can be substituted for the chicken stock, and the sauce served with seafood.

4 TBS butter **1/2 lb fresh mushrooms, sliced**	Saute over moderate heat until liquid is gone. Set aside for later use.
3 TBS butter **1 TBS bacon drippings** **3 TBS flour**	Blend and cook a light roux.
2 green onions, sliced **1 tsp dried parsley**	Add and saute for 3 minutes stirring constantly.
2 cups chicken stock **1/4 cup dry white wine** **1/2 tsp salt** **1/2 tsp white pepper** **1/2 tsp Worcestershire sauce** **1/8 tsp garlic powder** **mushrooms from above**	Add and simmer, stirring until thickened.
1 pint raw oysters	Add, stir, and simmer until the oysters curl on the edges. Serve immediately.

CHILI POWDER

Chili powder is a commercially available generic seasoning blend with no fixed composition, but normally contains red pepper, cumin, oregano, garlic, and salt. In this country, chili powder is not generally very hot (spicy), but in other countries it may be almost entirely chili pepper.

Caper Sauce

Makes 1-1/4 cups

1 TBS butter **1 TBS flour**	Blend and cook a light roux.
1 cup beef stock	Stir into the roux with a whisk until smooth and thickened.
1 TBS capers (cut in half if large) **2 TBS white wine vinegar** **1 tsp caper juice** **1/4 tsp white pepper** **1/4 tsp salt** **1/8 tsp dried dill weed**	Add, reduce heat, and blend ingredients thoroughly. Simmer for 10 minutes.

TERRARIUM

Nathaniel Ward invented the terrarium in 1829. It was originally called a Wardian Case. Mr. Ward noticed that a fern had sprouted and was growing in a tightly sealed glass jar containing soil. He was amazed at how well it grew in that environment, when ferns planted outside died from the intense London air pollution caused by coal fired fireplaces. The terrarium also allowed tender plants to survive long sailing voyages, which accounted for the sudden influx of new plants to North America and Europe from the Far East, especially China, during the mid and late 19th century.

Barbecued Beef

Barbecue is slow roasting with indirect, or very low direct, heat and abundant wood smoke. Roasts should be barbecued (roasted) in the same manner as the previous section, including spit roasting. In fact, about the only difference between barbecuing large cuts in this section and roasting in the previous section is the rather arbitrary distinction in basting sauces and requirement for wood smoke. The shortcut of leaving out the wood smoke and using liquid smoke flavor in a basting sauce is not recommended.

Most commercial barbecue sauces are thick and brown to red in color. They are almost all tomato based and are the most common style of barbecue sauce in this country. A review of published barbecue sauce recipes shows that most of them call for catsup, brown sugar, vinegar, and a relatively standard group of spices. This is the type of barbecue sauce presented in this section. However, these sauces should not be used until the meat is cooked, its fat rendered, and a smoky flavor acquired.

The richest and most tender cuts of beef are from the loin and rib sections, but these are generally reserved for broiling and roasting rather than barbecuing with thick red sauces. The most common cut of beef for commercial barbecue is the **brisket**. The flat-end half of the brisket is best for home use. Thick steaks (1 to 2 inches), or thin roasts, such as **strip** or **top sirloin** are good choices. Trim peripheral fat from these cuts prior to cooking. **Beef ribs** are an excellent choice for barbecuing. Other beef cuts suited to barbecue are: thick-sliced **top** and **bottom round, eye of round** roasts, medium-thick-sliced **chuck (chuck steak), chuck filet** and other small roasts from the chuck, **hanging tenderloin**, and the **flatiron** or **triangle roast**. Ground beef, or **hamburgers**, are generally broiled and not roasted, but they can be basted with a barbecue sauce toward the end of cooking.

CATSUP

The word catsup, or ketchup, currently implies tomato catsup. However, not many years ago mushroom and walnut catsup were commonly called for in recipes in this country. The English word comes from the Chinese word *ketsiap*, which means a sauce made from the juice of vegetables.

Barbecue Sauces

These barbecue sauces contain tomato catsup, sauce, or paste, and are generally high in sugar content. The meat should be cooked until done before basting. This allows the meat to acquire a good smokey flavor, permits the rendered fat to drip free, and prevents the sauce from burning or charring. Beef is best barbecued on either a covered grill (indirect) or a moist smoker, although an open grill can be used. Note that all tomato-based barbecue sauces are listed in this section (or under **Chicken**), while other fruit and non-fruit barbecue sauces are listed under **Barbecued Pork**. Virtually all of the beef and pork barbecue sauces are interchangeable.

All-Purpose
Barbecue Sauce

Makes 1-3/4 cups

1/2 cup catsup
1/3 cup chili sauce
1/3 cup brown sugar
1/3 cup vinegar
1/4 cup lemon juice
2 TBS vegetable oil
1 TBS Worcestershire sauce
1 tsp black pepper
1/2 tsp cayenne
1/2 tsp ground cinnamon
1/2 tsp salt
1/4 tsp ground allspice
1/4 tsp garlic powder
1/8 tsp ground clove
1/8 tsp ground cumin

Blend ingredients thoroughly, bring to a boil, and simmer for 30 minutes.

Simple Tomato Sauce

Makes 2-1/4 cups

1 can (6 oz) tomato paste
1 can (8 oz) tomato sauce
1/4 cup lemon juice
1/4 cup brown sugar
2 TBS Worcestershire sauce
1/4 tsp ground cinnamon
1/8 tsp ground allspice

Blend ingredients thoroughly, bring to a boil, reduce heat, and simmer for 30 minutes.

All-Purpose Barbecue Sauce No. 2

Makes 1-1/2 cups

1/2 cup catsup
1/2 cup water
2 TBS dark corn syrup
2 TBS vinegar
2 TBS Worcestershire sauce
2 TBS brown steak sauce
1/2 tsp celery seed, crushed
1/2 tsp chili powder
1/2 tsp ground paprika
1/2 tsp salt
1/2 tsp black pepper
1/2 tsp cayenne
1/2 tsp ground allspice

Blend ingredients thoroughly, bring to a boil, and remove from heat.

Dave's Barbecue Sauce

Makes 1-1/2 cups

1 can (6 oz) frozen pineapple juice   Blend ingredients thoroughly
1/2 cup catsup   and simmer for 30 minutes.
1/4 cup brown sugar
1 TBS lemon juice
1 TBS dry mustard
1/2 tsp ground ginger
1/4 tsp salt

Thick & Spicy
Barbecue Sauce

Makes 1-3/4 cups

1/2 cup dark corn syrup   Blend ingredients thoroughly and
1/2 cup catsup   simmer for 30 minutes.
1/4 cup Creole mustard
1/4 cup vinegar
1 bay leaf
2 TBS Worcestershire sauce
2 TBS soy sauce
1/2 tsp ground allspice
1/2 tsp black pepper
1/2 tsp cayenne

Jim's Barbecue Sauce

Makes 1-3/4 cups

1/2 cup catsup
1/2 cup water
1/2 cup apple butter
2 TBS vinegar
2 TBS Worcestershire sauce
1 small onion, chopped
1/2 tsp chili powder
1/4 tsp celery salt
1/4 tsp salt
1/4 tsp sugar
1/4 tsp Tabasco
1/4 tsp black pepper
1/8 tsp ground clove
1/8 tsp ground ginger

Blend ingredients thoroughly and simmer for 30 minutes.

Thick & Quick BBQ Sauce

Makes 1-1/4 cups

1 cup catsup
2 TBS American mustard
1 TBS vinegar
1 tsp Worcestershire sauce
1 tsp brown sugar
1 tsp lemon juice
1 tsp Tabasco
1/2 tsp allspice
1/2 tsp salt
1/4 tsp black pepper

Optional: 1 TBS molasses

Blend ingredients thoroughly.

Cajun Barbecue Sauce

Makes 2 cups

3 TBS bacon drippings 1 medium onion, chopped 1/2 green pepper, chopped 1 stalk celery, chopped 1 bay leaf	Saute until tender and remove from heat.
2 cans (6 oz) tomato sauce 2 TBS Worcestershire sauce 2 TBS lemon juice 2 TBS steak sauce 1 tsp cayenne 1/2 tsp white pepper 1/2 tsp black pepper	Add remaining ingredients, blend thoroughly, and simmer for 1 hour.

Uncle Harry's Barbecue Sauce

Makes 1-1/2 cups

2 cans (6 oz) tomato paste 1/2 cup vinegar 2 bay leaves 1 stick cinnamon 3 TBS brown sugar 1 TBS Tabasco	Blend ingredients thoroughly, simmer for 30 minutes, and let cool.
1 tsp Worcestershire sauce 1 tsp lemon juice	Add and blend.

Assorted Beef

Pulkoki

Serves 4

Trim the fat from a 2-1/2 pound slice of top or bottom round (approximately 1-3/4 inch thick slice) and slice the meat paper thin. Mix the sauce below and dip the meat to coat each piece. As each piece is coated, fold it accordion-style and skewer. Tightly pack the folded meat slices on the skewer and broil on direct heat over hot coals. Cook 2-1/2 to 3 minutes on each of the four sides for medium rare. Place remaining sauce on a heated platter. When meat is done, remove it from the skewers on to the platter, and serve.

1/2 cup onion, finely chopped   Blend ingredients thoroughly.
1/2 cup soy sauce
1/4 cup sesame seeds, toasted and still hot
1/4 cup sesame oil
1/4 cup sugar
2 TBS black pepper
1 TBS garlic powder
1/8 tsp cayenne

Chinese Beef

Serves 4

Trim the fat from 2 pounds of top or bottom round, loin, or rib steak (1/2 inch thick slices), and cut into 1-inch squares. Marinate the meat in the sauce below for 1 hour at room temperature. Skewer the meat so it will cook with its flat side to the fire. Cook approximately 2 minutes per side for medium.

2 TBS soy sauce   Blend ingredients thoroughly.
2 TBS gin
2 TBS hoisin
1 TBS sesame oil
2 green onions, chopped
5 cloves garlic, minced
1 tsp fresh ginger, grated
1 tsp Tabasco
1/2 tsp sugar

P.J.'s Carne Asado

Serves 4

Marinate 2 pounds of thin cut (1/4 to 1/2 inch thick) lean beef in the marinade below for 24 hours. Round steak and flank steak are recommended, but thicker cut steaks such as strip, T-bone, and sirloin can also be used. Remove the meat from the marinade and drain for 15 minutes. Broil directly over a hot fire with heavy mild smoke until done. Do not cook longer than about 3 minutes per side, only 2 minutes for medium to medium rare. This marinade can also be used for Fajitas.

1/4 cup dry red wine	Blend ingredients thoroughly.
1/4 cup beer	
1/4 cup Worcestershire sauce	
1/4 cup lime juice	
1 TBS olive oil	
1 tsp dried cilantro	
1/2 tsp black pepper	
1/2 tsp salt	
1/2 tsp chili powder	
1/4 tsp ground cumin	
1/4 tsp cayenne	
1/4 tsp garlic powder	

Boeuf en Brochette

Fry bacon until approximately three-quarters done. Cut cubes of beef (1 to 1-1/2 inches per side) and skewer them with a short piece of **bacon** between each piece. Brush the skewered meat with melted **margarine** and lightly salt and pepper. Sprinkle the skewers with very fine white **bread crumbs** (stale French bread) and sprinkle again with melted margarine Grill medium rare directly over hot coals for approximately 2-3 minutes on each of the four sides.

Beef Sausage

Beef sausages are an excellent choice for roasting. Roast them slowly on indirect heat of a covered grill or moist smoker with moderate-to-heavy wood smoke. If they swell with bubbles under the skin, pierce them with a fork to release rendered fat. A good grade beef sausage, however, does not generally have enough fat to cause much swelling. If you want them a bit dry for slicing to serve as appetizers, pierce their skin in a number of places with a sharp fork before cooking. This lets most of the rendered fat out, leaving them somewhat drier. If a basting sauce is not to be used, try moving the sausages directly over the coals to brown them for a few minutes before removing them from the grill. If basting sauce is desired, use any of the **Beef Barbecue** sauces. The easiest way to baste sausage is to put the sauce in a shallow pan. Take the sausages from the grill with tongs, lay them in the sauce and roll them to coat all sides. You can also brown the meat, and then baste with a sauce. Beef sausage is also excellent served like a hot dog on a bun or roll with a spicy mustard.

USDA

The United States Department of Agriculture (**USDA**) stamp on meat means that it has been inspected and graded according to quality (prime, choice, etc.). Inspections began in this country with the Meat Inspection Act of 1906. The **KOSHER** stamp on a meat carcass has no implication of health or quality of meat, only that it was slaughtered in accordance with Jewish religious doctrine.

Fajitas

Serves 4

Fajitas are similar to tacos, and like tacos have no fixed list of ingredients. The only two required ingredients are broiled beef (6 boned and skinned chicken breasts can be substituted for beef) and a tortilla (usually a flour tortilla). Marinate two pounds of beef skirt overnight in the marinade below. If you cannot find skirt meat, substitute flank steak or a thin slice of round steak. Broil the meat directly over a hot fire with large quantities of mild wood smoke. After cooking to medium rare or medium, slice the meat very thin across the grain. Place the sliced meat in the center of a soft tortilla, add any desired additional ingredients, such as chopped olives (green or black), chopped tomatoes, chopped onions, guacamole, grated Jack or cheddar cheese, and salsa.

MARINADE

1/2 cup dry white wine   Blend ingredients thoroughly.
1/4 cup vegetable oil
1 TBS Worcestershire sauce
2 cloves garlic, minced
1 tsp vinegar
1 tsp lemon juice
1 tsp dried oregano
1 tsp black pepper
1 tsp dried cilantro
1/2 tsp chili powder
1/4 tsp cayenne

SALSA

1 medium tomato, finely chopped   Blend ingredients
1/2 medium onion, minced   thoroughly and let stand at
3 banana peppers, minced*   room temperature for 1 hour.
1/3 cup water
2 tsp dried cilantro
1/2 tsp salt
1/4 tsp cayenne*

*NOTE: A wide range of chilies are available in the southwestern U.S. Serranos are recommended for this recipe; otherwise, use banana peppers and cayenne, or jalapenos. If you like it hot increase the amount of cayenne or chilies.

GUACAMOLE

2 medium avocadoes, skin and seed removed	blend
1/4 small onion, minced	ingredients thoroughly
2 banana peppers, minced	in a food processor
2 tsp lemon juice	
1 tsp salt	
3/4 tsp ground coriander	
1/8 tsp cayenne	
2 med. tomatoes, skinned	Add and blend,
and chopped	but leave the tomato chunky.

SCALLOPINE

Scallopine is veal top round sliced thinly across the grain. Cutting thin slices across the grain prevents the meat from curling, or crinkling, when it is cooked. Some butchers will erroneously label any thin cut of veal as scallopine.

Korean Short Ribs

Serves 2

Have two pounds of short ribs sawed into squares of 2-1/2 to 3 inches on a side. At home, place the ribs bone side down and slice 1/2 inch into the top of the meat with parallel cuts 1/2 inch apart. Turn one-quarter turn and make a similar set of parallel cuts perpendicular to the first set. Refrigerate the meat in the marinade below for 6-8 hours. After marinating remove the meat and let it drain for 15 minutes at room temperature. Brush the meat with **2 tablespoons of sesame oil** and sprinkle liberally with fresh ground black pepper. Broil the meat directly over moderate heat with moderate mild smoke, turning and basting if required with equal parts **vegetable oil** and **sesame oil**. Cook for approximately 15 minutes for medium rare and 20 minutes for medium, depending upon heat of the fire and thickness of the meat.

1/2 cup soy sauce   Blend ingredients thoroughly.
1/2 cup sherry
4 cloves garlic, crushed
1/2 tsp black pepper
1/2 tsp cayenne

Curried Kebabs

Serves 4

Cut 2 pounds of lean, tender beef into cubes of 1 to 1 -1/2 inch dimension. Skin and halve four small onions. Marinate the meat and onions for 2 hours at room temperature, in the marinade below. Skewer the meat and onions. Broil directly over moderate heat, with or without mild smoke, until done. Cooking time is 3 minutes per side (12 minutes total) for medium rare.

1/2 cup vegetable oil   Blend ingredients thoroughly and saute
2 cloves garlic, minced   for 5 minutes.
1 bay leaf
1 TBS jalapenos, minced
1-1/2 tsp curry powder
1 tsp ground paprika
1/2 tsp black pepper
1/2 tsp salt
1/4 tsp ground ginger

1/2 cup dry white wine   Add, blend thoroughly, simmer for 10
1/4 cup lemon juice   minutes, and let cool.

Spanish Kebabs

Serves 4

Cut 2 pounds of lean beef into 1 to 1-1/2 inch cubes. Marinate at room temperature for 2 hours. Skewer the meat, alternating it with small **onion** halves, sections of **bell pepper**, and **cherry tomatoes**. Broil directly over a hot fire, basting with the remaining marinade as necessary. Light to moderate amounts of mild wood smoke are recommended. Cook 3 minutes per side (12 minutes total) for medium rare.

1/2 cup sherry   Blend ingredients thoroughly, and let
6 TBS lemon juice   stand at room temperature for 1 hour.
1/4 cup olive oil
2 cloves garlic, crushed
1 TBS dried parsley
1 tsp dried chives

Hunan Kebabs

Serves 4

Cut 2 pounds of lean beef into 1 to 1-1/2 inch cubes. Marinate for 1 hour at room temperature. Remove from the marinade and alternately skewer marinated meat with fresh mushrooms brushed with the remaining marinade. Grill over moderate direct heat with mild wood smoke until done. Cook 3 minutes per side (12 minutes total) for medium rare.

1 TBS sesame oil	Saute on moderate heat until
1 TBS vegetable oil	garlic browns.
1 TBS fresh ginger, grated	
2 cloves garlic, minced	
2 tsp crushed chilies	
1/2 cup soy sauce	Add, blend, and simmer for 5 minutes.
1/2 cup sherry	
2 TBS hoisin	
2 TBS sugar	

CURRY POWDER

Curry powder is a generic spice blend which varies widely in composition, but commonly contains cumin, fenugreek, mace, clove, coriander, tumeric, ginger, and cardomom. Although ready blended curry powders are sold in Asian markets, there are several varieties (e.g., red, green, yellow), but no single type is used for all foods as is often done in this country.

Poultry

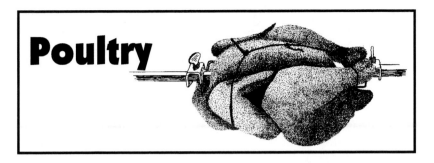

The **chicken** is the most popular and most commonly eaten bird in the world. It is thought to have been domesticated from wild jungle fowl in India. During Roman times the fattened hen became so popular that fear of its extinction led the Consul Fanius to ban its consumption. This decree quickly led to the development of the **capon**, a surgically neutered male chicken under eight months of age. More recently, crossing of the White Rock and Cornish breeds led to the **Rock Cornish Hen**, or **Cornish Game Hen**.

The chicken is popular in China, but the **duck** has been elevated to the pinnacle of foods. In Imperial China, duck was carefully prepared, hung, and roasted so the skin became golden brown and crispy. The nobles then ate the skin, leaving the meat for the kitchen servants. In Europe, the **goose** is the bird of choice for festive occasions, while in this country the turkey serves that purpose. Although the **turkey** is native to North America, it was probably first domesticated in Mexico and exported back to the United States by way of Europe. Most other fowl vary in popularity. The once popular **squab** (young pigeon) and **Guinea fowl** are now often difficult to find, as are domestic **pheasants**.

Most chickens are raised for egg production. These birds are called pullets. The most common chicken raised for meat is called a broiler, or fryer. These are young chickens of either sex, which are raised to an age of eight to ten weeks. Most are crossbreeds, or hybrids. Cornish Hens, are simply chickens of five to seven weeks age which have Cornish breed ancestry. Other classes of chicken are not satisfactory for grill or smoker cooking.

Fryer-roaster turkeys (under four months of age) and Young turkeys (five to seven months in age), either Hen or Tom, are suitable for grill or smoker cooking. However, hen turkeys are generally preferable to Toms because they are generally more tender. The major consideration with turkeys is size. Broiler Ducklings, Young Geese, Young Guineas, and squabs are all suitable for grill or smoker cooking.

The technique used for cooking poultry on grills and smokers depends upon the size and fat content of the bird. The basic principle of cooking fowl is to cook until the fat is rendered, primarily the layer directly beneath the skin, but to stop cooking before the bird can dry out. The goose and turkey are both large, and require hours to cook. Geese, ducks, and capons have a high fat content, which must be rendered and removed. A moist smoker is best for large or fat birds because of the slow moist cooking. Smaller birds can be cooked on indirect heat in a covered grill, and are an excellent choice for spit roasting. Small to medium-sized birds split in half, or pieces, such as wings and thighs, can be cooked on a grill with indirect or low direct heat. Boned turkey breasts can also be rolled, tied, and roasted using almost any recipe for veal roasts. Thin pieces of boned fowl, such as chicken or turkey, can even be broiled over a hot direct fire.

Basting sauces for poultry should normally contain a high oil or fat content, generally one-third the total volume. Thick barbecue sauce should be used only after a thin sauce has been applied and the meat is almost done. Most thin sauces designed for beef or lamb are made suitable for poultry simply by increasing the oil content.

Stuffing the body cavity of poultry with dressing should only be done with small birds, such as Cornish hens or squabs, or the bird will take forever to cook. However, the use of sliced onions, apples, celery, or lemon wedges in the body cavity will season whole birds without affecting the cooking time.

POPE'S NOSE

The tail of a bird, feathers removed, is commonly referred to as the Popes' Nose or Preacher's Nose. When roasting whole or split poultry, this part can be cut off prior to cooking. It can be used for stock, but few people care to eat it. Although it is not necessary, the wing tips of poultry can also be cut off at the first joint and saved for making stock. There is little meat on the wing tip.

Chicken

There are a variety of ways to cook chicken on a grill or smoker. The best method for moist smokers is to roast whole or split (halves) chickens. On covered grills, one can roast whole chickens with indirect heat on a grate or a rotisserie. Quarter chickens (thigh quarter or breast quarter), and pieces (wings, thighs, breasts, etc.) can be roasted on indirect or low direct heat on covered or uncovered grills. Chicken pieces can be skinned, boned, and broiled on direct heat on covered or uncovered grills. Finally, chicken can be skinned and ground for grilled burgers.

Tandoori Chicken

Serves 4

Traditionally, tandoori consists of chicken pieces cooked in a charcoal-fired cooker called a tandoor. However, it is most easily prepared and served as kababs. Bone and cut six chicken breasts into 1 inch chunks, and marinate in the refrigerator for 24 hours. Remove from refrigerator, brush excess marinade from the chicken, skewer, and brush with the basting sauce. Cook on the edge of a moderately hot indirect fire, with mild wood smoke for approximately 15 minutes (turning to cook all sides), basting as required.

MARINADE

2 cups yogurt   Blend ingredients thoroughly.
1/2 onion, chopped
2 cloves garlic, minced
2 TBS fresh ginger, grated
1 TBS ground coriander
1/2 tsp curry powder

BASTING SAUCE

4 TBS margarine, melted   Blend ingredients thoroughly.
1 tsp cayenne
1/2 tsp cumin
1/4 tsp red food dye

Basic Chicken Burger

Serves 3 to 4

This is a simple chicken burger recipe that is an excellent low-calorie low-cholesterol source of protein. Additional seasonings can be added, ground turkey can be substituted, and the burgers can be basted with a variety of sauces as is done with hamburgers. Remove the meat from chicken pieces. A food processor can be used to grind the meat, but an old fashioned meat grinder is better. This recipe uses yogurt for moisture because it does not include the chicken skin. If ready-ground turkey is used it commonly contains ground skin. The texture of ground chicken is considerably different from that of ground beef. Because it is sticky, put the patties on wax paper. Chicken burgers are soft and look like they will fall through the grate, but they do not. After they have cooked for a few minutes they can easily be turned with a spatula.

1 lb ground chicken
2 TBS plain yogurt
1/2 tsp salt
1/4 tsp black pepper

Blend ingredients thoroughly, and form into patties.

Spiced Chicken Burger

Serves 3 to 4

This recipe serves as an example of how the Basic Chicken Burger can be supplemented by additional ingredients. This recipe also uses yogurt for moisture because it does not include the chicken skin. If ready-ground turkey is used it commonly contains ground skin, and yogurt is not required.

1 lb ground chicken
1 slice onion, minced
1 clove garlic, minced
2 TBS plain yogurt
1 tsp lemon juice
1/2 tsp ground ginger
1/2 tsp salt
1/4 tsp ground coriander
1/4 tsp black pepper
1/8 tsp ground cumin

Blend ingredients thoroughly, and form into patties.

Mock Abalone

This will not taste like abalone, but is a tasty approximation. Skin and bone the desired number of chicken breasts. Pound them to a thin, uniform thickness (see discussion under **Boned and Broiled Chicken**). Marinate the chicken in the refrigerator for 3 days in canned clam juice. Although not commercially available, oyster juice can also be used for a slightly different flavor. After marinating let the chicken drain for 15 minutes at room temperature. Brush the chicken lightly with melted margarine and sprinkle lightly with salt, white pepper, and finely ground seasoned bread crumbs. Broil directly over a hot fire on a covered grill for approximately 3 minutes per side, depending upon the heat of the fire. Sprinkle lightly with lemon juice, or serve with lemon wedges.

BLOOD

The chuck is generally considered to be the most robustly flavored cut of beef. This is because a side of beef is hung upside down after slaughter, causing blood to drain to the chuck. The details of Kosher slaughter and meat preparation deal primarily with the bleeding and the removal of blood from meat with salt. Fishermen commonly bleed or field-dress fish soon after catching them, and then soak them in saltwater (then rinse prior to freezing). Some experienced hunters rinse venison in slow-running cold water until no color remains in the outflow (2 to 3 days). These hunters maintain this produces meat as mildly flavored as beef. Although it has not been documented by science, experience suggests that blood is responsible for much of the strong flavor associated with meats (including poultry and fish). Proper bleeding and marination in salt, or salt brine, for periods of several hours (rinsed thoroughly in cold water prior to cooking) will produce more mildly flavored meat, seafood, or poultry.

Grilled Pieces

The wing, thigh, and drumstick are the best pieces for grilling. These can be cooked with or without the skin. If cooked with the skin on, they should be cooked until the skin is golden brown. Cooking with the skin removed generally produces a drier piece of meat, with excellent flavor, and fewer calories. The recipes that follow are just as good with chicken quarters or halves, but require slower cooking. Hindquarters (drumstick plus thigh) are also a good choice for entertaining because they are approximately one adult serving and are relatively easy to eat with either a knife and a fork or by hand. Grilled chicken should be cooked with moderate indirect heat or very low direct heat on a covered or uncovered grill. Wood smoke is optional. Lightly salt and pepper chicken pieces, quarters, or halves (split chickens). Baste the chicken liberally with any of the basting sauces below. Oil and vinegar or Italian salad dressings can also be used. Pieces require 45 minutes to 1 hour cooking time on a covered grill with indirect heat. For chicken quarters and halves, allow 1 to 1-1/2 hour.

Sweet and Sour Baste

                                                           Makes 2/3 cup

1 TBS bacon drippings   Saute onion until translucent.
1 small onion, chopped

1/3 cup lemon juice   Add remaining ingredients,
1 TBS brown sugar   blend, and heat thoroughly.
1 tsp dry mustard
1 tsp Worcestershire sauce
1/2 tsp salt
1/2 tsp black pepper

Hawaiian Baste

Makes 2/3 cup

1/4 cup vegetable oil
3 TBS pineapple juice
2 TBS soy sauce
2 TBS sherry
2 tsp fresh ginger, minced
1 tsp Worcestershire sauce
1/4 tsp black pepper

Blend ingredients thoroughly.

Herb Baste

Makes 1-1/2 cups

1/2 cup vegetable oil
1 medium onion, minced
2 cloves garlic, minced

Saute until onion is translucent.

1/2 tsp dried thyme
1/2 tsp dried rosemary
1/2 tsp dried basil
1/4 tsp dried oregano

Add remaining ingredients, blend thoroughly, and saute for 3 minutes.

1/2 tsp black pepper
1/2 cup vinegar
1/4 cup water
1 tsp salt

Remove from heat, add remaining ingredients, and blend thoroughly.

Savory Baste

Makes 3/4 cup

1/4 cup water
1/4 cup vinegar
1/4 cup vegetable oil
1 TBS dried parsley
1 tsp dried savory
3/4 tsp salt
1/2 tsp black pepper
1/4 tsp dry mustard
1/4 tsp Worcestershire sauce

Blend ingredients thoroughly.

Teriyaki Baste

Makes 1-1/4 cups

1/2 cup soy sauce
1/3 cup sherry
1/4 cup vegetable oil
1 clove garlic, crushed
2 TBS sugar
1/2 tsp ground ginger
1/2 tsp black pepper

Blend ingredients thoroughly, let stand for 1 hour, and blend again.

Dill Baste

Makes 1 cup

1/2 cup vegetable oil
1/2 cup dry white wine
1 TBS lemon juice
1 TBS dried parsley
1 tsp dried dill weed
1/2 tsp salt
1/4 tsp dried tarragon
1/4 tsp white pepper

Blend thoroughly and let stand for 1 hour.

Mustard Baste

Makes 1-1/2 cups

1/2 cup vegetable oil
1/4 cup wine vinegar
1/4 cup water
1/4 cup Creole mustard
3 TBS catsup
1 clove garlic, minced
1 tsp dry mustard
1 tsp black pepper
1 tsp salt

Simmer for 30 minutes over low heat, then beat with a whisk to emulsify.

Piquant Baste

Makes 1-1/2 cups

1/2 cup vegetable oil
1 small onion, chopped

Saute in oil until onion is translucent, then remove from heat.

1 clove garlic, minced
1/2 cup vinegar
1/4 cup water
1 TBS Worcestershire sauce
1 tsp chili powder
1 tsp salt
1 tsp cayenne
1 tsp black pepper
1/2 tsp white pepper

Add remaining ingredients, and blend thoroughly.

Pepper Baste

Makes 3/4 cup

1/4 lb margarine
1 TBS vinegar
1 TBS lemon juice
1 tsp Worcestershire sauce
1 tsp black pepper
1 tsp dry mustard
1/2 tsp cayenne
1/2 tsp white pepper
1/2 tsp salt

Heat until butter is melted, and blend ingredients thoroughly.

BUTTER

Margarine was invented in 1870 and is simply vegetable oil with flavoring, additives, and dye. Butter browns and burns at lower temperatures than vegetable oils. For this reason, butter is not used in the basting sauce recipes of this book. Butter may be preferred in table sauces where the flavor difference between butter and margarine is noticeable, but this difference is not noticeable in a basting sauce after it has been applied to cooking meat. Use vegetable oil or margarine in basting sauce recipes to reduce the risk of burning the meat and to form a seal over the meat to prevent the loss of natural juices or marinades.

Barbecue Pieces

Thick barbecue sauces go well with chicken. However, they should be applied only after the chicken has been cooked. Chicken pieces, chicken quarters, or split chickens should be slowly cooked on indirect heat of a covered grill, or low direct heat of covered or uncovered grills. They should be basted with margarine, oil, or a high oil content thin sauce until cooked. Apply a thick sauce to form a coating or glaze just before removing from the cooker. This applies for chicken with the skin on or off. Wood smoke of any variety is desirable. Cooking times and procedures are the same as for grilled chicken pieces.

Baste the chicken pieces first with the **Oil and Vinegar Baste**, **Brady's Basting Sauce**, or any mildly seasoned thin basting sauce that contains a significant amount of oil. When the meat is done, or almost done, apply several coats of a thick barbecue sauce. Several such sauces are provided below. Thick barbecue sauces from the beef or pork barbecue sections can also be used, as can most commercial barbecue sauces. Commercially available French Salad Dressings are also good thick bastes for barbecued chicken.

THIN SAUCES

Oil and Vinegar Baste

Makes 3/4 cup

1/4 cup vegetable oil
1/4 cup distilled vinegar
1/4 cup water
1 tsp salt
1/2 tsp black pepper

Blend ingredients thoroughly.

Brady's Basting Sauce

Makes 1-1/4 cups

1 can (12 oz) beer
1/4 lb margarine, melted
1 tsp salt
1/2 tsp black pepper

Blend ingredients thoroughly.

Ken's Barbecue Sauce

Makes 1-2/3 cups

1 cup Coke Cola
1/2 cup catsup
1 TBS Worcestershire sauce
1 tsp Tabasco

Blend ingredients thoroughly.

NOTE: This thin sauce has a high sugar content and no oil. Basting with a high oil thin sauce can be done first, but is not necessary. If a high oil sauce is not used first, cook on lower heat and use caution not to burn.

THICK SAUCES

Catsup
Barbecue Sauce

Makes 2 cups

3/4 cup catsup
1/2 cup vinegar
1/2 cup water
1/4 cup brown sugar
1 TBS Worcestershire sauce
1 bay leaf
1/4 tsp celery salt
1/4 tsp chili powder
1/4 tsp ground allspice
1/4 tsp ground cinnamon
1/4 tsp black pepper
1/4 tsp cayenne
1/8 tsp ground cloves

Blend ingredients thoroughly, bring to a boil, reduce heat, and simmer for 30 minutes.

SHALLOTS

Shallots are a member of the onion family, with a flavor similar to a cross between onion and garlic. They are very common in French cooking. Shallots should not be confused with green onions (scallions); however, the terms are sometimes used synonymously in this country.

Tomato Barbecue Sauce

Makes 3/4 cup

6 TBS tomato sauce
2 TBS soy sauce
2 TBS water
2 TBS lemon juice
1 tsp Worcestershire sauce
1 tsp honey
1/2 tsp ground paprika
1/2 tsp black pepper

Blend thoroughly, and simmer for 30 minutes.

Chutney Barbecue Sauce

Makes 1-3/4 cups

2 TBS bacon drippings
1 medium onion, chopped

Saute onion until translucent.

1 cup apple cider
1/2 cup chutney*, pureed
2 TBS brown sugar
1 TBS Worcestershire sauce
1/2 tsp lemon juice
1/2 tsp cayenne

Add remaining ingredients, bring to a boil, and remove from heat.

*NOTE: Mango chutney is recommended, but other types can be substituted. Catsup or apple butter can also be substituted.

Whole, Half & Quartered

Whole or split chickens must be slowly roasted, and are ideally suited to smoke flavoring. The full range of woods, as well as any of the sauces from the previous section (**Barbecued Pieces**), can be used. Roast chicken is delicious eaten either hot or cold, at a sit-down dinner or for buffets and picnics. If the bird is to be eaten cold, the skin should be well cooked and all the fat not only rendered but removed. If you finish off with a tomato or other fruit based barbecue sauce, thin with water, wine, or half vinegar - half water, and do not baste the bird too heavily. If you use hickory wood smoke, do not use heavy smoke. A roasted chicken has a distinctive flavor that should not be overpowered.

Whole or split chickens (broiler or fryer size) must be roasted slowly on indirect heat using a grate or a spit to hold the bird. Small whole chickens are an excellent choice for spit roasting. Moist smokers are also well suited for cooking chicken. For this style of cooking, lay the chicken on its breast, or split side up to retain juice. This self-bastes the breast, which is the driest part of the bird. If you plan to carve a whole bird at the table, you may prefer to cook it breast side up for appearances.

The simplest recipe is to rub a whole bird inside and out with oil (vegetable, olive, or margarine), salt, and white pepper. Roast, basting lightly with margarine or olive oil, as required. Wedges or slices of apple, onion, celery, and lemon can be inserted in the body cavity for the addition of subtle flavor. Additional basting sauces are the **Oil and Vinegar Baste** or **Brady's Basting Sauce** given in the **Barbecued Chicken** section.

Additional basting sauces are listed below. With these, rub a whole chicken inside and out with salt and white pepper (1/2 tsp salt, 1/4 tsp pepper). Pour 1 TBS of basting sauce inside the bird and turn it to coat the inside. Brush the bird thoroughly on the outside and roast with moderate mild smoke. Use the remaining baste as necessary until done. If you plan to eat the chicken cold, empty the liquids in the body cavity 15 minutes before the bird is done and do not baste again. This procedure prevents the bird from being greasy.

MARANADE CAUTION

Marinades used on raw poultry, seafood, or pork should never be poured over cooked food or used for basting toward the end of cooking: bacteria such as salmonella are commonly present on uncooked food. If these marinades are used, bring them to a boil before re-use. Only beef, lamb, and game marinades are normally incorporated into basting or table sauces. Care should also be taken not to put cooked pork, poultry, or seafood on the same platter that the uncooked food was carried outside on. These platters should be thoroughly washed after the raw food is removed.

Rosemary Baste　　

Makes 1/3 cup

1/4 cup olive oil　　　　　Place in a jar with a tight lid, seal,
1 clove garlic, crushed　　　　and let stand 1 week or more.
1-1/2 tsp dried rosemary
1 tsp dried parsley

1 TBS lemon juice　　　　When ready for use, add and shake
1 TBS sherry　　　　　　　　to blend thoroughly.

Spice Baste　　

Makes 1 cup

1/2 cup vegetable oil　　　Saute over moderate heat for 5
1 tsp ground cardamom　　minutes and remove from heat.
3/4 tsp ground cumin
1/2 tsp onion powder
1/2 tsp garlic powder
1/2 tsp cayenne
1/2 tsp black pepper
1/2 tsp ground ginger
1/4 tsp ground cinnamon
1/4 tsp ground cloves

1/2 tsp salt　　　　　　　Add and blend thoroughly.
1/2 cup dry white wine

Oriental Chili Baste

Makes 3/4 cup

1/4 lb margarine, melted
1/4 cup red wine vinegar
3 TBS oriental chili sauce

Blend ingredients thoroughly.

Herb Baste

Makes 1-1/4 cups

1/2 cup olive oil
1 clove garlic, minced
1 TBS dried parsley
1/2 tsp black pepper
1/2 tsp dried rosemary
1/2 tsp dried basil
1/2 tsp dried marjoram

Saute over moderate heat for 5 minutes, and remove from heat.

1/2 cup dry white wine
1/4 cup wine vinegar
1/2 tsp salt
1/4 tsp Worcestershire sauce

Add and blend ingredients thoroughly.

MINCING GARLIC

To mince a garlic clove, place the clove on the edge of a cutting board and place the flat side of a knife blade (a cleaver is excellent) on top of it. Hit the knife blade and partially crush the garlic clove. The husk can then be easily removed. Repeat the process with the cleaned clove, but crush it completely. Thinly slice parallel to the long fibers of the crushed clove, then slice in a perpendicular direction. With practice, this is a simple and quick process which does not dirty a garlic press (most of which are hard to clean).

Boned & Broiled

The meat of a chicken leg is the tastiest part of the chicken. When boned with skin and fat removed, they are excellent broiled. Start with whole legs (thigh quarters), not just drumsticks. Insert your fingers between the skin and meat and pull the skin loose and down to the foot end of the drumstick. Remove the excess fat by pulling and cutting. Cut all the way around the foot end of the drumstick (to the bone) to sever the tendons and remove the skin. Place the leg on a cutting board with the inner side upward. Make an incision along the top of the leg and thigh bones so both bones are exposed. On the thigh-bone end, insert your fingers between the meat and bone and pull or cut the meat loose from the bone. The meat can now be pulled away from both bones (leg and thigh), with the exception of the knee region. The smaller of the two leg bones usually has to be cut out. Use a knife and cut the meat away from the knee. This will leave a skinned and boneless piece of meat with a thin spot or hole in the center (from the knee).

Chicken breasts are also excellent when marinated and broiled. Skin and bone the chicken breasts, and remove the small muscle from the bone side. Remove the tendon from this muscle. It will be difficult to flatten a boned breast with this muscle still attached. Use the side of a meat-tenderizing mallet or other flat object to pound the breast to a uniform thickness of approximately 1/4 inch. A good practice is to place the breast between two sheets of wax paper before pounding.

Once the meat has been skinned, boned, and excess fat removed, it is ready for marinading and broiling. A wide variety of marinades can be used on this lean meat. Oil and vinegar or oriental basting sauces, with soy sauce are excellent. Most of the basting sauces suggested for **Grilled Pieces** or almost any other marinade (or basting sauce) that will not burn on high direct heat can also be used. These marinades are specifically for boned chicken and are also good on chicken kebabs. Marinate the chicken for 2-4 hours in the refrigerator. Broil directly over a moderate fire on a covered or uncovered grill. Cooking time is approximately 5 minutes per side. This entre is relatively simple, tasty, low calorie, and high in protein.

Hoisin Marinade

Makes 1 cup

2 TBS vegetable oil
4 green onions, sliced
2 cloves garlic, minced

Saute over moderate heat for 5 minutes. Remove from heat.

1/2 cup dry white wine
1/4 cup Hoisin
1/4 cup soy sauce
2 tsp lemon juice

Add ingredients and blend thoroughly.

Sweet Vermouth Marinade

Makes 2/3 cup

1/3 cup white wine
3 TBS olive oil
2 TBS sweet vermouth
1 tsp dried parsley
1/4 tsp dried oregano
1/4 tsp dried basil
1/4 tsp black pepper
1/4 tsp salt
1/8 tsp bitters

Blend ingredients thoroughly, let stand for 30 minutes, and blend again.

Tarragon Marinade

Makes 2/3 cup

1/3 cup white wine
1/4 cup olive oil
2 TBS tarragon vinegar
1 TBS dried parsley
1 tsp dried tarragon
1/4 tsp dried thyme
1/4 tsp black pepper
1/4 tsp salt

Blend ingredients thoroughly, let stand for 30 minutes, and blend again.

David's Sweet Pineapple Marinade

Makes 3/4 cup

1 can (6 oz) pineapple juice
1/4 cup brown sugar
2 TBS soy sauce
1 TBS sherry
1 TBS fresh ginger, grated

Blend ingredients thoroughly, let stand for 30 minutes, and blend again.

Scallion Marinade

Makes 1 cup

3/4 cup dry white wine
1/4 cup olive oil
1 TBS lemon juice
3 green onions, chopped
1 clove garlic, minced
1 tsp jalapeno, minced
1/2 tsp salt
1/2 tsp black pepper

Blend ingredients thoroughly, let stand for 30 minutes, and blend again.

Turkey

Many people think of turkey as a bird filled with stuffing that is roasted for Thanksgiving or Christmas. However, there are a variety of ways by which turkey can be cooked outdoors on grills and smokers. Whole birds can be roasted or smoked. Turkey breasts can be roasted whole, or boned and roasted. Turkey breast meat can also be sliced and broiled. Turkey pieces can be barbecued, and ground turkey can be used for burgers. It is not advisable to stuff a whole turkey for outdoor cooking; it could take days to cook.

To bone a turkey breast, first remove the skin. The skin can usually be pulled loose, but you may need a knife to separate some of the skin from the meat. Lay the skinned breast on a cutting board rib side down. Make an incision along one side of the breast bone from front to back, all the way down to the ribs. Spread the incision open and make shallow cuts along the ribs to separate the breast meat from the ribs. This step is similar to filleting a large fish. Repeat the procedure on the other side of the breast. This produces two large pieces of lean white meat. These can be cooked using virtually any recipe for veal. Each half of the breast is composed of several large muscles. To cook the breast whole, as a roast, it should be tied with twine to hold these pieces together. Use a meat thermometer and baste with poultry basting sauces or oil based beef or lamb basting sauces.

An alternate method of cooking turkey is to cut the meat into steaks. Lay one of the boned breast halves flat and cut slices at approximately 30° to 45° from the vertical. Cutting on an angle like this produces a steak which is larger in diameter. Cut the steaks approximately three-quarters to one inch in thickness. These steaks can also be used with most veal recipes. These steaks can also be marinated in most beef or lamb marinades and broiled. The steaks can even be further cut into cubes and the meat used in kebabs.

Skinned and boned turkey breasts, whether cooked as roasts or as steak, are lean and mildly flavored. Care must be taken not to dry out the meat. As far as flavor, the turkey can either be mildly seasoned as with veal, or strongly seasoned using the turkey as a medium for holding the marinade flavor.

JUDGING DONENESS

Poultry is done when the joints (wing or leg) can be moved easily, and the juice no longer has a pink tint. Fish is done when the meat becomes opaque and can be flaked with a fork. However, some people feel that fish is overdone if it can be flaked. Whether or not a thin cut of beef, pork, or lamb is done must be judged on the basis of cooking time and appearance. A meat thermometer is recommended for roasts.

Roasted Whole Turkey

Most of the sauces listed under **Grilled Chicken Pieces** or **Roast Whole or Split Chickens** can also be used on turkey. The best basting sauces for turkey contain a significant oil content and not too much vinegar or sugar. Simple oil or butter basting sauces with herbs are excellent. However, there is less risk in using high sugar barbecue sauces because low heat is used. Hickory wood smoke is excellent, but if this is too pungent for your taste, try a milder wood, such as oak or mesquite. The simplest recipe is to rub the bird inside and out with oil, salt, and pepper. Finely ground white pepper is good because it sticks well. Cook with low indirect heat and baste periodically until done. Small whole birds, or breasts (5 to 10 pounds), can be cooked on covered grills, but a moist smoker is best. If you are cooking with indirect heat on a covered grill, hang a folded sheet of aluminum foil on a rung of the cooking grate. This will block radiant heat.

SAVORY BASTING SAUCE

2/3 cup vegetable oil	Saute until tender.
1 bell pepper, seeds and	
membranes removed, chopped	
1 medium onion, chopped	
2 TBS dried parsley	Add and saute for 3 minutes.
1 tsp dried savory	
1 tsp dried basil	
1 tsp black pepper	
1/4 tsp celery seed	
1 cup white wine	Add, bring to a boil, reduce heat, and
2/3 cup lemon juice	simmer for 30 minutes.
1 tsp salt	
1/4 tsp garlic powder	

SHERRY BASTING SAUCE

1/2 lb margarine, melted	Blend thoroughly and simmer for 5
1/2 cup water	minutes.
1/3 cup sherry	
1 TBS Worcestershire sauce	
1 TBS soy sauce	
1 clove garlic, minced	
1-1/2 tsp dried parsley	
1 tsp dried thyme	
1 tsp salt	

Turkey Roast with Fines Herbs

Serves 6 to 8

Bone a 5 to 6 pound turkey breast, and marinate the two halves refrigerated for 48 hours in the marinade below. Remove the turkey from the marinade. Remove the pieces of green onion and bay leaves and let it drain for 15 minutes. Place the two halves together with one reversed. Tie the pieces together with cotton string, as is done with boned and rolled beef or pork roasts. Brush the meat thoroughly with olive oil. Cover the outside with freshly ground black pepper. Cook on indirect heat on a covered grill or moist smoker. Baste as necessary with a mixture of equal portions of olive oil and dry white wine. Use light amounts of mild wood smoke, if desired. If the meat is not marinated long enough or is cooked too fast, it will be tough. It must absorb fluids and cook slowly. Cooking time is approximately 1 to 1-1/2 hours on a covered grill.

1 cup dry white wine
1 cup beef stock
1/4 cup olive oil
1 TBS wine vinegar
1 TBS dried parsley
2 tsp dried chives
1 tsp dried tarragon
1 tsp dried chervil
1 tsp salt
1/2 tsp white pepper
1 small bay leaf
1 green onion, chopped
1/8 tsp ground nutmeg

Blend ingredients thoroughly.

FINES HERBS

Fines Herbs is a blend of sweet herbs commonly called for in fish and poultry recipes, but not commercially available in blended form. *Fines herbs* consists of parsley, chives, tarragon, and chervil. Celery leaves are sometimes included.

Smoked Turkey

A smoked turkey is seasoned primarily by wood smoke. They are basted only if necessary to keep the meat moist. A moist smoker is preferable, but most large covered grills are adequate. If using a charcoal grill, build an indirect fire, and hang a folded sheet of aluminum foil over a rung of the grate, so it hangs below the grate and blocks radiant heat. Use low heat and wood smoke of almost any variety. Hickory or pecan are excellent, but mesquite and apple are milder in flavor.

Rub the bird inside and out with salt and white pepper. Blend a mixture of equal portions of **water**, **vinegar**, and **vegetable oil**. Pour 1/4 cup of the basting mixture into the body cavity and turn the bird to thoroughly coat the inside. Brush the outside of the bird thoroughly, but lightly, with this baste. Place the bird, breast down on the cooking grate and smoke. Breast down cooking will produce juicier breast meat. Be sure to allow plenty of time for cooking, a 10-pound bird will require 8-10 hours, and a 20-pound bird will require 12 to 14 hours on a moist smoker. Do not tend the bird too closely, check the fire every 3 to 4 hours to make sure there are adequate coals and wood. Add coals before the fire gets too low to ignite the new ones. Add new briquets around the edge, then once ignited move them to the desired location. Also, periodically check the bird and baste if necessary. A properly smoked bird has a black skin, but is not burnt. The color results from wood smoke.

Rotisserie Turkey Roast

This recipe can also be cooked with indirect heat on a covered grill or a moist smoker, but a rotisserie is best. Bone a turkey breast and marinate the two halves in the marinade below for 24 hours in the refrigerator. Remove from the marinade and let it drain on a plate for 15 minutes. Turn the two halves in opposite directions and tie them together with a series of half-hitches using cotton string, and skewer on the spit. Brush the meat liberally with olive oil, sprinkle with lemon juice, and liberally salt and pepper. Cook with moderate direct heat for the first 10 minutes without a drip pan, then place the drip pan underneath and continue cooking. This produces some browning of the meat and seals the juices. Mild wood smoke can be used if desired. Use a meat thermometer and cook until done (approximately 1 hour for a 4-pound breast).

1/4 cup olive oil	Saute until onions are tender,
1 onion, chopped	and remove from heat.
1 clove garlic, minced	
1 bay leaf	
1/2 tsp dried thyme	
2 cups beef stock	Add and blend ingredients thoroughly.
2 TBS cognac	
1/2 tsp salt	
1/2 tsp black pepper	
1/16 tsp clove	

POULTRY SEASONING

Poultry seasoning is a generic blend of herbs with no fixed composition or proportions, but usually contains thyme, marjoram, savory, and rosemary. It is commercially available in already mixed form, and can be used on a wide variety of foods in addition to poultry.

Turkey Burgers

Serves 3 to 4

Turkey burgers are similar to chicken burgers, but with a slightly different flavor. These burgers are designed for commercially available ground turkey, which contains more fat than that prepared at home by grinding lean turkey or chicken breast (skin and fat removed).

1 lb ground turkey   Blend ingredients thoroughly and form
2 TBS onion, chopped   into patties.
1 TBS dried parsley
1 tsp olive oil
1 tsp Foots' Seasoning Salt*
1/2 tsp dried thyme

* NOTE: See Roasted Beef

Table Sauces

Edgar's Caper Sauce

Makes 1-1/4 cups

This sauce can be served with the meat as a table sauce, and used as a sandwich spread the next day.

1 cup mayonnaise   Blend ingredients thoroughly.
2 TBS capers, cut in half
2 tsp caper juice
1 tsp soy sauce
3/4 tsp lemon juice

Beth's Cranberry Chutney

Makes 2 quarts

Prepare the mixture below, put it into sterilized jars (1/2 or 1 pint), and cover with melted paraffin as is done with jam or fruit preserves. Treat as you would with jam - store in a cool place and refrigerate after opening.

2 cloves garlic, minced **1 small onion, chopped** **2 TBS vegetable oil**	Saute until tender.
4 medium cans whole cranberry sauce **1 orange peel, chopped** **juice of one orange** **2 cups broken pecans*** **1-1/2 cup raisins** **1/2 cup vinegar** **1/2 cup brown sugar** **1 oz crystallized ginger, chopped** **1 tsp mustard seeds** **1/2 tsp black pepper** **1/2 tsp cayenne** **1/2 tsp ground allspice** **1/4 tsp salt** **1/8 tsp ground cinnamon**	Blend thoroughly and bring to a boil. Cook the mixture down until it is thick enough to slowly drop from a spoon (approximately 30 minutes). Stir frequently and be careful not to scorch.

***NOTE:** Walnuts can be substituted for pecans.

PARSLEY

Parsley is one of the few readily available fresh herbs primarily because it is used in large quantity as a garnish rather than as an herb. Italian parsley is a straight-leafed variety that is slightly more bitter. Chinese parsley is not parsley, but is the herb, cilantro (leaf of the coriander plant).

Other Poultry

With decreasing numbers of the family farms in this country came a reduction in the variety of poultry available for food. Ducks, geese, Guinea fowl, squab, and capons are no longer common fare. These specialty birds are still available in gourmet food stores and large supermarkets, but they are not commonly cooked outdoors. Many of these birds were not raised exclusively for food. Guinea fowl were kept in the hen house to awaken the sleeping hens if predators came in the night. Geese can rid a garden of insects without damaging a single plant, and their feathers are well suited to making pillows and feather beds. Ducks keep the farm pond in good condition.

These birds should be cooked using the same techniques as those used for chicken and turkey. If the bird is fat, be sure to remove rendered fat, and do not add too much oil or butter by basting. If the bird is dry, use a high oil content baste and take care not to overcook. If you choose the birds for their distinctive flavor, do not overpower them with highly seasoned sauces or intense wood smoke.

GUINEA FOWL

Guinea fowl were domesticated from wild fowl in West Africa (Guinea). They were imported to Europe by the Romans, who called them the Hen of Numidia. Although the distinction is seldom made outside of the poultry industry, "Guinea hen" is the term for a hen turkey. In lay conversation the terms "Guinea hen" and "Guinea fowl" are often used interchangeably.

Rock Cornish Hens

The Rock Cornish hen is a small, flavorful bird ideally suited to grill and smoker roasting as whole or split birds. They have ample fat to make them juicy and are small enough to be stuffed and roasted. Roast them on a grate or spit over indirect heat on a covered grill or on a moist smoker. If you choose to use split birds, have your butcher saw frozen birds in half to provide a clean, even split. Sweet basting sauces and glazes are excellent with Cornish hens. The herb and oil bastes, or barbecue sauces, listed under **Chicken** are also well suited to Rock Cornish hens.

Roasted Cornish Hens

Serves 4

Salt and pepper four whole birds inside and out. Place one-fourth of a small onion, a wedge of lemon, and a half strip of bacon inside each bird. Prepare any of the basting sauces below. Baste the birds when first placed in the cooker. If using a moist smoker cook for 1-1/2 hours before raising the lid. Continue to cook, basting every 30 to 45 minutes until done. If cooking with indirect heat on a covered grill, baste when first put on, but check after 30 minutes. Continue basting approximately every 30 minutes. Split birds can be cooked on indirect heat in a covered grill, or on very low direct heat of a covered or uncovered grill. Baste the birds as necessary, similar to chicken quarters. Any of the basting sauces for **Chicken Pieces, Whole or Split Chickens**, or **Roast Whole Turkey** can also be used. Wood smoke is suggested.

HERB BASTE

1/4 lb margarine	Melt margarine, blend, and simmer on low
1 clove garlic, minced	heat for 5 minutes.
1 tsp dried parsley	
1/2 tsp dried thyme	
1/4 tsp dried rosemary, crumbled	
2 TBS sherry	Remove from heat, add,
1/8 tsp cayenne	and blend thoroughly.

TABASCO BASTE

4 TBS margarine, melted	Blend ingredients thoroughly.
1/4 cup dry white wine	
1/2 tsp Tabasco	

GARLIC BASTE

1/4 cup olive oil	Saute for 5 minutes, but do not brown.
2 cloves garlic, minced	Remove from heat.
1/4 cup dry white wine	Add and blend thoroughly.

Barbecued Cornish Hens

Serves 4

Rub four hens inside and out with salt and white pepper. Cook on a moist smoker or indirect heat of a covered grill (grate or spit) with moderate amounts of mild wood smoke. Baste as required with **Vinegar and Oil Baste** or **Brady's Baste** (**Barbecued Pieces** under **Chicken**) until done and the skin begins to crisp. When the birds are almost done, begin basting with the sauce below.

2 slices bacon, diced	Saute until the vegetables are tender
1/2 small onion, chopped	and the bacon begins to brown.
1/4 bell pepper, chopped	
2 cloves garlic, minced	
3/4 cup vinegar	Add and simmer for 10 minutes.
1/2 tsp salt	
1/2 tsp black pepper	
1/4 cup catsup	Add, blend, and simmer on
1 TBS Dijon mustard	low heat for 10 minutes.
1/4 tsp cayenne	
1/4 cup dry white wine	Add, blend thoroughly,
	and strain entire mixture.

Oriental Cornish Hens

Serves 6

Have your butcher split (saw) three large Cornish hens in half, and let them thaw. Brush the birds with the sauce below and marinate refrigerate for 8 to 12 hours. Roast on a moist smoker until done (approximately 2 hours). This recipe can also be done on a covered grill with low indirect heat. If you use a covered grill, tend the birds carefully at first to make sure they do not cook too fast or burn. It may also be necessary to baste several times to prevent them from drying out, which is not generally necessary on a moist smoker.

3 cloves garlic, minced   Saute for 5 minutes, but do not brown.
3 TBS olive oil

1/2 tsp cayenne   Remove from heat and add.
1/2 tsp white pepper

3 TBS soy sauce   Add, blend, and let cool.
3 TBS oyster sauce
4 tsp sherry

Glazed Cornish Hens

Serves 3

Rub three small whole birds inside and out with salt and white pepper. Place two tablespoons of one of the glazes below inside each bird and turn to coat the inside. Baste the outside with the **Vinegar and Oil Baste**, or **Brady's Baste (Barbecued Pieces** under **Chicken)**, and place the birds on a moist smoker. Hickory wood smoke tends to overpower the flavor of these glazes, but moderate mild smoke is good. This recipe can also be done on a covered grill with indirect heat by placing the birds on a grate or rotisserie. Continue basting until the skin begins to brown and crisp. Stop basting and let the excess fat and basting sauce drip free of the birds. Begin basting with one of the glazes below, and baste heavily and thoroughly. Wait for the glaze to set then baste again. This can be repeated several times to build a thick glaze, but do not over cook.

ORANGE-SPICE GLAZE

1/4 cup brown sugar   Heat over low heat and stir until
4 TBS margarine   thoroughly blended.
3 TBS orange juice
1 tsp rum
1/4 tsp ground cinnamon
1/8 tsp ground nutmeg
1/8 tsp ground allspice
1/16 tsp ground cloves

PLUM GLAZE

1 cup plum jam   Blend ingredients thoroughly.
1 TBS brandy
1 TBS lemon juice
1/2 tsp Worcestershire sauce
1/4 tsp ground nutmeg
1/8 tsp ground cloves

Stuffed Cornish Hens

Serves 4

This is an excellent recipe for rotisserie cooking. The recipe makes approximately two quarts, which is adequate for stuffing four birds and have enough remaining to serve the birds on a bed of the rice stuffing. Salt and pepper four Cornish Hens inside and out. Prepare the stuffing below and fill the bird's body cavity, but do not pack it tightly. Skewer the birds so the two end ones have the neck end out. This prevents the stuffing from falling out. After the birds are stuffed and skewered, truss them with cotton twine so the wings and legs don't flop. Brush the birds with the basting sauce below and roast over moderate indirect or low direct heat. Light amounts of mild wood smoke can be used if desired. Cooking time with the stuffing is approximately 1 hour.

RICE STUFFING

1 cup rice — Boil and drain
2 cups mushrooms, finely minced — Saute until done.
1 TBS margarine
1 TBS olive oil

1/4 cup onion, finely chopped — Combine with ingredients above
1 TBS dried parsley — and bake covered in a 350° oven
1 TBS margarine — for 30 minutes.
1 tsp Foots' Season Salt*
1 tsp salt
1/2 tsp dried thyme

*NOTE: See Roasted Beef

BASTING SAUCE

3 TBS olive oil — Blend ingredients thoroughly.
1 TBS dry sherry
1 clove garlic, minced
1 tsp lemon juice
1 tsp Worcestershire sauce

Ducks

No one has raised the cooking of duck to a level comparable to the Chinese. Many of their recipes are quite elaborate; however, a few of the basic principles can be followed to provide a simple yet delicious entree. Duck is fatter than chicken and ducks larger than 4-1/2 pounds will be too fat. Parboiling will help remove some of this fat. The principle of roasting a duck is to carefully render the fat and remove it, leaving the skin crisp and the meat moist and sweet.

Chinese Roast Duck

Serves 4

Bring approximately one gallon of water to a boil. Immerse a four-pound duck in the water (be sure the duck is completely covered with water), let the water return to a boil, and boil for 5 minutes. Remove the duck, drain it, and pat the skin dry. Prick the skin in several places with a sharp fork. Prepare the cavity sauce below, pour 1/4 cup of it into body cavity. Turn the bird to coat the inside thoroughly. Set the remaining sauce aside. Roast on indirect heat in a covered grill, turning every 10 to 15 minutes until done (1-1/4 to 1-3/4 hours). A light amount of mild wood smoke is recommended. About 10 to 15 minutes before the duck is done, pour the liquids out of the body cavity, and thoroughly baste the outside with the basting sauce below. Serve accompanied by the table sauce below.

CAVITY SAUCE

2 TBS vegetable oil	Saute over medium heat for 5 minutes.
1-1/2 tsp orange zest, grated	
2 cloves garlic, minced	
2 green onions, sliced	
1/2 cup hoisin	Add and simmer for 20 minutes.
1/2 cup chicken stock	
2 TBS soy sauce	
1 tsp sugar	

BASTING SAUCE

3 TBS chicken stock   Blend ingredients thoroughly.
2 TBS soy sauce
2 TBS honey

TABLE SAUCE

1 cup chicken stock   Blend ingredients thoroughly and heat.
3/4 cup Cavity Sauce (above)

3 TBS cold water Thoroughly blend water and corn starch, and
2 TBS corn starch   slowly add to the sauce, stirring constantly
                                          until the sauce has thickened.

Orange Duck

Serves 4

Bring approximately one gallon of water to a boil. Immerse a four-pound duck in the water (be sure the duck is completely covered with water), let the water return to a boil, and boil for 5 minutes. Remove the duck, drain it, and pat the skin dry. Prick the skin in several places with a sharp fork. Rub the inside and outside of the duck with **salt** and fine ground **black pepper** (1/2 tsp each). Prepare the basting sauce below, pour 1/4 cup of it into body cavity, and turn to coat the inside of the duck thoroughly. Set the remaining sauce aside. Roast on indirect heat of a covered grill, turning every 10-15 minutes until done (1-1/4 to 1-3/4 hours). A light amount of mild wood smoke is recommended. About 10 to 15 minutes before the duck is done, pour the liquids out of the body cavity and thoroughly baste the outside with the basting sauce below. Heat the remaining basting sauce and serve it as a table sauce with the duck.

2 cups orange juice   Blend thoroughly and simmer on
1/4 cup brown sugar   low heat for 20 minutes.
1 TBS fresh orange zest, grated
1 TBS fresh ginger, grated
2 tsp soy sauce

1/4 cup Orange Curacao   Remove from heat, let cool,
                                              add, and blend thoroughly.

Capons & Geese

Capons and geese are fat birds. The primary concern when cooking them is to not have a greasy final result. Birds under ten pounds are easiest to handle. Even then, they are best done on a moist smoker; however, covered grills can be used with low indirect heat and caution. Lightly brush the bird inside and out with **melted margarine** and rub with the Sage Mix or Poultry Seasoning given below. These mixtures are easier to apply to the bird if it is thoroughly ground in a mortar with a pestle. Place **1/2 small onion, 1/4 fresh lemon**, and **1 stalk celery** (cut in sections) in the body cavity. Roast with moderate to heavy wood smoke. Baste as necessary with **Vinegar and Oil Baste** or **Brady's Baste** (**Barbecued Pieces** under **Chicken**). If the sage blend or poultry seasoning is omitted, any of the basting sauces from **Chicken Pieces** can be used.

Sage Mix

Makes 1-1/2 TBS

1 TBS rubbed sage
1 tsp salt
1/2 tsp white pepper

Poultry Seasoning

Makes 2-1/2 tsp

1 tsp dried thyme
1/2 tsp dried marjoram
1/2 tsp dried savory
1/2 tsp dried rosemary, crumbled

Seafood

A wide variety of seafood is well suited to grill and smoker cooking, but fish is the most common. **Fish** steaks and fillets are excellent when broiled. Whole fish can be roasted. Whole fish, filets, or steaks can all be smoked. Many species of **shark** are excellent for grill and smoker cooking because they are lean, firmly fleshed, and have no bone. Shark is sometimes referred to as a nonboney fish, but they are not closely related to fish. The word fish is not a biological term and has no specific meaning in terms of biological classification.

Certain species of fish have a strong flavor associated with their meat, skin, or lateral line. The **skin** of a trout has a characteristic flavor which many people enjoy. Removing the skin of a trout before cooking provides a more mildly flavored fish. Some species of saltwater fish have dark-colored or **red meat**, which is strongly flavored. Red-meat sport fish, such as Atlantic Bonito and Crevalle Jack are edible if properly bled and handled. Marinate thin slices of these fish in salt brine for two to three hours, then rinse thoroughly in fresh water and pat dry before cooking. This is essentially Kosher-style cooking. Some varieties of saltwater fish have dark-colored, strongly flavored meat associated with their **lateral line**. The lateral line is a pressure sensing canal in the skin of the fish that is often marked on the skin by color variations. Dark-colored lateral line meat should be removed before marinating or cooking.

Shellfish are biologically classified as **mollusks,** and include scallops, clams, oysters, and mussels. The entire clam, oyster, or muscle is generally eaten, while only the adductor muscle of the scallop is commonly eaten. The scallop's muscle is firm and easily skewered for broiling. Clams, oysters, and mussels can also be skewered, with slightly more difficulty. They are also excellent roasted in the shell or smoked on the half-shell.

Crustacea is the biological order that includes lobster, shrimp, and crab. Lobsters can be broiled in their shell, or the tail meat removed, sliced, skewered, and broiled. Shrimp are best when shelled, skewered, and broiled. Crab is not commonly cooked on grills or smokers, but broiled soft-shell crab is a tasty variation.

The muscle tissue of seafood has very little connective tissue, it is most tender when raw. The longer it is cooked the tougher it becomes, so exercise caution not to overcook. Crustaceans have very little fat distributed through their muscle, but often have concentrations of quite flavorful fat around the viscera. Fish, however, are divided into lean and fatty varieties, the latter having in excess of 5% fat by weight. The fat in fish is generally distributed throughout the meat, with some concentration around the viscera and backbone. One concern with fish is that its fat is polyunsaturated and will quickly go rancid. Rancid fish fat produces the so-called **"fishy" taste**. The fat of seafood has little effect on how it should be cooked; however, broiling is an excellent method of cooking fatty fish.

Broiled Seafood

Fish fillets can be broiled with or without skin and scales. In general, remove the skin of firm-fleshed fish. Small **sharks** can be filleted or steaked for broiling. **Catfish**, both fresh and saltwater varieties, should always be skinned. For less firmly fleshed fish, or thin fillets, leave the skin on to add strength. Broil these skin side down without turning. **Coarse-scaled fish** can be broiled with the scales on. Cooking scale side down protects the fish from radiant heat. This allows the fish to cook more slowly with conductive heat, even though it is directly over a hot fire. **Steaks** are usually cut thick enough to hold together while cooking. Steaks also have backbone, ribbone, and skin to hold the steak together.

Broiling shellfish (mollusks) can pose technical problems. Adductor muscles, such as with **scallops**, can be easily skewered. Whole animals, such as **oysters** or **clams**, are hard to keep on a skewer and too small to lay directly on the grate of most grills. The easiest way to broil them is to skewer them alternately with vegetables or pieces of fish for support. The concave side of a mushroom cap is ideal for this purpose. A slice of vegetable, such as zucchini or summer squash, can also be hollowed out slightly on the ends for this purpose. Another method is to wrap them in pieces of bacon that have been fried or microwaved until one-half to three-quarters done. Canadian bacon or sliced ham can also be used for wrapping. **Lobster** poses no problem in broiling, because their shell contains them nicely. However, lobster can also be removed from the shell, sliced and broiled or skewered, and broiled. **Shrimp** are best when peeled and skewered. Broiling soft-shell crab is slightly more difficult, because the legs tend to hang down through the grate.

Garlic Fish

Serves 4

Blend the basting sauce below and let it stand at room temperature for 1 hour. Marinate 2 pounds of fish fillets in a mixture of **1/2 cup lemon juice** and **1/2 cup dry white wine** for 30 minutes at room temperature. Remove from the marinade, let drain for 5 minutes, pat dry with paper towels and baste with the basting sauce. Let the fish marinate at room temperature for an additional 30 minutes. Broil over moderate direct heat until done.

1/4 cup catsup	Blend thoroughly and let stand at room temperature for 1 hour.
1/4 cup dry red wine	
6 cloves garlic, minced	
1 tsp dried cilantro	
1/2 tsp Tabasco	

Fish with Vegetable Sauce

Serves 6 to 8

Marinate 3 to 4 pounds of lean fish fillets in **1/2 cup lemon juice** for 1 hour in the refrigerator. Remove and pat dry with a paper towel. Brush lightly with olive oil. Sprinkle (lightly) with **salt, pepper**, and **fine bread crumbs**. Broil over direct heat until done. Remove to a heated serving platter, pour the sauce below evenly over the fillets, and serve. This makes a relatively large quantity of sauce, but it is difficult to reduce the quantities and retain the proper proportions.

2 TBS olive oil	Saute until vegetables are tender.
1 medium onion, chopped	
2 fresh semi-hot peppers, minced	
1 clove garlic, minced	
1/4 tsp dried rosemary, crumbled	
1/4 tsp dried thyme	
2 med. tomatoes, skinned, seeded, and chopped	Add and saute for 2 minutes.
3/4 cup mushrooms, sliced	
3/4 tsp black pepper	
1/2 tsp salt	
1/2 cup black olives, chopped	Reduce heat, add, and heat
1/3 cup dry white wine	until thoroughly warm.

Fish with Green Sauce

Serves 4

Sprinkle 2 lbs lean fish fillets with **lemon juice** and marinate refrigerated for 1 hour. Remove fillets, brush with **melted margarine** and lightly **salt and pepper**. Broil over direct heat until done and remove to a heated serving platter. Cover fillets with the sauce below and serve immediately.

1/4 lb butter or margarine   Saute for 5 minutes.
3 TBS dried chives
4-1/2 tsp dried parsley
1-1/2 tsp dried tarragon
3/4 tsp dried mint

3 cups fresh spinach,   Add and simmer until cooked down.
   deveined and chopped
1 tsp lemon juice
1/2 tsp salt

4 tsp lemon juice   Remove from heat, add,
                       and blend thoroughly.

Fish with Tomato Sauce

Serves 4

This recipe is suitable for any cut of firm, mild fish (catfish, swordfish, shark, etc.). The sauce is adequate to cover 2 lbs of fish. Prepare the sauce below, and thoroughly drench the fish with **lemon juice**. Let the fish sit at room temperature, in the juice, for 20 minutes. Then brush with **olive oil**, and lightly **salt and pepper**. Broil directly over a hot fire. Transfer the fish to a heated serving platter, and pour the tomato sauce over it.

3 slices onion, chopped   Saute until tender.
l clove garlic, minced
2 TBS butter or margarine
2 TBS olive oil

l jalapeno, minced*   Add and saute for 5 minutes.
l TBS dried parsley
1/4 tsp dried oregano
1/4 tsp dried basil

l can (8 oz.) Italian plum   Add, bring to a boil, reduce heat,
   tomatoes, chopped   and simmer for 30 minutes.
1/3 cup red wine
1/2 tsp black pepper
1/2 tsp sugar
1/2 tsp salt

***NOTE:** This item is optional, but it is not hot enough to make the sauce very spicy. Both the tomato and jalapeno can be added with or without their seeds.

CRAB BOIL

Crab boil is a commercially available seasoning blend used on the Louisiana and Mississippi Gulf Coasts for boiling shrimp, crab, and crawfish. Crab boil contains mustard seed, coriander seed, cayenne, bay leaves, dill seed, and cloves. Pickling spice can be substituted for Crab Boil.

Blackened Shark

Blackened fish is normally cooked in a cast iron skillet which is so hot it glows red. A similar procedure can be used on a grill, but the fish used must be quite firmly fleshed. Steaks or fillets (approxmately 1 inch thick) of large, lean firmly fleshed fish are recommended. The need for thick cuts of a firm fleshed fish is to allow quick handling over a very hot fire. Combine the ingredients below to form a dry seasoning. This makes enough for about three 1 x 4 x 12 inch fillets. It is easiest to make a larger quantity and store it in an old spice bottle with a shaker top inside a screw-on lid.

Sprinkle the fish (shark) with lemon juice and let it stand at room temperature for 15 minutes. Brush the fish thoroughly with olive oil and sprinkle liberally with the seasoning. Broil directly over a very hot fire. With a good hot fire, the fish will slightly char, or blacken. Cook 5 minutes on each side for a 1-inch-thick fillet. This seasoning, mixed with melted margarine or olive oil, can also be used to baste virtually any lean fish whether broiled or roasted.

1 TBS salt　　　　　　Blend ingredients thoroughly.
1 tsp cayenne
1 tsp white pepper
1 tsp dried oregano
1/2 tsp onion powder
1/4 tsp ground cumin
1/8 tsp garlic powder

Charcoal Broiled Alligator

This recipe is modified from an old Louisiana recipe for alligator. If you have access to alligator meat, try it, but if not, it is an excellent recipe for broiling lean fish. Marinate the alligator (fish) refrigerated for 3 to 4 hours in a liberal amount lemon juice. Remove the alligator (fish) from the marinade and let it drain for 5 minutes. Baste liberally with the sauce below. Broil the alligator (fish) directly over a hot fire. Rebaste when you turn the alligator (fish) and again when you remove it from the grill. Broiling time depends upon thickness of the alligator (fish).

2 TBS bacon drippings, melted	Blend
2 TBS vegetable oil	ingredients thoroughly.
l tsp Worcestershire sauce	

Grilled Fish with Jalapeno Bernaise

Serves 4

Sprinkle 2 pounds of fish fillets liberally with lemon juice and brush lightly with olive oil. Lightly salt and pepper to taste, or sprinkle with **Foot's Season Salt** (see **Roasted Beef**). Broil directly over a hot fire until done and remove to a serving platter. Lay slices of **very ripe avocado**, thinly sliced, on top of each fillet. Cover the fillets with the Bernaise Sauce below and serve immediately.

3 egg yolks	Blend thoroughly in a food processor or
3 TBS lemon juice	blender.
1 TBS jalapenos, minced	
1 tsp dried parsley	
1/4 lb butter or margarine,	Slowly add to food processor
melted and still bubbling	while blending.

Broiled Fish with Shrimp Salt

Brush fish fillets lightly with olive oil or melted margarine, and sprinkle with pepper and Shrimp Salt. Use approximately twice as much Shrimp Salt as you would normally use with ordinary salt. Broil fish directly over a moderately hot fire.

NOTE: This seasoning has a strong smell when bottled, too strong for some palates. However, when used lightly as a seasoning salt, it is mild and can be used on a variety of foods, including green salads.

Shrimp Salt

Makes 1/2 cup

Take approximately two quarts of heads and shells from cleaned fresh shrimp. This quantity will cover a cookie sheet. Dry the heads and shell thoroughly in a 250° F oven (2 to 3 hours) or in a microwave (5 to 10 minutes). The heads will take longer to dry than the shell from the tails. After drying, thoroughly pulverize the shells in a food processor. This will produce a wide range of particle size. Sift the ground shells in a strainer to remove the coarser particles. The final yield will be approximately 1/2 cup of finely powdered shell. Mix three parts powdered shell to one part salt (5 TBS powdered shell to 5 tsp salt).

Broiled Catfish with Vegetable Baste

Serves 4

A variety of fish can be used for this recipe, but catfish are especially good for grill cooking. Take 2 pounds of fish fillets and brush them liberally with the basting sauce below. Lightly salt and pepper them and let them stand for 15 minutes at room temperature. Broil directly over a moderate to hot fire, basting liberally when turned and just before removing them from the fire. This produces a very mild flavored fish which can be served plain, or with any of the table sauces under **Roasted Fish**.

1 cup dry white wine   Bring almost to a boil, reduce the heat,
1 clove garlic, crushed   and simmer covered for 1 hour.
1 stalk celery, sliced   Remove from stove and strain.
1/2 med. onion, chopped   Do not include the pepper and thyme
1 bay leaf   dregs in the bottom of the pan.
1 tsp salt
1/2 tsp dried thyme
1/2 tsp black pepper

2 TBS olive oil   Add to the strained vegetable stock and blend
2 TBS lemon juice   ingredients thoroughly.

Swordfish and Eggplant Kebabs

Serves 4

Cut 1/2-inch thick slices of eggplant into 1-inch squares. Remove the seeds and membranes from four semi-hot peppers and cut them into 1-inch squares. Blanch eggplant, peppers, and two crushed garlic cloves in lightly salted water for 5 minutes. Remove the eggplant and peppers from the water and set aside to drain. Cut 2 pounds of 3/4- to 1-inch thick swordfish steaks, or other firm lean fish, into one inch squares. Skewer the fish, alternating with pieces of pepper and eggplant. Baste thoroughly with the sauce below and broil directly over a hot fire with heavy mild wood smoke. Cook for 2-1/2 to 3 minutes per side (10 to 12 minutes total).

1/4 cup lemon juice   Blend ingredients thoroughly.
4 TBS margarine, melted
1 tsp Worcestershire sauce
1/4 tsp salt
1/4 tsp Tabasco

Broiled Shrimp

Serves 4

Shell and devein 2 to 2-1/2 pounds of large (10 to 15 per pound) shrimp. If they are frozen, thaw them before marinating. Prepare the marinade below, pour it over the shrimp and toss them, taking care to coat each shrimp. Marinate refrigerated for 1 to 2 hours. Remove shrimp from refrigerator and skewer so the skewer passes through each shrimp twice. Align shrimp so the skewers will lay flat on the grill. Broil directly over a hot fire on a covered grill. Cook approximately 3 minutes on each side. Bring the remaining marinade to a boil, reduce heat and keep it warm. Remove from grill, baste with remaining marinade and serve.

1/2 cup olive oil **1 medium onion, chopped** **3 cloves garlic, minced**	Saute until onion is translucent.
1 TBS dried parsley **1 tsp dried basil** **1 tsp dry mustard** **1 tsp salt**	Add, blend ingredients thoroughly, and saute on low heat for 15 minutes.
1 TBS lemon juice **2-3 dashes Tabasco**	Remove from heat, add, and blend ingredients thoroughly. Let stand for 15 minutes.

Barbara's Shrimp

Serves 3

This recipe calls for more black pepper than most, so use caution if you do not like spicy food. Prepare the sauce below and pour it, still warm from the stove (not hot), over 1-1/2 lb of large (l0 to 15 per pound) cleaned shrimp. Toss the shrimp and let them stand in the sauce for 30 minutes at room temperature. Remove the shrimp and skewer them, with the skewer passing through each shrimp twice. Align the shrimp so the skewers will lay flat while cooking. Brush additional sauce on the skewered shrimp so they are heavily coated. The sauce should be rather thick from congealing margarine and sticks to the shrimp. Broil the shrimp on a covered grill directly over a hot fire for 3 minutes on each side.

l/4 lb margarine	Saute for 5 minutes.
2 cloves garlic minced	
1 TBS black pepper	Add and saute for 1 minute.
l/4 tsp dried rosemary, crumbled	
l/8 tsp cayenne	
l/4 cup dry white wine	Remove from heat, add, and blend
4 tsp Worcestershire sauce	ingredients thoroughly.
l TBS lemon juice	
l/2 tsp salt	

Shrimp Hoisin

Serves 4

Shell and devein 2 to 2-1/2 pounds of large (10 to 15 per pound) shrimp. Prepare the marinade below. Marinate the shrimp in the refrigerator for 2 hours, but do not pour hot marinade over the shrimp or it will cook them. Drain the shrimp and pour the marinade into a sauce pan. Bring the marinade barely to a boil, reduce heat, and leave the sauce on a low heat to keep it warm.

Skewer the shrimp with the skewer passing through each shrimp twice. Align them on the skewers so they lay flat on the grill. Broil directly over hot coals on a covered grill for 3 minutes on each side. Slightly longer cooking time may be required on an open grill. Do not overcook the shrimp or they will become tough and lose their delicate flavor. Remove the shrimp from the skewers for serving. They can be served several ways. Simply put the shrimp on a platter and pour the reheated marinade over them and serve. A second way is to put the shrimp on a bed of boiled white rice. Pour the reheated marinade over the shrimp and rice, then top with a liberal amount of chopped green onions (including the tops) and serve. These shrimp can also be combined with the reheated marinade and served in a chafing dish as hot hors d'oeuvres.

1 TBS vegetable oil   Saute over high heat until garlic is
2 cloves garlic, minced   golden brown.
2 slices fresh ginger, minced

1/3 cup hoisin   Reduce heat, add, and blend ingredients
1/3 cup soy sauce   thoroughly. Simmer for 10 minutes.
1/2 tsp cayenne

Sweet and Sour Shrimp

Serves 4

This recipe has a sweet and sour flavor, but is not served in a large quantity of sauce as is commonly done with many "sweet and sour" dishes. Shell and devein 2 to 2-1/2 pounds of large (10 to 15 per pound) shrimp. Pass the skewer through each shrimp twice, and align the shrimp so they will lay flat for cooking. Baste the shrimp thoroughly with the sauce below, and broil directly over a hot fire for 3 minutes on each side.

5 TBS margarine   Blend ingredients thoroughly.
1 TBS honey
1 tsp lemon juice
1 tsp Worcestershire sauce
1 tsp Dijon mustard
1/4 tsp Tabasco

Lobster (Langosta)

The term lobster as used here is meant to include all of the "lobster-like" decapod crustaceans. There are three species of true lobster. One is found off the northeastern United States and Canada, one off northern Europe, and one off South Africa. More readily available in much of this country are various species of the "spiny lobster," which is commonly referred to by its Hispanic name, langosta, or variations of this word. Also included are the mantis shrimp (family Squillidae), sometimes caught and sold by shrimpers on the Gulf Coast. Frozen imported varieties such as a langostina and rock lobster can also be used.

Whole fresh lobsters of approximately 1 to 1-1/2 pound size are preferred, but frozen tails from comparable-sized ones are satisfactory. For live lobsters, insert a sharp knife into the back between the tail and body sections and sever the cord to kill them prior to cooking or preparing them for cooking. Put the whole lobster, or tail, on its back and split the underside lengthwise with a sharp knife. Do not cut through the back shell, but all the way through the meat. Virtually all of the lobster is edible except for the stomach or "lady," which is near the head. The gills (on the sides of the body inside the shell) will not hurt you, but are not especially flavorful. The bright red "coral" and the greenish "tomalley" are highly prized for their flavor. These can be either left intact and the entire lobster cooked, or they can be removed and mixed into a stuffing. For stuffing, remove the coral and tomalley and prepare the stuffing below for each lobster. Remove the black vein in the body cavity, rinse the cavity, and fill it with the stuffing mixture.

coral   Mash and blend thoroughly.
tomalley
2 TBS seasoned bread crumbs
1 TBS soft butter
1 tsp lemon juice

Brush the tail meat and stuffing, or body cavity with melted butter or lemon butter. Broil directly over a moderate fire, or on indirect with a hot fire. Cook for 10-15 minutes on each side and serve if not stuffed. If stuffed, cook the lobster on its back for approximately 20 to 30 minutes, depending upon size. Use caution; overcooking will make the meat tough. If smaller tails are used, reduce the cooking time.

Rather than a plain butter baste, lobster can also be marinated. Blend the mixture below, brush the split lobster with it and marinate refrigerated for 1 hour. After marinating, broil the lobster as previously directed. It can also be marinated and then stuffed. Split them and remove the tomalley and coral. Baste and marinate the tail and empty the body cavity. After marination, stuff as described above and broil. Be sure to also refrigerate the coral and tomalley while the lobster marinates.

1 TBS soft butter or margarine   Blend ingredients thoroughly.
1 TBS olive oil
1 TBS lime juice
1 TBS green onion, minced
1/2 tsp black pepper

Broiled Soft-Shell Crabs

Serves 4

These are slightly difficult to broil, because the legs tend to hang down through the grate. The difficulty is in cooking the body without burning the legs. Because of these difficulties, it is not easy to cook them in large numbers. Try a few for appetizers or a first course before attempting them in quantity for a party. Their flavor is excellent, so do not let these remarks prevent you from trying them. Clean one dozen crabs by removing their gills and cutting off the face (eyes and mouth parts). Marinate them refrigerated for 2 to 3 hours in the marinade below and broil them directly over a moderately hot fire until done (3 to 5 minutes per side).

1/2 cup olive oil   Blend ingredients thoroughly.
1/2 cup dry white wine
1/4 onion, minced
2 cloves garlic, minced
2 TBS lime juice
1 tsp Worcestershire sauce
1/2 tsp Tabasco

Spiced Oysters en Brochette

Serves 2

Fry or microwave four slices of bacon three-quarters done, then drain. Cut the bacon into thirds. Alternately skewer one dozen oysters, pieces of bacon, and fresh mushroom caps. You may also substitute thin squares of lightly browned ham or Canadian bacon. When skewering, start with a mushroom cap, insert the skewer through the top. Skewer an oyster next (pushing it into the cavity of the mushroom cap), then add a square of bacon. This will help to hold the skewered oyster. Apply basting sauce after each item is skewered. Repeat this sequence to fill the skewer. Reverse the order of the ingredients on the last one to help hold the last oyster on the skewer. Baste the filled skewer thoroughly with sauce, and broil over direct moderate heat for 8 minutes. Turn the skewers to cook for 2 minutes on each side. These can also be served as an appetizer.

3 TBS olive oil	Saute until translucent.
1 thin slice onion, minced	
2 cloves garlic, minced	
1/2 tsp salt	Add, blend ingredients thoroughly, and
1/2 tsp ground paprika	saute for 5 minutes.
1/2 tsp cayenne	
1/2 tsp black pepper	
1/2 tsp white pepper	
1/4 tsp dried thyme	
1/8 tsp dried oregano	
1/8 tsp dried basil	

Grilled Scallops

Serves 4

Marinate 2 pounds of scallops refrigerated for 2 hours in the marinade below. Skewer the scallops and grill directly over a hot fire for 6 to 8 minutes, depending on size. Turn the scallops at least two times during cooking. This recipe is also good for pieces of lean fish.

1 medium onion, chopped   Blend ingredients thoroughly.
1/2 cup olive oil
1/2 cup dry white wine
1 clove garlic, minced
1/2 tsp black pepper
1/4 tsp salt

Scallops en Brochette

If you have access to fresh scallops, they do not need much seasoning. Sprinkle the scallops lightly with lemon juice, toss them, and let them stand refrigerated for 30 minutes. Brush them lightly with melted margarine and skewer them. Lightly salt and pepper the skewered scallops and sprinkle them liberally with unseasoned bread crumbs. Broil the scallops directly over a hot fire on a covered grill for 6 to 8 minutes, turning several times to cook evenly. Very light mild wood smoke is good, but do not over do it.

SHARK

If you fish saltwater, do not overlook the shark as a source of food for outdoor cooking. Mako and Thresher sharks are highly prized for their meat, but other varieties are also delicious. However, some species do not freeze as well as others, and shark must be carefully handled. Shark blood is high in ammonia, and if a shark is not bled soon after catching, the meat will taste like ammonia. It is a good practice to soak shark fillets in salt brine for 1 to 2 hours, then rinse in cold water before cooking or freezing. If a faint ammonia smell is still present on cleaned fillets or steaks, marinate in the Shark Marinade for 48 hours. Marination in equal portions of dry white wine and lemon juice for 1 to 24 hours is also good, or highly season the meat (Blackened Shark).

Broiled Fish Fillets & Steaks

Broil fish directly over a moderately hot fire on a covered or uncovered grill. Baste one side of the steak or fillet and place it basted side down. Baste the top and cook. Most steaks or fillets take 4 to 10 minutes total cooking time, depending upon the fire's heat and thickness of the meat. After turning, rebaste the cooked side and continue cooking until the fish is done. If you have doubts about the fish being done, test it with a fork. It should flake.

Most lean fish are mildly flavored and go well with mild herbs. Stronger flavored or fatty fish can withstand flavors of stronger herbs and spices. Bear in mind, however, that there is a wide range in the fat content of fish; the division between lean and fatty is not sharp. Below are basting sauces for broiled fish. These can be used both as marinades or simply baste and broil. The sauces with oil do not congeal as much when marinated in the refrigerator as those containing margarine. These basting sauces also go well with roasted whole fish.

Garlic-Parsley Baste

Makes 3/4 cup

1/2 cup olive oil	Saute for 3 minutes.
3 cloves garlic, minced	
1 TBS dried parsley	
1/4 cup lemon juice	Remove from heat, add remaining
1/2 tsp salt	ingredients, and blend thoroughly.
1/8 tsp black pepper	

Vermouth-Dill Baste

Makes 1 cup

1/4 lb margarine
2 tsp dried dill weed

Saute for 2 minutes and remove from heat.

1/3 cup lemon juice
1/4 cup dry vermouth
l tsp salt
l tsp black pepper

Add, blend ingredients thoroughly.

Lemon Baste

Makes 2/3 cup

4 TBS margarine, melted
1/4 cup dry white wine
2 TBS lemon juice
zest of 1 lemon, grated
1/2 tsp salt
1/4 tsp black pepper
1/4 tsp Tabasco

Blend ingredients thoroughly.

Mixed Herb Baste

Makes 1/4 cup

4 tsp olive oil
1/4 tsp dried savory
1/4 tsp dried tarragon
1/4 tsp dried parsley
1/4 tsp white pepper
1/8 tsp dried dill weed

Saute for 2 minutes.

zest of 1/2 lemon, grated
2 tsp lemon juice
1/2 tsp salt

Remove from heat, add, and blend ingredients thoroughly.

Marinara Baste

Makes 1/4 cup

3 TBS margarine
l clove garlic, minced

Saute for 3 minutes.

l TBS dried parsley
1/2 tsp dried basil
1/2 tsp dried thyme
1/4 tsp salt
1/8 tsp dried oregano
1/8 tsp cayenne

Add, blend ingredients thoroughly, and saute for 3 additional minutes.

Sage Baste

Makes 1/3 cup

2 TBS olive oil
1 TBS rubbed sage

Saute for 3 minutes.

1/4 cup lemon juice

Remove from heat, add, and blend ingredients thoroughly.

Dill Baste

Makes 1 cup

4 TBS margarine
2 tsp dried parsley
l tsp dried dill weed
1/4 tsp salt
1/4 tsp black pepper

Saute for 3 minutes.

1/2 cup dry white wine
1/4 cup lemon juice

Remove from heat, add, and blend ingredients thoroughly.

Tabasco Baste

Makes 1/2 cup

6 TBS margarine l TBS dried parsley 1/2 tsp dried basil 1/4 tsp white pepper 1/4 tsp black pepper	Saute for 3 minutes.
2 TBS lemon juice 4-6 dashes Tabasco	Remove from heat, add, and blend ingredients thoroughly.

Picante Baste

Makes 1-1/4 cup

3 slices onion, minced l clove garlic, minced l can (8 oz) tomato paste 1/4 cup dry white wine 2 TBS jalapeno, minced l tsp ground paprika l tsp lemon juice 1/2 tsp sugar 1/2 tsp horseradish powder 1/4 tsp salt 1/8 tsp cayenne 1/8 tsp dried oregano 1/8 tsp ground cumin	Blend ingredients thoroughly, and simmer for 15 minutes.

NOTE: Use caution, this sauce burns easily. Use it only on the top of fillets which are not turned (with skin or scales left on), or baste only the top after turning.

Sweet Vermouth Baste

Makes 1/3 cup

3 TBS olive oil
2 TBS dry white wine
1 TBS sweet vermouth
1/4 tsp black pepper
1/8 tsp dried basil
1/8 tsp dried rosemary, crumbled
1/8 tsp salt

Blend ingredients thoroughly, let stand for 1 hour, and reblend.

Bahama Baste

Makes 1/2 cup

1/4 cup olive oil
1/4 cup lime juice
1/4 tsp bitters

Blend ingredients thoroughly.

Oriental Baste

Makes 1 cup

1/2 cup dry white wine
1/4 cup vegetable oil
2 TBS oyster sauce
1 TBS prepared horseradish
1 TBS Creole mustard
1 TBS chili sauce
1 TBS soy sauce

Blend ingredients thoroughly, let stand for 30 minutes, and reblend.

Seasoned Lemon Baste

Makes 1 cup

1/2 cup dry white wine
1/4 cup vegetable oil
1/4 cup lemon juice
1 tsp fresh onion, grated
1 tsp lemon zest, grated
1 tsp Worcestershire sauce
1/2 tsp Tabasco
1/2 tsp salt

Blend ingredients thoroughly, let stand for 30 minutes, and reblend.

CITRUS ZEST

Zest is the outer (colored) part of the skin of a citrus fruit. The inner (white) pithy portion of the skin has a bitter taste. When grated citrus skin is called for, use care to grate only the zest. In recipes where a bitter flavor is desired, use sliced or chopped fruit.

Marinated Fish Fillets & Steaks

Marinate 2 pounds of fish (or shark) fillets or steaks for 12 to 48 hours in the refrigerator. Remove the fish from the marinade and drain for 15 minutes. Brush the fish liberally with vegetable oil, olive oil, or melted margarine. Broil directly over a hot fire until done.

Soy-Lime Marinade

Makes 3/4 cup

1/4 cup dry white wine
1/4 cup soy sauce
1/4 cup lime juice

Blend ingredients thoroughly.

Citrus-Jalapeno Marinade

Makes 2 cups

1 cup grapefruit juice
1/2 cup orange juice
1/2 cup olive oil
2 TBS jalapenos, minced
1 clove garlic, crushed
1/2 onion, sliced
1 tsp dried cilantro
1/2 tsp salt

Blend ingredients thoroughly.

Shark Marinade

Makes 3 cups

2 cups dry white wine
1/2 cup olive oil
1/4 cup brown sugar
2 TBS soy sauce
1 TBS lemon juice
1/2 onion, sliced
1 clove garlic, crushed
1/4 tsp ground ginger

Blend ingredients thoroughly.

Seafood Kebabs

A variety of fish are suitable for skewer broiling, as are shellfish and crustaceans. Cubed fillets or steaks of firm-fleshed fish, shrimp, scallops, and slices of lobster can be alternated with vegetables or fruit, as done with lamb and beef shish kebabs. The same procedures should be followed for parboiling or microwaving and marinating vegetables as is outlined under **Seasoning**. Try constructing your own kebabs using the ingredients and basting sauces below.

Most fish is mildly flavored and goes well with the items listed under **Mildly Flavored Ingredients**. Mild fish can also be alternated with scallops, shrimp, or bacon-wrapped oysters. The Onion Baste, Oriental Baste, and Picante Baste listed below are recommended for mild fish. The sauces for **Grilled Fish (steaks and fillets)** can also be used.

Some fish are more strongly flavored and go well with more strongly flavored vegetables. Selected saltwater sport fish are quite edible, if properly prepared. Crevalle Jack and Bonito are examples of seldom eaten "red meat" sport fish that can be delicious. Cut their meat into 1-inch cubes and marinate them (refrigerated) for 2 hours in salt brine (1 cup water, 2 tsp noniodized salt). Remove the fish from the refrigerator and thoroughly rinse it in cold water. Pat dry and skewer, interspersed with items listed under **More Strongly Flavored Ingredients**. These can be basted with the Curry Baste, or any milder flavored basting sauce for fish.

MILDLY FLAVORED INGREDIENTS
large pitted ripe olives
avocado cubes
canned artichoke hearts (water packed)
canned hearts of palm
pineapple chunks
cubes of melon (cantaloupe or honeydew)
zucchini squash
summer squash
eggplant cubes
raw onion, slices or quarters
apple slices
cherry tomatoes

lemon slices
lime slices
fried bacon slices

MORE STRONGLY FLAVORED INGREDIENTS
pickled onions
large stuffed green olives
sweet pickles
pickled semi-hot peppers
whole bay leaves

Onion Baste

Makes 3/4 cup

1/4 lb margarine **l tsp dried chervil** **2 green onions, sliced**	Saute until tender.
l TBS lemon juice **1/2 tsp salt** **1/4 tsp white pepper**	Remove from heat, add, and blend ingredients thoroughly.

Oriental Baste

Makes 1/3 cup

2 TBS vegetable oil **2 TBS soy sauce** **2 TBS sherry** **l tsp sugar** **2 slices fresh ginger, minced**	Blend ingredients thoroughly, and let stand for 1 hour.

Picante Baste

Makes 1/3 cup

2 TBS margarine, melted
2 TBS lemon juice
1-1/2 tsp oriental chili sauce
1/2 tsp Worcestershire sauce

Blend ingredients thoroughly.

Curry Baste

Makes 1/2 cup

1/4 lb margarine
1 tsp curry powder
1/2 tsp salt
1/4 tsp white pepper

Saute for 3 minutes.

REFRIGERATION

The Egyptians manufactured ice for the Pharohs by setting pans of water (insulated on the bottom) in the desert at night. Radiation to the sky reduced the water temperature to the freezing point. In Europe and North America ice has long been cut from ponds in the winter, packed in sawdust, and stored underground for use during summer. There is debate about who developed the first mechanical refrigeration device. Oliver Evans is reported to have tested the first machine in 1805. In 1834, Jacob Perkins appears to have built the first operational refrigeration machine. In 1877, Joel Tiffany patented the refrigerated railroad car. In 1929, Clarence Birdseye was first to develop a process for quick-freezing foods. The development of refrigeration and frozen food have dramatically increased the variety and quality of foods available to people.

Roasted Fish

Roasting (baking) fish over smoky indirect heat is a good technique for whole fish and thick fillets. They should be cooked on indirect heat in a covered grill, but can withstand a relatively hot fire. Fish are fragile and handling them with tongs is tricky. They can be handled with a combination of spatula and tongs, which are adequate if you just want to experiment, but a fish holder is a good investment. If cooking whole fish, it is advisable to get one of the hinged wire fish holders. Make sure that the handles of the fish holder are heat-proof (metal), and that the holder will fit under the cover of your cooker.

Seasonings will not penetrate large fish; so a simple baste to keep it from drying out is adequate. Lemon butter (margarine) is good, but olive oil is recommended because of its lighter flavor. An equal quantity of margarine and olive oil is also a good combination. The fish should also be lightly salted and peppered. If more seasoning is desired, any of the basting sauces from **Broiled Seafood** can be used. Since larger pieces of fish need to be cooked longer, there is time to acquire a smoke flavor, and mild wood smoke adds a delightful taste. Since fish has a delicate flavor, do not overpower it with pungent wood smoke, such as hickory. Fresh herbs provide a delicate smoke flavor if thrown on the fire just before removing the fish from the cooker. Fennel is commonly used in France. Bay leaves are good and are available from wild trees in the southeastern United States. Roasted whole fish also goes well with a dressing (stuffing) and table sauces. Bread dressing with chopped onion and herbs is the most common, but seafood stuffings and chopped or sliced vegetables can also be used. If highly seasoned stuffings are used, a simple basting sauce is suggested. Dressing does not have to be used on whole fish; they can simply be basted inside and out and roasted. Sliced onions, lemons, or limes are also good for the inside of whole fish.

Scales should be removed, but leave the skin on whole fish with the exception of catfish. All species of catfish (fresh and saltwater) should be skinned before cooking. Before marinating or cooking, score whole fish by making cuts perpendicular to their long dimension every 1 -1/2 to 2 inches. Cut all the way to the bone. This allows seasoning to penetrate, reduces the cooking time, and simplifies serving at the table. Thoroughly baste fish, making sure to get spices or herbs in the cuts on the sides. If stuffing is to be used, stuff the fish and close the body cavity before scoring. A fish holder will help to hold the fish and stuffing together. A larger quantity of stuffing can be used if the head is left on the fish, and the gills and tongue removed. A fish holder can also be used to hold two small stuffed fish, or for containing stuffed fillets. Lay out a large skin-on fillet (skin side down), and put a layer of dressing on top of it. Place the second fillet skin side up on the top. Either place these directly in the fish holder, or tie with cotton string. Cook the fillets the same as with whole fish, basting as necessary.

┌────── JUICING CITRUS FRUIT ──────┐

Place a whole lemon, lime, or orange in a microwave for 45 seconds on full power before juicing it. You will extract more juice much more easily.

Dressings (Stuffing)

Vegetable Dressing

Makes 2-1/2 cups

1/2 cup onion, chopped	Saute until tender.
1/2 cup celery, chopped	
1/2 cup bell pepper, chopped	
3 TBS butter or margarine	
1 clove garlic, minced	
1 cup mushrooms, chopped	Add, saute until tender,
1 cup tomato, skinned, seeded, and chopped	and remove from heat.
1 TBS dried parsley	
1/2 tsp dried basil	
1/2 tsp dried thyme	
1/2 tsp salt	
1/2 tsp black pepper	
3/4 cup bread crumbs	Add and blend thoroughly.
1 TBS Romano cheese, grated	

Cheese Dressing

Makes 2 cups

1 cup bread crumbs
1/2 cup mushrooms, chopped
1/4 cup Romano cheese, grated
1/4 cup water
3 TBS butter or margarine, softened
2 TBS olive oil
1 small onion, chopped
1 tsp dried parsley
1/2 tsp dried basil
1/2 tsp salt
1/2 tsp black pepper

Blend ingredients thoroughly.

Bread Dressing

Makes 1 cup

6 TBS butter or margarine
2 green onions, sliced
2 stalks celery, chopped
2 tsp dried parsley
1 tsp white pepper
1/2 tsp salt
1/2 tsp dried thyme
1/4 tsp cayenne

Saute until tender.

3/4 cup bread crumbs
1/4 cup water

Add and blend thoroughly.

Shrimp Dressing

Makes 2 cups

2 TBS butter or margarine
2 green onions, sliced
1 stalk celery, chopped
1 clove garlic, minced
1/4 bell pepper, chopped

Saute until tender.

1/2 tsp salt
1/2 tsp dried basil
1/4 tsp dried oregano
1/4 tsp dried thyme
1/4 tsp cayenne
1/4 tsp black pepper
1/4 tsp white pepper

Add, blend thoroughly, and saute for 5 minutes.

1/2 lb shrimp, diced
1 tsp Worcestershire sauce

Add, saute until shrimp are pink, and remove from heat.

3/4 cup bread crumbs
3 TBS water

Add and blend thoroughly.

Crab Dressing

Makes 1-2/3 cups

1/4 cup olive oil
3 TBS butter or margarine
6 green onions, sliced
3/4 tsp dried thyme
1/2 tsp dried basil
1/2 tsp dried oregano
1/2 tsp black pepper
1/2 tsp salt

Saute for 15 minutes on low heat, and remove.

1-1/2 cups crab meat
1/3 cup bread crumbs

Add and blend thoroughly.

Table Sauces

Many people prefer to season their fish at the table with a sauce. Prepare the fish using only light smoke and a butter (margarine) or olive oil baste, possibly thinned with dry white wine and lemon juice. When preparing whole fish to be served with sauce, put sliced onion and lemon in the body cavity and possibly a few herbs, such as dill, thyme, or basil. **Tabasco Butter** or **Garlic Oil** (see **Cornish Hens**) are also good choices for basting. The table sauces below go equally well with broiled fish steaks and fillets.

Guacamole

Makes 2-1/3 cups

2 cups mashed avocado   Blend ingredients thoroughly.
1/4 cup mayonaise
6 slices bacon, fried crisp and crumbled
2 TBS lemon juice
1 TBS onion, minced
1/4 tsp chili powder
1/4 tsp salt
1/8 tsp garlic powder
1/8 Tabasco

Granny's Dill Sauce

Makes 1 cup

1/2 cup sour cream   Blend ingredients thoroughly,
1/2 cup plain yogurt   refrigerate for 24 hours, and
1 tsp Creole mustard   reblend.
1/4 tsp dried dill weed
1/4 tsp salt
1/8 tsp Tabasco

Yellow Remoulade Sauce

Makes 1-1/4 cup

6 TBS olive oil	Combine and let stand at room temperature
2 green onions, sliced	for 24 hours. Blend in a food processor.
1/2 cup Creole mustard	Add, blend thoroughly, let stand
3 TBS catsup	for 30 minutes and reblend.
1 TBS vinegar	
1 TBS lemon juice	
1/4 tsp Tabasco	

White Remoulade Sauce

Makes 1-3/4 cups

1/2 cup dill pickles, minced	Blend ingredients thoroughly in a
1 TBS Dijon mustard	food processor.
1 TBS dried parsley	
1 TBS dried tarragon	
1 TBS dried chervil	
1 tsp horseradish	
2 cups mayonnaise	Add and reblend.

Elaine's Tartar Sauce

Makes 1-1/2 cups

1 cup mayonnaise	Blend ingredients thoroughly in a
1/4 cup dill pickles, chopped	food processor.
3 TBS Creole mustard	
1 tsp lemon juice	

Jalapeno-Garlic Sauce

Makes 1 cup

3/4 cup mayonnaise
2 green onions, chopped
1 clove garlic, minced
2 tsp pickled jalapenos, minced
1 tsp lemon juice
1/2 tsp chili powder
1/4 tsp salt
1/8 tsp ground cumin

Blend ingredients thoroughly in a food processor.

COOKING WINE

Cooking wines, including sherry, contain salt and are of a very poor quality. For cooking, use a dry wine or sherry of a quality suitable for drinking.

Smoked Seafood

Smoking seafood includes an extremely wide range of techniques, which can be subdivided into hot smoking and cold smoking. **Hot smoking** cooks the fish (temperatures above 120°F). For **cold smoking** the fire is removed from the food and only the smoky dry air reaches the fish (temperatures below 90°F). Cold smoking does not cook. Salt is also used in conjunction with cold smoking to extract even more moisture. Hot smoking uses less heat than required for roasting, and the fish is cooked slower and is drier than roasted fish. Hot smoking can be done on a large, covered grill by putting a small fire at one end of the grill and fish at the other. It is advisable to fold a piece of aluminum foil over one rung of the grate so that it extends down between the fish and fire, and protects the fish from radiant heat. Leave some room below and on the ends of the foil to allow convection around it. A moist smoker is preferred because it allows no radiant heat, and the moist heat keeps the fish from drying too rapidly.

Florida-style smoking is commonly used for mullet, but the technique serves equally well for most small salt or fresh-water fish. The fish are split and smoked with salt and butter. A second style of hot smoking uses no basting, but the fish are marinated in brine before cooking. Brine marination and smoking can make many fish palatable that are otherwise considered unworthy of cooking. This is particularly true of dark-meat, oily, or strong tasting fish.

There are several ways to split a fish. The crude, but simplest, method is to remove the head and viscera, then lay it belly up and cut along one side of the backbone. Cut through the rib bones, but not through the back skin. Extend the cut all the way to the tail. Spread the two halves apart and press them flat. Leave the skin and scales on.

Florida Style Smoked Fish

Use plenty of mild wood smoke, such as apple or bay. Mesquite can also be used. Split the fish, leaving the skin on and sprinkle the meat lightly with salt, especially along the backbone. Place skin down and smoke for approximately 1 hour. Brush away the white juice that has started cooking out of the meat and lightly resalt. After another hour of smoking, baste with butter and lightly resalt. At this point the meat should be starting to darken. Continue basting and salting until the fish is done (about 4-5 hours). Be careful not to use too much butter, or the fish will become greasy.

RED HERRING

Smoked salmon (lox) has long been an expensive delicacy. Because of this, the herring common to northern European waters has long been dyed, smoked, and sold as a lox counterfeit. Hence, the term "red herring" means "something less than expected." The addition of red and yellow food dye to the brine recipes for smoked fish will achieve the same effect, if you want to experiment.

Smoked Shellfish

Shuck oysters, mussels, or clams; drain their juice, and leave them on the half-shell. Place the shells over very low, indirect heat on a grill or moist smoker. Use moderate to heavy amounts of mild wood smoke. You can double up by putting several on each shell. As they begin to dry on the surface, baste lightly with butter and lightly salt. Smoke up to 3 to 4 hours, turning occasionally. These can also be smoked along with fish. If you want them in quantity for a party or as ingredients for other dishes, place them in rows on a sheet of aluminum foil instead of their shells.

BRINE

Brine is a mixture of salt and water. The strongest brine normally used in cooking is a 10% solution, which is formed by dissolving 4-1/2 teaspoons of salt in 1 cup of water. This solution will float a raw egg, which is an old kitchen technique for testing the concentration of a brine. Marination in salt or salt brine will toughen meat. Sugar is usually added to a brine to counteract the toughening effect of the salt. The sugar is not added for flavor.

Brine Marinated

This style of smoking produces a dry fish, but one much lower in oils or fats (butter) than Florida style. This is an excellent recipe for fatty fish and the stronger flavored red meat fish. Fish done in this style are good as snacks, hors d'oeuvres, or ingredients in other dishes. The following recipes for brines should be used to prepare the fish for hot smoking. Use small whole skinned fish or skinned fillets. Marinate the seafood for 24 hours, refrigerated, in one of the following brines.

Simple Brine for Fish

Makes 1 quart

1 quart water
1/3 cup kosher salt (noniodized)
1/4 cup sugar
1 tsp black pepper

Blend ingredients thoroughly.

NOTE: This is a good basic brine recipe for fish. It is recommended for smoked fish that are to be used as an ingredient in other recipes.

Seasoned Brine for Fish

Makes 1 quart

1 quart water
1/3 cup kosher salt (noniodized)
1/4 cup brown sugar*
2 TBS lemon juice
2 cloves garlic, crushed
1 med. onion, chopped
1/4 tsp dried dill weed

Blend ingredients thoroughly.

*NOTE: Molasses can be substituted for the brown sugar.

Seasoned Brine for Other Seafood

Makes 1 quart

1 quart water
1/3 cup kosher salt (noniodized)
1/4 cup brown sugar
4 TBS soy sauce
1-1/2 TBS lemon juice
2 cloves garlic, minced
1 med. onion, chopped
2 slices ginger, minced

Blend ingredients thoroughly.

NOTE: Although this recipe was developed primarily for other seafood, it is also good for fish.

Table Sauces

Smoked fish can be served either as an appetizer or an entre. Either way it is good served with a table sauce. These two table sauces are designed specifically for brine-smoked fish.

Cucumber Sauce

Makes 1 cup

1 cucumber, peeled, seeds removed, and chopped **1/2 cup sour cream** **3 TBS white wine vinegar** **1 TBS dried chives** **1/2 tsp salt** **1/2 tsp dried dill weed** **1/4 tsp white pepper**	Blend thoroughly in a blender or food processor.

NOTE: This sauce is also a good substitute for tartar sauce. Try it with broiled or roasted fish. Another variation is to substitute plain yogurt for the sour cream, which alters the flavor and reduces the calories.

Curry Sauce (serve hot)

Makes 1 cup

2 TBS butter **2 TBS flour**	Blend over low heat and cook a light roux.
1 cup milk **1/2 tsp curry powder** **1/4 tsp salt** **1/8 tsp white pepper**	Increase heat to medium, add ingredients, and stir with a whisk until thick and smooth.

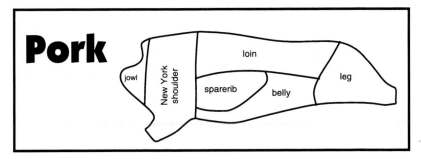

Only one-third of a hog is used for whole meat. The remainder is processed for lard and sausage. Because the bulk of a hog goes to processed meat, packing houses seldom distribute pork carcasses. They are usually butchered into primal cuts for fresh meat distribution or processing. The carcass is divided into six primal cuts: the jowl, New York shoulder, loin, spareribs, belly, and leg. The jowl is mostly fat, and the belly is bacon. The New York shoulder, loin, spareribs, and leg are butchered for fresh meat. The leg is also processed for ham.

Large cuts of the loin are termed **bone-in loin roasts**. With this roast, be sure the butcher cuts the chine (backbone) at regular intervals to facilitate carving. If the loin is sliced, the result is **pork chops**. The **boned loin roast** and **tenderloin** are the choicest roasts of pork. The boned loin usually comes with a modest amount of peripheral fat, while the tenderloin usually has almost no peripheral fat. The rib bones, when removed from the loin, are termed **back ribs**. **Spareribs** are the lower section of ribs below the loin. **Country ribs** are not ribs at all, but are slices from the shoulder end of the loin.

The New York shoulder is subdivided into the **Boston butt** or **blade shoulder**, which is the upper section, and the **picnic shoulder**, which is the leg end. The butt contains the shoulder bone and first few ribs. Its lean meat is interspersed with fat. These are available bone-in, or boned, rolled, and tied. Although tasty and tender, there is much more fat on a butt than on a loin roast. However, there are two excellent uses for the butt. One is to cut **pork steaks**, also known as **blade steaks**, by slicing a bone-in butt at right angles to the shoulder bone. The steaks can be cooked on low direct or indirect heat until the fat is rendered and eaten fat and all, just like bacon. The second is to buy a **boned butt** and trim all possible fat. The result of the latter is several small (3"-5" by 1") pieces of lean meat that have excellent flavor and are good for small quantities of lean pork. The lean pieces are excellent for Chinese roasted, or barbecued, pork. The butt and shoulder are excellent cuts for very slow cooking and heavy smoke (barbecue) on a moist smoker.

Fresh ham is unprocessed, is available boned or bone-in, and should be cooked well done, similar to other pork roasts. A number of techniques are used for processing hams, but only the imported Prosciutto and Wesphalian, or sliced and packaged sandwich ham, can be eaten "as is." Other processed hams should not be eaten without cooking to an internal temperature of at least 170° F. The "old-style" cured, or "country," hams are not suitable for grill or smoker cooking. They are tough and salty, and a different style of cooking is recommended. Hams, or pieces of ham, are available in a variety of sizes. It is generally preferable to chose a piece of the desired size and cook it as a roast, remembering that processed ham tastes like "ham" and fresh ham tastes like a pork roast. Slices of **processed ham** can also be broiled on direct heat, if not too thick.

Pork **link sausages** are an excellent choice for grilling. **Bulk sausage** is not commonly cooked on grills or smokers; however, patties can be cooked like hamburgers.

HOT SAUCE PRIMER

The most popular style of hot sauce used in this country is the thin, red, vinegar-based type which has become synonymous with the brand name *Tabasco*. Pepper sauce is the name commonly applied to the small green chilies bottled in vinegar. Oriental-style hot sauces are less common. Oriental chili sauces are thick and red, and are made from fruit, vinegar, and chilies. These usually come from Southeast Asia and are available in oriental groceries and selected supermarkets. American-style chili sauce is quite mild and similar to catsup. Chili oil consists of chili pepper flakes in oil, is very hot, and is often served with Hunan-style food. Oil in a hot sauce makes it appear hotter. Salsa and Pica de Gillo are relatively mild Mexican sauces consisting of chopped onions, tomatoes, chilies, and cilantro. There are also a variety of red pepper or chili pastes which are generally quite hot. Harissa, used in Arabic cooking, is an example of this type. Harissa is available in many specialty food stores, and comes in small cans and toothpaste-type tubes.

Barbecued Pork

Pork should be barbecued very slowly with moderate to heavy wood smoke. Marinades and either dry rubs or thin basting sauces are recommended. Thin barbecue sauces for pork are predominantly vinegar, salt brine, and spices. Dry-rub recipes are included in this book, but they are not commonly found in most cookbooks, magazines, or newspapers. Thick basting sauces should not be used until after the meat is completely cooked. Thick sauces for pork are generally made from fruit, such as peach or apricot, or consist of a combination of mustard and syrup (molasses or sorghum). Thick tomato basting sauces can also be used (see **Barbecued Beef**). Oriental-style barbecue marinades and basting sauces usually contain hoisin, are moderately thick, and should be used only on lean pork. Many varieties of wood are satisfactory for smoke flavored pork barbecue, but hickory or pecan (a variety of hickory) are traditional. Oak is also a good choice for pork barbecue.

Spareribs can be cooked as a whole side, or cut into strips approximately 2 inches wide. The latter is common for Chinese-style ribs. **Back ribs** are smaller, but have excellent flavor. **Country ribs** are thicker and have more meat. **Pork steaks** (butt slices through the shoulder blade) are not butchered in all parts of the country, but most butchers will cut them for you. The best technique for barbecuing spareribs, other thin cuts of pork, or lean pork barbecued Chinese style is to hang them in a moist smoker. This allows the rendered fat to drip free. Pork steaks are a good choice for picnics (sliced 1/2 inch thick) because they can be cooked on low direct heat of an open grill, but indirect heat on a covered grill is best. The peripheral fat along the edge of steaks, chops, or fresh ham slices does not pose a problem. With these thin cuts, fat can be rendered until it is as crisp as fried bacon. **Loin chops** or slices of

VINEGAR

Vinegar is produced by the acetic fermentation of alcohol. There are several major varieties, each with slightly different flavors. Distilled vinegar is clear and colorless, has an acidity of approximately 4%, and is used primarily for "barbecue" type sauces. Wine vinegars, both red and white, have a mild flavor and an acidity of approximately 5%. They are used primarily in marinades and table sauces. Malt vinegar has a stronger flavor with an acidity of 5-6%. Malt is simply grain that has sprouted. When sprouted grain is used to make fermented products such as beer or vinegar, it produces a distinctly different flavor from that of unsprouted grain. Malt vinegar is traditionally sprinkled over fish and chips. If you have trouble procuring it try one of the national chains of fish-and-chip restaurants. Herb vinegars are wine vinegar in which herbs have been soaked.

fresh ham are also good, as are pork **link sausages**. For Chinese-style barbecue, pieces of meat can be cut from the **Boston butt** and trimmed of fat. For sliced barbecue, a **boned loin roast** is good. **Pork shoulders** and **butts** are roasts that require longer to cook, but yield tender juicy meat. Large cuts, such as roasts or **fresh hams**, are good if sliced meat is desired. These larger cuts can be cooked on covered grills with indirect heat, but moist smokers are recommended.

Barbara's BBQ

Serves 4

Baste 4 pounds of lean pork with the mixture below, and marinate in the refrigerator for 8 to 24 hours. Cook on very low direct or low indirect heat of a covered grill, or moist smoker. Use moderate to heavy wood smoke preferably oak, hickory, or pecan. Baste as necessary with the remaining sauce until the meat is done.

1 cup vinegar   Blend and simmer over
1 small onion, sliced   low heat for 1 hour.
1/2 lemon, sliced
1/4 cup brown sugar
4 TBS margarine
1-1/2 tsp Worcestershire sauce
1 tsp salt
1 tsp black pepper
1 tsp cayenne
1/2 tsp ground allspice

Vinegar Spiced BBQ

Serves 4

Marinate 4 pounds of lean pork in the refrigerator for 4 to 8 hours in the marinade below. Remove the meat from the marinade and let it drain on a plate for 15 minutes. Pat the meat dry with a paper towel and brush lightly with vegetable oil. Rub it thoroughly with the dry rub and roast with heavy smoke.

MARINADE

1 cup water
1 cup vinegar
4 TBS brown sugar
4 tsp salt

Blend ingredients thoroughly.

DRY RUB

1 tsp black pepper
1 tsp chili powder
1 tsp dry mustard
1 tsp ground paprika
1/2 tsp cayenne
1/2 tsp ground cumin
1/8 tsp ground allspice

Blend ingredients thoroughly.

BBQ with Brown Sauce

Serves 4

Prepare the sauce below. Roast 4 pounds of lean meat over indirect heat with moderate to heavy wood smoke and baste with the sauce below as necessary. Depending on the size of the cuts of meat and the heat of the fire, cook until only 1/2 hour cooking time remains. Add **1 can (8 oz) tomato paste** to the remaining basting sauce, and blend thoroughly. Continue basting the meat until done. Caution should be used not to burn or char the meat once the tomato paste has been added to the basting sauce.

1/2 cup vegetable oil	Saute until translucent.
1 medium onion, chopped	
1 clove garlic, minced	

1/2 cup water	Remove from heat, add, and blend the
1/2 cup vinegar	ingredients thoroughly.
3 TBS Pickapeppa sauce	
2 TBS lemon juice	
1 TBS Worcestershire sauce	
1 tsp black pepper	
1/2 tsp cayenne	
1/2 tsp salt	

Beer Ribs

Serves 4

Trim excess fat from 4 pounds of spareribs and marinate in the mixture below for 4 to 24 hours refrigerated. Remove the meat after marinating and drain on a plate for 15 minutes. Brush the meat lightly with vegetable oil and sprinkle the meat liberally with black pepper. Cook on very low direct or low indirect heat of a covered grill, or moist smoker. Use moderate to heavy wood smoke.

1 cup beer
1/2 cup lemon juice
1/2 cup soy sauce

CHINESE SEASONING

The Chinese seasonings called for in this book are; hoisin or sweet bean sauce (Hoi Sin Deung), yellow bean sauce (Yeun Shoai She Deun), oyster sauce (Ho Yau), plum sauce (So Mooi Tseung), and five-fragrance powder (Mm Heung Foon). Plum sauce is also commonly referred to in this country as duck sauce. These are all readily available in oriental grocery stores and many supermarkets.

Spicy Oriental Ribs

Serves 4

Trim excess fat from 4 pounds of spareribs. Marinate 2 to 6 hours in the mixture below. Remove ribs from the marinade, drain on a plate for 15 minutes, and baste thoroughly with the sauce below. Cook the ribs with indirect heat of a covered grill, or a moist smoker, with mild wood smoke.

MARINADE

1/3 cup soy	Blend ingredients thoroughly.
1/3 cup sherry	

BASTING SAUCE

2 TBS vegetable oil	Saute for 3 minutes.
2 TBS sesame oil	
4 cloves garlic, minced	
2 tsp fresh ginger, grated	

1/2 tsp cayenne	Add, blend thoroughly,
1/2 tsp black pepper	saute for 1 minute.
1/8 tsp ground clove	

1/4 cup water	Remove from heat, add, and blend
1/4 cup vinegar	thoroughly.
1 tsp salt	

Five-Fragrance Ribs

Serves 4

Trim excess fat from 4 pounds of spareribs and brush them thoroughly with the marinade below. Marinate 6 to 12 hours in the refrigerator. Cook the ribs with indirect heat of a covered grill, or moist smoker, with mild wood smoke.

1/3 cup soy sauce   Blend thoroughly and
1/3 cup sherry   simmer for 10 minutes.
2 TBS vinegar
6 cloves garlic, minced
1 TBS fresh ginger, grated
1 TBS sesame seed oil
1/4 tsp five-fragrance seasoning

Indonesian Ribs

Serves 4

Trim excess fat from 4 pounds of spareribs and brush them thoroughly with the marinade below. Marinate 6 to 12 hours in the refrigerator. Cook the ribs with indirect heat of a covered grill or a moist smoker, with mild wood smoke.

2 TBS soy sauce   Blend ingredients thoroughly.
2 TBS sherry
2 TBS brown sugar
2 tsp curry powder
1 tsp five-fragrance powder
1 tsp black pepper
1/2 tsp cayenne
1/2 tsp garlic powder

Thick Sauces

For thick sauces, pork should first be rubbed with vegetable oil and lightly salted and peppered (black pepper). If you prefer barbecue a bit spicy, add cayenne. Roast the meat slowly on very low direct heat or low indirect heat of a covered grill, or best of all a moist smoker. Use moderate to heavy wood smoke of almost any variety. When the meat is cooked, begin basting with the thick sauce. Several applications over a period of 15 to 30 minutes is adequate. Tomato-based sauces and commercial barbecue sauces are also good. See **Barbecued Beef** and **Barbecued Pieces** (under **Chicken**).

Apricot Sauce

Makes 2 cups

1 can (16 oz) apricots, drained
3/4 cup vinegar
1 TBS Worcestershire sauce

Puree in blender
or food processor.

1 TBS Dijon mustard
1/2 tsp cayenne
1/4 tsp ground cinnamon
1/4 tsp ground nutmeg
1/8 tsp ground cloves

Add additional ingredients and
blend thoroughly.

Peach Sauce

Makes 1-1/2 cups

2/3 cup peach preserves, pureed
1/3 cup apple butter
1/3 cup vinegar
1/4 cup brown sugar
1 TBS Worcestershire sauce

Blend ingredients thoroughly.

OPTIONAL

1/2 tsp ground ginger
1/4 tsp garlic powder

Molasses Sauce

Makes 1 cup

1/3 cup molasses
1/3 cup Dijon mustard
1/3 cup distilled vinegar

Blend ingredients thoroughly.

Sorghum Sauce

Makes 1 cup

1/2 cup sorghum*
1/4 cup Dijon mustard
1/4 cup distilled vinegar
2 TBS Worcestershire sauce
1/2 tsp salt
1/2 tsp cayenne
1/2 tsp black pepper

Blend ingredients thoroughly.

*NOTE: Molasses or dark corn syrup can be substituted for sorghum, but will produce a slightly sweeter sauce.

Hunan Sauce

Makes 1 cup

1/4 cup honey
1/4 cup soy sauce
1/4 cup dry white wine
2 TBS distilled vinegar
2 TBS orange marmalade
1/2 tsp black pepper
1/2 tsp cayenne
2 cloves garlic, minced
1/4 slice ginger, minced

Blend over low heat until it begins
to bubble; remove from heat.

Thin Sauces

The sauces below can be used as both marinades and basting sauces. They do not burn easily and can be applied at any time during cooking. Thin basting sauces can also be followed by thick basting sauces, after the meat is cooked.

Pepper Baste

Makes 1 cup

4 TBS margarine, melted
2 TBS brown sugar

Melt margarine and blend ingredients thoroughly.

1/2 cup vinegar
1 tsp Worcestershire sauce
1 tsp cayenne
1/2 tsp salt

Remove from heat, add, and blend ingredients thoroughly.

All Purpose Baste

Makes 1-1/4 cups

1/2 cup water
1/2 cup vinegar
2 TBS Worcestershire sauce
2 tsp salt
1 tsp chili powder
1/2 tsp black pepper
1/2 tsp cayenne
1/2 tsp celery seed, crushed
1/2 tsp ground paprika
1/2 tsp onion powder
1/4 tsp garlic powder

Blend ingredients thoroughly, and let stand for 1 week or more.

NOTE: If using this recipe for barbecued chicken add 1/4 cup vegetable oil for a basting sauce.

Dry Rubs

Blend one of the dry rubs below and rub it evenly over 4 pounds of pork, trimmed of excess fat. Marinate refrigerated for 12 to 24 hours. Roast the meat with indirect heat and moderate to heavy wood smoke. A moist smoker is ideal, especially if the meat is hung from hooks. If you like peppery ribs, increase the amount of pepper for the same quantity of salt and meat. If you prefer more moist meat, brush it lightly with vegetable oil just before cooking. These seasonings can also be followed by thick basting sauces, after the meat is cooked.

Mild Dry Rub

Makes 1-1/2 TBS

1-1/2 tsp salt
1-1/2 tsp ground paprika
3/4 tsp cayenne
1/2 tsp black pepper
1/4 tsp garlic powder
1/8 tsp dried oregano
1/8 tsp celery seeds

Blend ingredients thoroughly.

Seasoned Dry Rub

Makes 1-3/4 TBS

1-1/2 tsp salt
1 tsp black pepper
1 tsp onion powder
1/2 tsp cayenne
1/2 tsp ground paprika
1/2 tsp garlic powder
1/2 tsp ground allspice
1/8 tsp ground cumin

Blend ingredients thoroughly.

Pepper Dry Rub

Makes 2 TBS

2 tsp salt
2 tsp black pepper
2 tsp cayenne

Blend ingredients thoroughly.

Sweet Dry Rub

Makes 1-1/2 TBS

1 TBS brown sugar
1-1/2 tsp salt
1 tsp cayanne
1/2 tsp black pepper
1/2 tsp white pepper
1/2 tsp dried oregano
1/4 tsp garlic powder
1/4 tsp ground cumin

Blend ingredients thoroughly.

SOY SAUCE

There are two types of soy sauce, dark and light. Dark soy has a salt content of 12%, and is the type most commonly found in grocery stores. Light soy is milder flavored, has a salt content of approximately 16 to 18%, and is often available only in oriental grocery stores. In Chinese cooking, light soy is used most commonly in sauces and soups, while dark soy is more common in dark gravies. Soy sauce is saltier than most salt brines, so use caution when adding salt to recipes containing soy sauce.

Roasted Pork

Cooking a pork roast is much the same as a beef roast. They should be cooked slowly on indirect heat of a covered grill or a moist smoker. Boneless roasts are good choices for rotisserie cooking. Even bone-in roasts can be spitted if the bones are to the side, such as with a loin roast. Wood smoke flavoring of almost any variety goes well with pork.

Seasoning the thick layer of fat that surrounds a pork roast will have no effect upon the final result. The seasoning will not penetrate to the meat, most people will only cut off the fat (with the seasoning). Slicing through the fat will let some seasoning through to the meat. A diamond pattern of slices is commonly made in the peripheral fat of hams before cooking. However, the preferred method for grill and smoker cooking is to trim the peripheral fat layer to a uniform thickness of approximately 1/8 inch. The exact thickness depends upon the size of the roast and heat of the fire. With experience, the final result will be a well-seasoned, crisp outer crust and a juicy interior. It takes some practice to have the fat layer rendered and crisp just as the meat finishes cooking. If the roast does not have a peripheral fat layer, such as a tenderloin, thick sauces or glazes are good when applied toward the end of cooking. When no peripheral fat is present, caution should be used not to overcook and dry the meat. Some basting with oil or a sauce containing oil is recommended. Deep seasoning is best accomplished by marinating for 1 to 2 days.

A **sirloin roast** is from the ham end of the loin, and is available bone-in, or boned rolled and tied. Boned roasts consist of two halves, from opposite sides of the backbone, which are tied together. The **center cut loin roast** is also available bone-in or boned. The **blade end loin roast** is available bone-in, or boned with the two pieces (one from each side of the backbone) reversed, rolled, and tied. The latter is known as a **bladed pork roast.** Thick **chops** (two or more inches) from any section of the loin are good choices for roasting. The choice cuts from the loin are center cut.

The **Boston Butt** is a fat, but tasty roast from the front end of the back, similar to the chuck of a beef. The **pork shoulder** is the lower cut of the New York shoulder, which includes the front leg. It is quite fat, but has good flavor. Small lean pieces of the shoulder (3-5 inches by 1 inch thick) trimmed of fat, are an excellent choice for Chinese style roast pork or barbecue.

The **pork leg**, or **ham**, is a large lean cut of meat well suited to roasting. Both fresh and processed hams are good choices. **Fresh hams** have a taste similar to other pork roasts, while **processed hams** have a distinctive "ham" taste. Whole hams are often too large for most outdoor cooking and are often butchered into smaller roasts. These are the butt end toward the hip; the **shank** or **hock**, which is toward the foot; and the center cut. The large lean center cut of fresh ham is often cut into two boneless roasts; the **knuckle** and the **cussion**. Both of these are rolled and tied, and have a peripheral layer of fat. These cuts are somewhat like the top and bottom round roasts of beef. With large hams the cussion roast is sometimes further divided into the **inside ham roast** (the top half) and the **outside ham roast** (bottom half). These are also rolled and tied, with a layer of peripheral fat covering them. The hock is not a meaty cut suitable for roasting. The ham butt can be used, but the more common roast is the **completed fresh ham butt** roast. This roast is two boned fresh ham butts rolled and tied together.

Processed hams are normally subdivided into the hock, the center cut, and the butt. These are often further subdivided into smaller prepackaged or **canned hams**, known by a variety of names. These are usually quite lean and well suited to roasting. Thick (2 to 3 inch) slices of either fresh or processed ham are also good choices for roasting.

GINGER

Ginger is available as ground ginger (dry powder), as fresh roots, and as candied root slices. All three forms are called for in this book. Ground ginger is readily available in a small can or bottle and lasts for a long time at room temperature. Fresh ginger is available in most supermarkets. Wrap fresh ginger in aluminum foil and freeze it. When it is needed simply grate it, still frozen, and return the unused portion to the freezer. Candied ginger is generally available only in specialty stores, but will keep refrigerated in a sealed container for months.

Hickory Roast Pork

Serves 4 to 6

This is a simple, tasty recipe. Trim excess fat from any 2 to 3 pound boneless cut of fresh pork, and rub with the mixture below. A loin roast is an excellent choice. This mixture provides a tasty outer crust and juicy lean pork in the center. Roast very slowly with low indirect heat on a covered grill or a moist smoker. Use heavy hickory smoke and a meat thermometer to insure the proper degree of cooking.

2 cloves garlic, minced   Blend ingredients thoroughly.
2 tsp salt
1 tsp coarse ground black pepper

Cajun Pork Loin

Take a bone-in pork loin sliced at regular intervals. Insert **1 clove garlic** crushed, a 2 inch length of **green onion** split lengthwise and flattened, and a sliver (1/8"-1/4") of a **jalapeno pepper** between each cut. Make sure all of the cuts are closed; if necessary use cotton string to tie the roast. Place the roast on a moist smoker with heavy hickory or pecan wood smoke. Cook until thoroughly blackened by smoke and the meat is done. The use of a low fire will require longer cooking, but will produce more smoke flavoring. The addition of coals will be required, or put the meat on overnight and rebuild the fire in the morning. Cooking time will vary between 8 and 12 hours, depending upon conditions.

Herb Roasted Pork

Serves 4 to 6

Trim a 2 to 3 pound loin or tenderloin roast of excess fat. Mix one of the seasoning mixes below, rub the meat thoroughly with **vegetable oil**, and then with the seasoning mix. The meat should be slowly cooked on low to moderate indirect heat, either on the grate or on the spit of a covered grill. A moist smoker is also good. Use wood smoke of almost any type, depending upon taste.

SAGE MIX

1 tsp black pepper   Blend ingredients thoroughly.
1 tsp salt
1/2 tsp dried rubbed sage
1/4 tsp ground ginger
1/4 tsp ground nutmeg
1/4 tsp dried thyme
1/4 tsp cayenne

FENNEL MIX

1 tsp lemon zest, grated   Blend ingredients thoroughly.
1 tsp salt
1/2 tsp black pepper
1/2 tsp cayenne
1/2 tsp fennel seeds, crushed
1/4 tsp ground coriander
1/4 tsp garlic powder

Oriental Marinated Pork

Serves 6 to 8

Marinate a 3 to 5 pound pork roast in the marinade below for 12 to 24 hours refrigerated. After marinating, remove the roast and let it drain on a plate for 15 minutes. Brush meat lightly with **vegetable oil**, and rub with a mixture of **1/4 tsp cayenne** and **1/8 tsp five-fragrance seasoning**. Roast on moderate indirect heat with moderate mild wood smoke.

1/4 cup soy sauce	Blend ingredients thoroughly.
1/4 cup dry red wine	
1/4 cup sherry	
2 cloves garlic, minced	
2 TBS vegetable oil	
1 TBS Worcestershire sauce	
1/4 tsp cayenne	

ALLSPICE

Allspice is not a blend of spices, but comes from a specific plant native to the Caribbean region. It's the only spice grown exclusively in the Americas. For a long time allspice was ignored by early explorers and colonists who mistakenly thought it was a variety of pepper.

Glazed Pork Roast

Serves 4 to 6

Trim a 2 to 3 pound boned pork loin or tenderloin roast of fat. Brush with vegetable oil, and liberally sprinkle it with finely ground black pepper. Cook on indirect heat of a covered grill, or a moist smoker. Mild wood smoke can be used, if desired. When the roast is done, thoroughly brush it with one of the glazes below. Place the roast as far back from the fire as possible and let the glaze set. Two coats of glaze over a period of 10 minutes is recommended.

APRICOT GLAZE

1/4 cup apricot jam   Blend ingredients thoroughly
2 TBS honey   in a blender or food processor.
1/4 tsp Creole mustard
1/4 tsp ground cinnamon
1/8 tsp ground allspice
1/16 tsp ground nutmeg

ORANGE GLAZE

1/2 cup orange marmalade   Mince any large pieces of fruit,
1/2 cup bourbon whisky   and blend ingredients thoroughly.

Pepper Jelly for Roast Pork

This jelly is good served with many foods, but especially with roast pork. It is slightly sweet and slightly spicy. Prepare the mixture below, pour it through a fine strainer, skim the foam, add **1 tsp food coloring** and blend thoroughly. If you want red jelly, use red bell peppers, red chilies, and red food coloring. For green jelly, use green bell peppers, green chilies, and green food coloring. Pour the hot liquid into 6 small jelly jars and cover with melted paraffin to seal, as is done with fruit jellies.

1 jar (4 oz.) pimento   Blend ingredients thoroughly
1-1/2 cup cider vinegar   in a food processor of blender.
1 cup bell pepper, chopped
3 fresh chili peppers, minced

6-1/2 cups sugar   Add, blend thoroughly, and bring to a boil.

1 bottle Certo*   Add, blend thoroughly, and boil for 1 minute.

***NOTE**: Certo is the trade name of a product used in making jellies. It causes the mixture to jell.

Marinated Pork Tenderloin

Serves 6 to 8

Marinate a 3-pound pork tenderloin roast for 48 hours refrigerated in the marinade below. Drain on a plate for 15 minutes and rub thoroughly with vegetable oil, salt, and a good amount of black pepper. Cook the meat on indirect heat of a covered grill or moist smoker. Boneless pork roasts are ideal for spit roasting. Use moderate amounts of almost any wood smoke.

3/4 cup beer　　　　　　Blend ingredients thoroughly.
1/4 cup vegetable oil
1 TBS lemon juice
1 TBS Worcestershire sauce
1 TBS distilled vinegar
1 TBS prepared horseradish
1 TBS Dijon mustard
1 tsp Tabasco
1/2 tsp salt
1/2 tsp onion powder
1/2 tsp cayenne
1/2 tsp black pepper
1/4 tsp garlic powder

Mustard Pork Roast

Serves 6 to 10

Marinate a 3 to 5 pound pork roast, preferably trimmed of fat, for 24 to 72 hours refrigerated. After marinating let the roast stand on a plate to drain for 15 minutes. Rub the meat thoroughly with a liberal amount of fresh coarsely ground **black pepper**. Cook on a moist smoker or a covered grill with indirect heat from a low to medium fire. Spit roasting is also a good means of cooking. Use heavy smoke with the wood of your choice.

1/3 cup distilled vinegar　　Blend ingredients thoroughly.
1/3 cup water
1/3 cup vegetable oil
3 TBS Creole mustard
2 TBS molasses
1 TBS Worcestershire sauce
2 tsp salt

Orange Marinated Pork

Serves 4 to 6

Marinate a 2 to 3 pound roast trimmed of fat in the marinade below for 12 to 24 hours refrigerated. After marinating, let the roast drain on a plate for 15 minutes, then brush the meat thoroughly with vegetable oil. Roast on indirect heat of a covered grill or moist smoker. When the meat is almost done, begin brushing it with the glaze below. Be careful not to burn the glaze. If the fire is still hot, you may need to move the meat farther from the fire before applying the glaze.

MARINADE

3/4 cup distilled vinegar   Blend ingredients thoroughly.
3/4 cup orange juice
2 tsp salt
1 tsp black pepper
3 slices fresh ginger, minced
1 clove garlic, crushed

GLAZE

1/2 cup orange juice   Blend ingredients thoroughly.
1/4 cup honey
zest of one orange, grated
1/2 tsp fresh ginger, grated
1/4 tsp ground cinnamon
1/8 tsp ground clove
1/8 tsp ground allspice

Marinated Pork Roast

Serves 6 to 8

Marinate a 3 to 5 pound pork roast in the marinade below for 3 days, refrigerated. After marination, remove the roast from the marinade and let it drain on a plate for 15 minutes. Brush the meat with vegetable oil and rub with coarsely ground black pepper. Roast on moderate indirect heat with moderate to heavy amounts of wood smoke.

1 can (12 oz) flat beer
2/3 cup vegetable oil
2 TBS lemon juice
1 TBS prepared horseradish
1 TBS Creole mustard
1 TBS distilled vinegar
1 tsp salt
1 tsp cayenne
1/2 tsp onion powder
1/2 tsp garlic powder

Blend ingredients thoroughly.

SYRUP

Un-sulphured molasses is made directly from sugar cane. Sulphured molasses is a by-product of the sugar industry, and contains sulphur from the sugar making process. Sorghum is made from sorghum cane, and is thinner and less sweet than molasses. Maple syrup is made from sugar maple sap, and to carry the maple syrup label it must (by law) contain at least 35% natural maple syrup. Honey is made by bees. Light and dark "generic" commercial syrups are commonly formulated from corn sugars.

Polynesian Pork

Serves 4 to 6

Marinate a 2 to 3 pound boneless pork roast for 12 to 24 hours refrigerated in the marinade below. For a stronger flavor the meat can be marinated for a longer period of time (24 to 48 hours). Remove the meat from the marinade and set it on a plate to drain for 15 minutes. After the meat has drained, brush it thoroughly with vegetable oil and sprinkle with a liberal amount of black pepper. Cook the meat with indirect low to medium heat on a covered grill or a moist smoker with moderate to light mild wood smoke. After the meat is almost done, begin brushing with the glaze below. This glaze will burn easily because of the sugar.

MARINADE

1/2 cup soy sauce   Blend ingredients thoroughly.
1/2 cup sherry
1/2 cup chicken bouillon

GLAZE

1 can (8-1/4 oz) crushed   Blend thoroughly in
** pineapple, drained**   a blender or food processor.
2 cloves garlic, minced
1 TBS fresh ginger, grated

1/4 cup honey   Add, blend, and simmer on low heat
                                              for 15 minutes.

Chinese Roast Pork

Pork roasted over a charcoal fire has been a Chinese favorite for centuries. Small amounts of mild wood smoke add considerably to the flavor of this recipe. The red food dye is optional, but is characteristic. The best choice of meat for this recipe is pieces of pork shoulder trimmed of fat. The pieces will be approximately 1x3x5 inches. Several of these pieces can be cut from a shoulder roast. Marinate the meat in the marinade below (refrigerated) for approximately 12 hours. These can be roasted on low indirect heat of a covered grill, but a moist smoker is preferred. In fact, hanging the meat in a moist smoker is best. When this style of meat is done let it cool before serving. It is never sold hot in Chinese markets. A good technique is to wrap it in aluminum foil and freeze. When sliced pork is desired, simply slice it still frozen and thaw the slices by placing them in hot chicken broth for 30 seconds. These are excellent for topping noddles boiled in broth, drained and tossed with a few drops sesame oil. Top with pork, chopped green onions, and sprinkle with soy sauce.

1/2 cup hoisin   Blend ingredients thoroughly.
1/2 cup soy sauce
1/2 cup sherry
3 TBS sugar
1 TBS red food dye

Stuffed Pork Roast

Serves 6 to 8

Trim a 3 to 5 pound boneless loin roast of all but a thin layer (1/8 inch) of peripheral fat. Push a sharp long-bladed knife through the center of its long dimension, and cut to within 1/2 inch of the outside edge. Rotate the blade 1/2 turn and extend the cut to within 1/2 inch of the opposite side of the roast. The roast now has a hollow center pocket all the way through its long dimension which can be filled with stuffing. Almost any pork stuffing can be used. Bread dressings with sage or diced apple are especially good. Canned sauerkraut can be squeezed dry of juice, mixed with caraway seeds, and white wine or beer added until the proper moisture content is achieved. A recipe for cornbread dressing is provided below. Stuff the roast. If necessary tie it with string or use poultry skewers on the ends to keep the stuffing from coming out. Rub the outside of the roast with the seasoning mix below, and roast on moderate indirect heat with or without wood smoke.

CORNBREAD STUFFING

1/2 cup onion, chopped — Saute on low heat until reduced in
1/4 cup celery, chopped — volume until reduced volume
1/4 cup green onion, chopped — (approximately 30 minutes),
1 clove garlic, minced — remove from heat.
2 TBS butter or margarine

1 cup cornbread, crumbled — Add to cooked vegetables
1/3 cup seasoned bread crumbs — and blend all
1/3 cup saltine crackers, crumbled — ingredients thoroughly.
1/3 cup white bread toast, crumbled*
1 egg, beaten
1 cup chicken stock

***Note:** Make very dry toast in the oven, a toaster will not make it dry enough.

SEASONING MIX

2 tsp green peppercorns, crushed — Blend and mash
1 tsp salt — to a paste with a fork.
1 tsp dried thyme
1 clove garlic, minced

2 TBS vegetable oil — Add to seasoning paste
and blend thoroughly.

Dee's Baked Ham

If you like ham sandwiches, try this recipe. Cook a lean boneless ham as directed below, then slice it very thin as soon as it cools. Use a meat slicer or have a butcher slice it for you.

Take an ice pick, and repeatedly stab a 4 to 5 pound ham. Stab all sides thoroughly and evenly to a depth of several inches. Spread the paste below over the meat and seal tightly in heavy duty aluminum foil. When the ham cooks the mixture will melt and boil, so be careful that there are no leaks in the foil or the seasoning will run out onto the fire. Place the meat on a cooker with moderate direct heat. Cook for two hours turning after one hour, then open the foil and add a mild wood to the fire for smoke. Continue cooking until done (approximately 4 to 5 hours total). The outside of the meat will get dark, but take care not to burn it.

1 cup brown sugar   Blend ingredients thoroughly
4 TBS butter or margarine, softened   into a smooth paste.
1/2 tsp ground allspice

Kentucky Ham

For this recipe, use a small boneless processed ham. Prepare the seasoning blend below, place the ham in an ovenproof dish, and pour the seasoning over it. Cook the ham on low heat (direct of indirect) of a covered grill with heavy wood smoke. Baste the ham with the juice in the pan, and turn the ham at least once.

1/2 cup bourbon whisky   Blend ingredients thoroughly.
1/2 cup honey
1/4 cup Dijon mustard

Assorted Pork

Bratwurst and Beer

Perforate **bratwurst** or other mild pork link sausages repeatedly with a fork. Marinate the sausages in **beer** for 24 hours refrigerated. Remove from the beer and broil on a covered grill directly over low heat or on indirect medium heat. Watch them closely and turn often so they do not burn. If the skin bulges, pierce with a fork to release rendered fat. Serve on hot dog buns or rolls with a spicy mustard.

Sweet and Sour Spareribs

Serves 4

Trim excess fat from 4 pounds of spareribs, brush them liberally with **soy sauce**, and marinate at room temperature for 30 minutes. Cook on a covered grill with indirect heat or on a moist smoker. It is preferable to hang the ribs as discussed in the **Barbecued Pork** section. Use moderate to heavy smoke from a mild wood. Cook until done, remove from the grill, cut into individual ribs, and place them in an ovenproof dish. Prepare the sauce below, pour it over the ribs, and place them in a warm oven (250° F) for 15 minutes.

1 cup wine vinegar **1/2 cup honey** **1/2 cup Port wine** **1/2 cup brown sugar** **2 TBS soy sauce** **2 green onions, sliced** **1 green pepper, thinly sliced** **2 cloves garlic, minced**	Blend and bring to a boil, then reduce heat.
1 TBS corn starch **1 TBS water**	Blend together and add to thicken the mixture above.
1 can (8 oz) crushed pineapple, drained **1/4 cup sweet pickles, sliced** **1-1/2 tsp preserved ginger, minced** **1 tsp dry mustard** **1/4 tsp five-fragrances powder**	Add remaining ingredients, remove from heat, and blend thoroughly.

Inihaw

This Philippine dish is tasty and simple. It can also be served as an hors d'oeuvres. Cut 1/4 -inch thick pork chops or fresh ham slices into 3/4- to 1-inch squares. Marinate refrigerated for 4 hours in either **soy sauce**, or equal portions of **soy sauce** and **sherry**. Skewer the meat through the side so it will lay flat and cook quickly. Broil over moderate direct heat, with or without wood smoke. These can also be roasted on indirect heat.

Sausage Kebabs

Serves 4

Peel and cube (1 to 1-1/2 inch) **1 medium size eggplant**. Place the eggplant in a covered dish with **2 TBS water** and **1/4 tsp salt** and microwave on full power for 4 minutes, turning once. Place the eggplant, still hot, in a plastic bag with the marinade below. Toss, then marinate for 1 hour at room temperature. Skewer the eggplant, alternating with 1-inch lengths of Italian sausage (1 lb). What is commonly referred to as Italian sausage in this country is salsiccia. It is flavored with fennel seeds and is available in mild or spicy varieties. Place the skewers on hot indirect heat, but close to the fire of a covered grill. Turn as necessary (cooking time is approximately 20 minutes). Use a moderate amount of mild wood for smoke. Baste if necessary with the remaining marinade.

1/2 cup olive oil
1/4 cup lemon juice
2 cloves garlic, minced
1 TBS dried parsley
1 tsp dried marjoram
1/2 tsp black pepper
1/4 tsp dried oregano

Blend ingredients thoroughly.

Broiled Pork with Garlic

Serves 4

Use four thick (approximately 1/2 to 3/4 inch) pork chops or other lean cuts of pork. Prepare the paste below and thoroughly rub it onto both sides of the meat. Let the meat stand covered in the refrigerator for 6 hours. Broil the meat directly over moderate heat.

5 cloves garlic, minced	Mash with a spoon until
1 tsp vegetable oil	a smooth paste is formed,
1 tsp salt	and the ingredients
1/2 tsp black pepper	are thoroughly blended.

Four Kinds of Pork

Serves 10

These recipes can be served as hot appetizers or in combination as the main course. Oriental meals usually consist of a variety of small portions. Use 1 lb of meat (trimmed of fat and bone) for each recipe. The best choice is a loin roast; pork chops, fresh ham, and country ribs can also be used. Trim the meat and cut into 1-inch cubes (smaller if used for hors d'oeuvres). Marinate the meat refrigerated in one of the sauces below for 2 to 3 hours. After marinating, bring the remaining marinade to a boil, reduce the heat, and let it simmer while you skewer the meat. Skewer the meat and cook on indirect or very low direct heat with light to moderate mild wood smoke. Use care not to burn the meat. Baste as necessary with the remaining sauce.

PEANUT SAUCE

1 green onion, chopped	Blend ingredients thoroughly,
2 TBS peanut butter	let stand at room temperature
2 TBS vegetable oil	for 1 hour, and
2 TBS soy sauce	blend again.
2 TBS distilled vinegar	
2 tsp sugar	
1/2 tsp sesame oil	
1/2 tsp cayenne	
1/4 tsp garlic powder	

NOTE: If you like peanuts, also add finely chopped unsalted roasted peanuts to the sauce.

SESAME SAUCE

2 TBS hoisin
1 TBS oyster sauce
1 TBS soy sauce
1 TBS sherry
1 tsp sesame oil
1 tsp fresh ginger, grated
1 tsp sugar

Blend ingredients thoroughly.

CHILI SAUCE

2 TBS oriental chili sauce
1 TBS hoisin
2 tsp soy sauce
1 tsp sherry
1 tsp ginger, grated
1/4 tsp five-fragrance powder

Blend ingredients thoroughly.

GARLIC SAUCE

2 TBS soy sauce
1 TBS sherry
1 TBS brown sugar
1 TBS vegetable oil
1 TBS cornstarch
5 cloves garlic, minced
2 green onions, minced

Blend ingredients thoroughly
and simmer over low heat
until thickened.

MSG

Monosodium glutamate (MSG) is a white powder which is used to enhance the flavor of other foods. Large quantities of MSG will make you thirsty, a common side-effect of eating Chinese food. It was originally produced by evaporating the liquids from cooked seafood, but is now synthesized from soybeans. MSG is not used in the recipes of this book.

Oriental Meatballs

Serves 4

This recipe uses ground lean pork with a small amount of vegetable oil added for moisture. Care should be taken not to cook the meatballs too long, or they will dry out. Use a loin roast, tenderloin, shoulder roast, or fresh ham trimmed of fat. If you buy pork already ground it will already have fat included, so leave out the vegetable oil. Blend the ingredients below and form meatballs of approximately 1-inch diameter. If they are being served as hors d'oeurvers they can be smaller. Skewer the meatballs, brush them lightly with vegetable oil, and cook with indirect heat on a covered grill with moderate heat, and mild wood smoke. Cook for approximately 20 minutes, depending upon size and heat of the fire.

1-1/2 lb ground lean pork   Blend ingredients thoroughly.
10 water chestnuts, minced
1 green onion, minced
1 clove garlic, minced
1 TBS soy sauce
2 tsp vegetable oil
1-1/2 tsp lemon juice
1 tsp oyster sauce
1 tsp oriental chili sauce
1 tsp fresh ginger, grated
1/4 tsp sugar
1/4 tsp salt

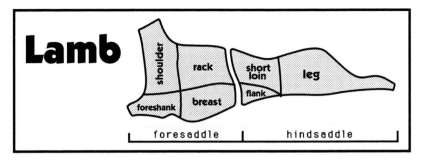

During the first half of this century, **mutton** was almost eliminated from the American diet. However, the popularity of lamb has increased significantly in recent years. **Lamb** is defined as an ovine (sheep) of less than 1 year in age with a live weight of less than 90 pounds. The most highly prized lamb was originally known as a **hothouse lamb**, which was under 60 pounds and generally born between October and January. **Spring lambs** weighed between 60 and 90 pounds, were born in the spring, and were usually sold the following winter. However, changes in production methods have now extended the lambing season. These definitions are no longer used officially by the wholesale meat industry, but are still used for marketing.

A lamb carcass is not split down the backbone like beef, but is divided into the foresaddle and the hindsaddle by cutting it between the 12th and 13th ribs. The foresaddle is subdivided into four primal cuts: shoulder, rack, foreshank, and breast. The hindsaddle is subdivided into three primal cuts: short loin, flank, and leg. Since one-third of a lamb's dressed weight is in the hind legs, **leg of lamb** is the most common retail cut. The leg is retailed whole, or with the sirloin (end toward the short loin) removed, leaving a smaller leg and a **sirloin roast**. This usually depends upon the size of the lamb. **Leg steaks**, or **chops**, are also cut from the sirloin end of the leg.

The primal cuts containing the choicest cuts are the rack and the short loin. The **rack of lamb** is the back and rib section toward the shoulder; the **short loin** is the back section toward the hind legs. Note that with lamb the sirloin is included in the leg and the short loin is similar to the loin of beef, while the rack of lamb is comparable to the rib section of beef. The rack is usually split in half down the back, and the halves trimmed to form a **crown roast** or is sliced into **rib chops**. The short loin is either boned and sold as a **rolled roast** or is split and sliced into **loin chops**. Chops are sometimes trimmed to the bone on the rib end and labeled **Frenched chops**. The shoulder is normally retailed as a **square cut shoulder**, boned and tied as a **rolled shoulder**, or sliced into **arm chops, blade chops**, and **boneless shoulder chops**. Shoulder meat is also **cubed** for kebabs. Much of the rest of the lamb carcass is ground for **lamb loaf** or **lamb patties**. Other lamb cuts are generally less desirable for grill and smoker cooking, although barbecued breast of lamb is relatively common.

Leg of Lamb

Cooking a leg of lamb can be accomplished by one of three basic techniques: roasting a **whole leg** (bone in), roasting a **boned leg** (rolled and tied), and grilling a **butterflied leg** (boned and spread out). The butterflied leg of lamb is not as common, but is the best technique for grill cooking. In fact, if you like broiled beef but are not sure of lamb, the butterflied and broiled recipes of this section are a good introduction.

Roasting a bone-in leg is the most common technique for leg of lamb. Most recipes designed for oven roasting can be easily adapted for covered grill or moist smoker cooking. However, some practice is required in carving a whole leg of lamb because of the way the leg bone is shaped. Use a whole (bone-in) leg of lamb trimmed of excess fat. However, some people prefer to leave the fat (feld) on. Season the meat and roast it on a moist smoker or indirect heat of a covered grill. A variety of table sauces are good served with a whole leg of lamb. See **Assorted Lamb & Goat** and **Steaks & Burgers** (under **Beef**).

A boned and rolled leg is easy to carve, is just as tasty as a whole leg, and an excellent choice for rotisserie cooking. Occasionally recipes call for spreading a stuffing or a seasoning mixture on the meat before it is rolled and tied, but a boned leg of lamb is not easily stuffed because of its shape. However, simply seasoning a butterflied leg and rolling and tying it produces a good technique.

The butterflied and broiled leg of lamb technique is emphasized in this section because it is not commonly found elsewhere, is easy to prepare and carve, and has excellent flavor. Open a boned leg of lamb trimmed of excess fat. Marinate or season as directed in the recipes that follow. For cooking, build a hot fire to only one side of a covered grill. Leave the meat spread out, and sear it directly over the fire for 5 minutes on each side. Move the meat back until it is just over the edge of the fire and cook. Cook as desired, but if you do the thick end medium rare, the small end will be medium. This provides something for all tastes. Cooking time is approximately 45 minutes for medium rare. For well done, cook the meat on indirect heat. Indirect cooking takes slightly longer than direct, and a meat thermometer in the thick portion is advised.

FELD

The feld is the layer of slightly crystalline fat that covers a leg of lamb. Some prefer to leave it on during cooking to seal in juice and flavor. However, leaving on the feld prevents flavoring by marinating, by applying basting sauces, and from wood smoke. The only means of seasoning a feld-on leg of lamb is to make slits through the feld and into the meat with a sharp knife, then inserting slivers of garlic. Slivers of onion (green onions are the easiest) and jalapeno pepper can also be inserted in slits.

Traditional

Serves 6 to 8

Start with a whole leg of lamb, trimmed of excess fat. Slice two **cloves of garlic**. Make cuts by inserting the tip of a sharp knife into the meat, and push the garlic slices into cuts. Distribute the garlic slices evenly over the meat. **Green onions** can also be inserted into cuts and then trimmed flush. Thoroughly brush the lamb with olive oil or melted margarine, and sprinkle it with freshly ground **black pepper**. Let the meat sit at room temperature for 4 hours. Roast on a moist smoker or indirect heat of a covered grill. Baste as necessary with olive oil or melted margarine if the meat appears to be drying out. Use a meat thermometer to judge doneness. Moderate amounts of mild wood smoke are recommended but not necessary.

Slightly Seasoned

Serves 6 to 8

Use a whole (bone-in) leg of lamb trimmed of excess fat. Blend the basting sauce below, and thoroughly baste the meat. Let it stand at room temperature for 4 hours. Roast on a moist smoker or indirect heat of a covered grill with light to moderate mild wood smoke. Baste as necessary with the remaining sauce.

2 TBS margarine, melted   Blend ingredients thoroughly.
2 TBS olive oil
1 tsp fresh ginger, grated
1 tsp dried rosemary, crumbled
1 tsp dried thyme

Mary Lou's Lamb

Serves 6 to 8

Trim excess fat from a boned leg of lamb and rub it with a liberal quantity of **garlic powder** and freshly ground **black pepper**. Marinate at room temperature for 3 to 4 hours in the marinade below. Leave butterflied and cook as directed in the beginning of this section. Baste with remaining marinade each time the meat is turned, taking care that the meat does not burn or char. Pour a liberal amount of heated marinade on a serving platter, slice the meat, and serve.

3/4 cup olive oil   Blend ingredients thoroughly.
6 TBS red wine vinegar
1 tsp dried thyme
2 bay leaves

Near East Lamb

Serves 6 to 8

Trim excess fat from a boned leg of lamb, and marinate at room temperature for 3 to 4 hours in the marinade below. Leave butterflied and cook as directed in the beginning of this section.

2/3 cup olive oil   Blend ingredients thoroughly.
1/3 cup wine vinegar
2 TBS Worcestershire sauce
2 tsp dried mint
1 tsp ground cumin
1 tsp black pepper

Creole Lamb

Serves 6 to 8

Trim the excess fat from a boned leg of lamb and rub it with a liberal amount of **garlic powder** and freshly ground **black pepper**. Marinate refrigerated in the marinade below for 3 days. Drain the meat for 15 minutes and save the marinade. Brush the meat with olive oil. Leave the meat butterflied, and cook as directed in the beginning of this section. Heat and pour the remaining marinade over the sliced meat, or thicken it with a mixture of equal portions of water and corn starch. Heat and serve the thickened marinade as a table sauce.

3 TBS olive oil	Saute until onion is translucent.
1 onion, chopped	
2 cloves garlic, minced	
1/2 tsp dried thyme	Add, and simmer for 2 minutes.
2 bay leaves	
1/2 tsp salt	
1/2 tsp black pepper	
1-3/4 cup beef stock	Add, blend thoroughly, bring to a boil,
1/4 cup chili sauce	then let cool.
3 TBS vinegar	
3 TBS Worcestershire sauce	

Foots' Leg of Lamb

Serves 6-8

Use a boned leg of lamb which has been trimmed of excess fat. Marinate refrigerated in the marinade below for 1 to 2 days. Remove the lamb from the refrigerator and let it drain for 15 minutes before cooking. Cook the meat with a moderate amount of mild wood smoke. Baste as necessary with the remaining marinade.

1 cup olive oil	Blend ingredients thoroughly.
1/2 cup red wine vinegar	
1 onion, chopped	
4 cloves garlic, crushed	
2 TBS Creole mustard	
1 TBS dried rosemary	
1 bay leaf	
1-1/2 tsp cayenne	
1 tsp dried basil	
1 tsp dried thyme	
1 tsp salt	

Lamb with Dry Rub

Serves 6-8

Use a boned leg of lamb, trimmed of excess fat. Rub it thoroughly with with the dry rub below. Marinate at room temperature for 2 to 3 hours. Cook as directed in the beginning of this section using moderate amounts of mild wood smoke. Baste with the sauce below as required.

DRY RUB

2 tsp black pepper	Blend ingredients thoroughly.
1 tsp salt	
1 tsp ground cumin	
1/2 tsp garlic powder	

BASTING SAUCE

1/4 cup sherry	Blend ingredients thoroughly.
1/4 cup dry white wine	
1/4 cup olive oil	

Burgundy Leg of Lamb

Serves 6 to 8

Marinate a boned leg of lamb, trimmed of fat, for 1 to 2 days refrigerated in the marinade below. Cook as directed in the beginning of this section. Use heavy mild smoke. Baste often with the remaining marinade until done.

1/2 cup olive oil   Saute until tender.
1 medium onion, chopped
3 cloves garlic, minced

1 cup dry red wine   Blend ingredients thoroughly.
1 cup water
2 TBS chili sauce
1 TBS salt
1 TBS dried parsley
1 tsp black pepper
1/4 tsp dried marjoram
1/4 tsp dry mustard
8 to 10 drops Tabasco

Moroccan Lamb

Serves 6 to 8

Trim the excess fat from a boned leg of lamb and rub it liberally with the dry rub below, and let it stand at room temperature for 2 to 3 hours. Cook the meat as directed at the beginning of this section with moderate amounts of wood smoke. Baste with the sauce below and turn as necessary.

DRY RUB
2 tsp ground paprika   Blend ingredients thoroughly.
2 tsp ground coriander
1/2 tsp ground cumin
1/2 tsp salt
1/2 tsp black pepper
1/2 tsp cayenne

BASTING SAUCE
1/4 lb margarine   Saute on low heat for 5 minutes.
5 cloves garlic, minced

Mustard Leg of Lamb

Serves 6 to 8

Trim a boned leg of lamb of excess fat. Marinate at room temperature for 2 to 3 hours in the marinade below. Cook as directed in the beginning of this section. Baste with the remaining marinade as required.

1/4 cup red wine	Blend ingredients thoroughly.
1/4 cup vegetable oil	
1/4 cup Creole mustard	
4 cloves garlic, minced	
2 TBS Dijon mustard	
2 TBS soy sauce	
2 TBS wine vinegar	
1 TBS lemon juice	
1 tsp black pepper	

PEPPER

Black pepper is the ground dried seed of the pepper plant (Piper nigrum). White pepper comes from the same seed, but the outer covering is removed before drying and grinding. Green peppercorns are simply the same seeds picked while still green. They are either dried or pickled in brine or vinegar. These peppers are all true spices. Red pepper, including cayenne, is the ground dry seed pod of the chili pepper plant (family Capiscum). These are not spices, but are classified as dried vegetables. Family Capiscum also includes the mild bell pepper and semi-hot peppers. Semi-hot (banana) peppers are elongated with a pointed end and are usually green or yellow. There are also mild varieties of chilies. Szechwan pepper is not a true pepper, but a dried berry from China. It has a pepper-like flavor, but is distinctly different and not as spicy.

It is common to combine several of these peppers, since each has a different flavor (discernible only to those who like spicy food). Red pepper is for heat, white pepper for bite, and black pepper for aroma. Black pepper also tends to have a cumulative effect which slowly builds in intensity, while the effect of red pepper is instantaneous. White pepper is a good choice for rubbing poultry because it will stick better than black pepper. White pepper is also used in table sauces so that they will not have black specks. The combination of red, black, and white pepper is characteristic of many Cajun dishes.

Shish Kebab

Shish kebab is the Turkish term for skewered meat broiled over coals. Shish means to skewer and kebab means to grill or barbecue. In Turkey "meat" implies lamb. For shish kebab the meat should be cut into cubes of 1 to 1-1/2 inches. A boned leg of lamb is the easiest cut of lamb to work with, and is the most readily available. The shoulder is often retailed already cubed. Almost any cut that yields lean pieces will do. Lamb meatballs are also delicious when skewered and broiled. Grind leftover scraps for meatballs or lamb patties.

Meat cubes are commonly marinated, while meatballs commonly have seasoning blended into them. Both meat cubes or meatballs are often interspersed with vegetables or herbs. The most commonly used vegetables for kebabs are onions, tomatoes, bell peppers, and mushrooms. Eggplant, zucchini, and artichoke hearts are also good choices. Vegetables can be blanched or microwaved and marinated, or they can be skewered raw without marination.

A leg of lamb will serve approximately 6 to 8 people, depending upon its size and the appetite of the diners. However, a leg of lamb does not produce large cuts of lean meat like beef. A 5 to 6 pound leg of lamb will produce approximately 4 to 5 pounds of lean meat. About half of this meat can be cut into large cubes, 1 to 2 inches per cube. The other half will have smaller pieces and lean scraps that can be ground for meatballs.

The following recipes were designed for approximately 2 to 2-1/2 pounds of lamb, or approximately one-half leg. If lamb is readily available in your area, many cheaper cuts such as neck meat or shanks can be used for meatballs. The meatball recipes in this book are for very lean ground lamb. If you desire, fat can be added, but it is not necessary. Ready-ground lamb will have fat included. In that case, the amount of oil should be reduced in the recipes.

An important consideration for skewered meatballs is keeping the meatballs on the skewer. Too much oil mixed with the meat, or too large a meatball, will cause them to split and fall off the skewer. With a little practice one can determine if the meat will hold. If it is too soft, try slowly adding fine, unseasoned bread crumbs and kneading until the consistency becomes stiffer. Cracked bulgur wheat and chopped nuts can also be added. Too much dry material, such as bread crumbs or dry herbs, can make the mixture crumbly. The latter will also cause the meatballs to break apart and fall off the skewer when turning. A good practice when cooking skewered meatballs is to keep a spatula and pair of tongs handy. If the meat tends to stick to the grill, run the spatula under it before trying to turn the skewers. If a meatball falls off, use tongs to retrieve it. Tongs are also handy to hold the pointed end of a skewer, while a mittened hand lifts and turns the handle.

Herb Kebabs

Serves 4

Marinate 2 pounds of lamb (cut into 1 to 1-1/2 inch cubes), a dozen or so fresh mushroom caps, one blanched or microwaved bell pepper (with seeds and membranes removed, and cut into 1 to 1-1/2 inch squares), and 3 small onions cut in halves or quarters in the marinade below. Marinate for 1 to 2 hours at room temperature. Skewer, alternating meat and vegetables, and cook directly over hot coals. Cook for 2-1/2 to 3 minutes on each of the four sides for medium rare.

3/4 cup olive oil **1 clove garlic, minced** **2 slices onion, chopped** **1-1/2 tsp dried rosemary, crumbled** **1/2 tsp dried thyme**	Saute until onion is translucent.
1/4 cup red wine vinegar **1 tsp salt** **1/2 tsp black pepper**	Remove from heat, add, and blend ingredients thoroughly.

Persian Kebabs

Serves 4

Marinate 2 pounds of lamb (cut into 1 to 1-1/2 inch cubes) refrigerated for 12 hours in the marinade below, skewer, and cook. Cook directly over hot coals (cook for 2-1/2 to 3 minutes on each of the four sides for medium rare). Reserve the marinade and place it in a sauce pan. Heat and blend it thoroughly with **1/2 cup** of **beef broth**, or lamb stock. If it curdles blend it with a wire whisk or in a blender. Serve the marinade as a table sauce with the kebabs. Vegetables can also be grilled on separate skewers if desired, but this marinade is not well suited to skewered vegetables interspersed with the meat.

1 cup yogurt	Blend ingredients thoroughly.
1 medium onion, chopped	
1 clove garlic, minced	
1 tsp ground cardamom	
1/2 tsp black pepper	
1/4 tsp ground ginger	
1/4 tsp cayenne	
1/4 tsp ground cumin	
1/4 tsp salt	
1/4 tsp ground cinnamon	
1/8 tsp ground clove	

Greek Kebabs

Serves 4

Cut 2 pounds of lamb into 1 to 1-1/2 inch cubes. Rub the meat with the spice and herbs mixture below. Skewer the meat, alternating it with fresh mushroom caps. Sprinkle with **1 tsp salt** and **1/4 cup lemon juice**, let stand at room temperature for 30 minutes, then baste with **olive oil**. Grill directly over hot coals on a covered or uncovered grill until done, basting with olive oil each time the meat is turned. Cook 2-1/2 to 3 minutes on each of the four sides for medium rare. When the meat is served, sprinkle it lightly with additional lemon juice, or serve with lemon wedges.

1 tsp black pepper   Blend ingredients thoroughly.
1 tsp dried thyme
1/2 tsp dried oregano

Eastern Kebabs

Serves 4

This recipe tastes a little more spicy and is stronger in taste than others. Skewer raw mushroom caps, onions, and bell peppers. Brush them with olive oil. Cut 2 pounds of meat into 1 to 1-1/2 inch cubes and marinate in the mixture below for 1 hour at room temperature. Skewer the meat and broil both meat and vegetables directly over hot coals on a covered grill for 2-1/2 to 3 minutes on each of the four sides.

1/4 cup olive oil   Saute until onion is translucent.
2 slices onion, chopped

2 cloves garlic, minced
2 tsp dried red pepper flakes   Add, blend, and
1-1/2 tsp ground turmeric*   saute for 1 minute.
1/2 tsp ground coriander
1/2 tsp ground ginger
1/2 tsp salt

2 TBS lemon juice   Remove from heat, add, blend and let cool.

***NOTE:** The turmeric will stain fingers yellow, especially around the fingernails.

Sosaties

Serves 4

This is a South African shish kebab. Marinate 2 pounds cubed lamb (cut into 1 to 1-1/2 inch cubes) in the marinade below for 1 hour at room temperature. Fry or microwave **4 slices** of **bacon** approximately three-quarters done but not crisp. Reserve the bacon drippings for the marinade. Drain and cut the bacon into squares. Cut **2 onions** into eights. Skewer the bacon, marinated lamb, and onion sections. Remove the bay leaves from the marinade and bring it to a boil. Add **1 cup** of **chicken stock**, and heat. Use this as either a basting sauce, a table sauce, or both. Broil the skewered meat directly over hot coals until medium rare to medium. Cooking time should be approximately 10 to 12 minutes (2-1/2 to 3 minutes per side), depending upon the desired degree of cooking and heat of the fire.

2 TBS bacon drippings **1 medium onion, chopped** **3 cloves garlic, minced**	Saute until onion is translucent.
2 tsp curry powder **1/2 tsp ground coriander** **1/2 tsp ground turmeric*** **1/2 tsp dry mustard**	Add and saute for 5 minutes.
1 can (16 oz) apricot **halves, drained and pureed** **3 bay leaves** **1/2 cup lemon juice** **2 TBS brown sugar** **1 tsp cayenne** **1/2 tsp salt**	Add, blend, and simmer for 30 minutes.

*NOTE: The turmeric will stain fingers yellow, especially around the fingernails.

Mary Lou's Kebabs

Serves 4

Mix the marinade listed for **Mary Lou's Lamb** and add **2 minced cloves of garlic**. Marinate 2 pounds of cubed lamb (cut into 1 to 1-1/2 inch cubes), blanched or microwaved onions, bell peppers, and mushroom caps for 2 hours at room temperature. Add quartered raw tomatoes when the meat and marinated vegetables are skewered. Baste with the remaining marinade while cooking. If you like your meat done medium or more, it is best to skewer and cook the vegetables separately to prevent the vegetables from being over-done. Medium rare should take 2-1/2 to 3 minutes on each of the four sides.

Shish Kebab Supreme

Serves 4

Flaming shish kebabs are seen in old movies, but seldom found in cookbooks. It is less dramatic, but safer, to flame the food on a platter after it is removed from the skewers. Cut **two medium onions** into eights, and **two small zucchini** into one inch thick sections. Microwave the vegetables for four minutes on a power setting of 10. Marinate two pounds of cubed lamb (1 to 1-1/2 inches square), and the microwaved vegetables in the mixture below for two hours at room temperature. Broil directly over a hot fire for 2-1/2 to 3 minutes on each of the four sides. Remove the food from the skewers to a heated platter. Heat **1/4 cup brandy** (preferably Cognac), until it can be ignited with a match. Once ignited, pour the flaming brandy over the food, and serve immediately. If you want to leave the food on the skewers, stack them on a platter and flame them together.

1/2 cup olive oil	Blend ingredients thoroughly,
1/4 cup red wine vinegar	and let stand for 1 hour.
1 TBS lemon juice	
1 clove garlic, minced	
1 tsp Worcestershire sauce	
1 tsp brown sugar	
1 tsp black pepper	
1/2 tsp salt	

Meatballs with Herbs

Serves 4

Blend the ingredients below and form into meatballs approximately 1 to 1-1/2 inch in diameter. Skewer the meatballs and broil directly over hot coals on a covered grill. Cook for a total time of approximately 12 minutes, depending upon the fire. After the meat is cooked, remove from the skewers to a serving platter and liberally sprinkle with **lemon juice**, or serve with wedges of lemon. Lemon juice adds significantly to the flavor of this dish.

1-1/2 lbs ground lamb   Blend ingredients thoroughly.
1 TBS olive oil
2 tsp dried parsley
1 tsp lemon juice
1 tsp dried thyme
1/2 tsp dried oregano
1/2 tsp salt
1/2 tsp black pepper

Meatballs with Tomato Sauce

Serves 4

First prepare the tomato sauce below and set it aside. Then, combine and thoroughly blend the ingredients for the meatballs. Let the mixture stand at room temperature while you make the remaining preparations. Slice **1 eggplant** into circular slices approximately 3/4 inch thick, lightly salt both sides, and set aside for 30 minutes. Take **8 semi-hot (banana) peppers**, cut off the stem end and slit them lengthwise. Remove the seeds and membranes. After 30 minutes rinse the eggplant in cold water and pat dry with a paper towel. Build an indirect fire with the coals to one side of a covered grill. Moderate amounts of mild wood smoke are recommended. Baste the eggplant and peppers with the Garlic-Oil below, sprinkle the eggplant with black pepper, and put them on the indirect side of the cooker. Turn and baste the vegetables as required. They will require 20 to 30 minutes cooking time.

Form meatballs approximately 1 to 1-1/2 inches in diameter and skewer. Broil them directly over the coals, turning to brown all sides. The meatballs will require 10 to 12 minutes total cooking time, depending upon the fire and desired doneness. When the meat and vegetables are done, remove them to a warm serving dish or platter. Pour the remaining tomato sauce (heated) over the top and serve.

GARLIC-OIL

4 TBS olive oil   Saute over moderate heat
3 cloves garlic, minced   until garlic is tender.

TOMATO SAUCE

3 TBS olive oil   Saute over low heat until
1/2 medium onion, chopped   peppers are tender.
1/4 bell pepper, minced
2 cloves garlic, minced

1 tsp dried parsley   Add and saute for 2 additional minutes.
1/2 tsp dried basil
1/4 tsp dried thyme
1/4 tsp dried oregano

1 can (8 oz) tomato sauce   Add and simmer over low heat
1 can (6 oz) tomato paste   for 15 minutes. Remove from
1/4 cup dry red wine   heat and let stand for 30 minutes.
1/4 cup water
1/2 tsp salt
1/2 tsp black pepper
1/4 tsp cayenne

MEATBALLS

2 lbs lamb, ground   Blend ingredients thoroughly.
2 TBS tomato sauce (above)
1 TBS olive oil
1 TBS parmesan cheese
1 tsp dried parsley
1/2 tsp salt
1/4 tsp dried thyme
1/4 tsp black pepper
1/8 tsp dried oregano

Spiced Meatballs

Serves 4

Grind lamb scraps (trimmed of fat) with the vegetables below. An old fashioned food grinder works much better than a food processor, but is more trouble. If you use a food processor mince the onion, pepper and garlic. Processing them turns them to mush. The nuts should be processed to a coarse grind. Form the mixture into meatballs of approximately 1 to 1 -1/2 inch diameter and skewer. Broil directly over a hot fire for a total of 10 to 12 minutes. Turn the skewers several times to cook the meat on all sides. Because of the olive oil, it is best to use a covered grill. If using an uncovered grill, use only one tablespoon of olive oil and lightly brush the meatballs with the second tablespoon of oil after they are cooked. Serve with lemon wedges, or sprinkle them with lemon juice just before serving.

2 lbs lamb	Grind.
1 small onion	
2 semi hot peppers, seeds and membranes removed	
1 clove garlic	
1/3 cup walnuts	
2 TBS olive oil	Add and blend thoroughly.
1 TBS dried parsley	
1 tsp dried mint	
1 tsp dried basil	
1 tsp salt	
1/2 tsp ground allspice	
1/2 tsp black pepper	

Meatballs and Eggplant

Serves 4

This recipe calls for **Chinese eggplant** which are small, long, and thin. If these are not available, cubes of common eggplant can be substituted. First, prepare the meatballs approximately 1 to 1-1/2 inch in diameter and let stand at room temperature for one hour. While these are standing, combine **1/2 cup olive oil** with **2 minced cloves of garlic** and heat on moderate heat for a few minutes. Remove the oil from the heat and let it stand until needed for basting. Cut the eggplant crosswise into 1-1/2 inch lengths. Lightly salt the ends of the sections and set them aside for 30 minutes. Rinse the eggplant in cold water and pat dry. Baste the ends of the eggplant with the garlic oil and skewer, alternating sections of eggplant and meatballs. Baste the skewered meat and eggplant thoroughly with the garlic oil. Grill with moderate indirect heat and mild wood smoke. Cook approximately 20 minutes until the meat is medium and the eggplant is soft. If you want the meat less done and the eggplant more done, you may want to cook the eggplant first, then broil the meatballs.

2 lbs lamb, ground	Blend ingredients thoroughly.
2 tsp dried parsley	
1 tsp salt	
1/4 tsp ground cinnamon	
1/4 tsp ground allspice	
1/4 tsp black pepper	
1/8 tsp ground clove	

Seekh Kebab

Serves 4

This is a variation of a Hindu recipe for skewered meatballs. Prepare the mixture below and add it to **1-1/2 to 2 pounds of ground lamb**, and **1/2 cup of very fine unseasoned bread crumbs**. Kneed the mixture until well blended and form into meatballs of approximately 1 to 1-1/2 inch diameter. Skewer the meatballs without vegetables and baste thoroughly with melted margarine. Broil directly over hot coals on a covered or uncovered grill for approximately 10 to 12 minutes total time for medium, turning at least two or three times and basting with margarine.

2 onions, chopped	Saute until translucent.
2 TBS margarine	
2 cloves garlic, minced	
1 tsp curry powder	Add and saute for 2 minutes.
1/2 tsp ground ginger	
1/2 tsp dried red pepper flakes	
1/2 tsp ground cumin	

KEBABS

Kebabs, or more properly shish kebabs, were taken from Persia to India by the Mogul Emperors during the period 600-1000 A.D. The spread of Islamic culture by Arab traders also introduced kebabs to Indonesia, where they are now known as sate. Kebabs were probably introduced to the United States in the mid-19th century by a sea captain named Riley (they were originally called cububs).

Assorted Lamb & Goat

Loin chops are the choice cut of the lamb, but rib and shoulder chops are also good. Lamb chops have a delicate flavor that can be easily overpowered. They are good grilled with very little seasoning and served with a table sauce. More practical, yet just as delicious, is lamb steak. Have your butcher cut a small leg of lamb or lamb sirloin into 1/2 to 3/4 inch thick slices (or your preferred thickness). Chops and steaks can also be more highly seasoned with the basting sauces in this section or most beef steak marinades and basting sauces.

Goat is highly prized by a few and carefully avoided by most. In many areas it is often hard to obtain, but if young animals are available, try it. Old animals are tough. **Cabrito**, the Spanish word for **kid** or young goat, is often served at festive occasions by Hispanic peoples. Barbecued goat is also a 4th of July tradition in many parts of the South. If you do try goat and it is tough, grind the leftovers for chili, it is excellent. If you find goat as butchered cuts, the chops are recommended.

─── WORCESTERSHIRE SAUCE ───

Many officers in the military or members of the East India Company brought spices and a taste for seasoned food back to England from India. It is said the Sir Marcus Sandys of county Worcester (Worcestershire) brought back a recipe for Worcestershire sauce. However, it is also claimed that Worcestershire sauce originated in Ancient Rome. Recipes for homemade Worcestershire sauce can be found in old English (or commonwealth) cookbooks, but they are not usually as strongly flavored as the commercial varieties now available.

Marinated Steaks

Serves 4

Blend the marinade below and marinate 2 pounds of lamb leg steaks cut 1 inch thick, for 2 hours at room temperature. Remove the lamb from the marinade and let it drain for 5 minutes. Broil directly over a hot fire on a covered or uncovered grill.

1/2 cup cognac	Blend ingredients thoroughly
2 TBS olive oil	and let stand for 1 hour.
1 TBS lemon juice	
2 cloves garlic, minced	
1 tsp dried rosemary, crumbled	
1/2 tsp white pepper	
1/2 tsp black pepper	

Grilled Lamb Chops (or steaks)

Brush rib or loin chops lightly with olive oil or melted margarine and salt and pepper to taste. The chops can also be rubbed with a crushed clove of garlic and sprinkled lightly with **dried thyme** or **rosemary**. If herbs are used, let the chops stand at room temperature for 1/2 to 1 hour. Sprinkle the chops with very **fine unseasoned bread crumbs** (it is best to make your own bread crumbs from stale French bread), and grill directly over a hot fire. For more seasoning serve with a table sauce.

Karsky Shashlik

This recipe is Russian in origin and uses dill, as do many Russian recipes. Carefully trim all fat from a boned leg of lamb. Cut the lean meat into 6 to 8 equidimensional pieces of about 3 to 5 inches by 1 inch thick. Try to get all of the pieces approximately the same thickness so they will all cook in the same amount of time. Prepare the marinade below and marinate the meat refrigerated for 24 hours. Broil the meat directly over a hot fire on a covered grill until medium rare (about 15 minutes). Turn the meat to sear both sides, as with beef steak. This marinade is equally good for shish kebabs.

3/4 cup olive oil   Blend ingredients thoroughly.
1/3 cup lemon juice
1-1/4 tsp dried dill weed
1 tsp salt
1 tsp black pepper
2 cloves garlic, minced
2 bay leaves

Cabrito Asado (Roast Kid)

Serves 6 to 8

Rub 5 to 6 pounds of goat meat with the dry rub below. Let the meat stand for 1 hour at room temperature. Grill the meat on a covered grill on indirect heat with moderate to heavy wood smoke. Baste with the basting sauce below.

DRY RUB

1 TBS chili powder
1/2 tsp cayenne
1/2 tsp black pepper
1/2 tsp salt
1/2 tsp ground paprika
1/4 tsp ground cumin
1/4 tsp rubbed sage
1/4 tsp sugar
1/4 tsp celery seed
1/4 tsp garlic powder
1/4 tsp onion powder
1/4 tsp dried oregano

Blend ingredients thoroughly.

BASTING SAUCE

1-1/2 cups dry white wine
1/2 cup olive oil
2 TBS sherry

Blend ingredients thoroughly.

Cabrito Asado II

Serves 6 to 8

Rub approximately 5 to 6 pounds of goat meat with wedges of **fresh lemon**. Sprinkle the meat with **1 tsp garlic powder** and **1 tsp black pepper**. Sprinkle with additional lemon juice if desired and cover the meat or place it in a sealed plastic bag. Refrigerate for 24 hours. One half hour before cooking, remove meat from the refrigerator and sprinkle with the seasoning mixture below and let it stand. Cook the meat on indirect heat with a moderate amount of wood smoke. Baste as required with the **basting sauce from the previous recipe**.

3/4 tsp dried marjoram   Blend ingredients thoroughly.
1/2 tsp cayenne
1/2 tsp dried oregano
1/2 tsp salt

Basting Sauces

These basting sauces are designed for lamb chops and steaks. The marinades and basting sauces from **Steaks & Burgers** (see **Beef**) can also be used with lamb.

Mustard Baste

Makes 1 cup

1/2 cup Creole mustard
2 TBS vegetable oil
1 TBS soy sauce
1 tsp Worcestershire sauce
1 tsp lemon juice
1/2 tsp black pepper

Blend ingredients thoroughly.

Ginger and Herb Baste

Makes 1/2 cup

2 TBS olive oil
1 clove garlic, minced
1 TBS lemon juice
1 tsp fresh ginger, grated
1 tsp dried rosemary, crumbled
1/4 tsp black pepper
1/4 tsp salt

Blend ingredients thoroughly.

Oriental Baste

Makes 1-1/4 cups

1/2 cup water
1/4 cup hoisin
2 TBS oyster sauce
2 TBS brown sugar
1 TBS soy sauce
1 TBS catsup
1 TBS sherry
1 tsp fresh ginger, grated
1 clove garlic, minced

Blend ingredients, bring to a boil, and remove from the heat.

Green Curry Baste

Makes 1-1/2 cups

3 TBS vegetable oil
3 TBS pickled jalapenos, minced
2 cloves garlic, minced
1/2 small onion, chopped
1 tsp lemon zest, grated
1 tsp crystallized ginger, minced
1/2 tsp ground coriander
1/2 tsp ground nutmeg
1/8 tsp ground clove

Saute on low heat for 5 minutes and remove from the heat.

1 cup beer
1 TBS lemon juice
1/2 tsp salt

Add and blend ingredients thoroughly.

Table Sauces

Lamb chops have an excellent flavor and require little or no seasoning. Listed below are several table sauces for grilled lamb. Many of the table sauces listed under **Steaks & Burgers** (see **Beef**) can also be served with lamb chops.

Bernaise with Mint

Makes 1-2/3 cups

4 egg yolks
3 TBS lemon juice
1 tsp dried mint
2 green onions, sliced

Blend thoroughly in a food processor.

1/4 lb butter, melted and still bubbling

Add very slowly while blending.

Blue Cheese Sauce

Makes 1-1/2 cups

1 cup cream   Bring almost to a boil, and reduce the heat to low.

8 oz Blue cheese, crumbled   Add stirring constantly until smooth
1/4 tsp cayenne   and thoroughly blended.

Pepper Sherry

Makes 1 cup

1 cup dry sherry*
1 tsp red pepper flakes

Let stand for 1-2 weeks at room temperature before using.

*NOTE: Use a good quality sherry.

Green Pepper Corn Sauce

Makes 1-1/3 cups

2 TBS flour 2 TBS vegetable oil	Cook a light to medium dark roux.
2 green onions, minced 2 TBS green pepper corns	Add, blend, and simmer until thickened, stirring constantly.
1 cup cream 2 TBS Dijon mustard	Add, blend thoroughly, and simmer for 5 minutes, stirring constantly.

Worcestershire Sauce

Makes 1 quart

Worcestershire sauce was prepared long before it was bottled and sold commercially. This recipe is milder than the commercial variety. Serve it heated as a table sauce, or use as a marinade.

1 qt cider vinegar 1 onion, chopped 1 large apple, chopped 1/2 orange sliced 1 clove garlic, minced 1/2 cup sugar 1/2 cup molasses 1 TBS salt 1-1/2 tsp ground ginger 1-1/2 tsp ground clove 1/2 tsp cayenne	Bring to a boil, reduce heat, and simmer for 2 to 3 hours. Strain, let cool, and bottle.

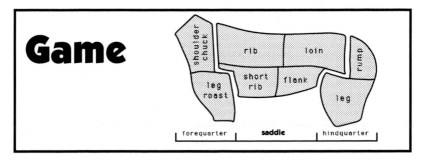

Game

This section is not extensive, because many people neither hunt nor have ready access to game. Even if you do not hunt, game is available in specialty stores and from friends or neighbors who hunt. The selected game recipes included can provide variety for your table. For those unfamiliar with butchering antlered game, the carcass is divided into two sides by splitting down the backbone. It is then cut into the forequarter, saddle, and hindquarter. The forequarter is subdivided into two primal cuts, the shoulder chuck and leg roast. The saddle is subdivided into four primal cuts; the rib, loin, short rib, and flank. The hindquarter is subdivided into the rump and leg. Like beef, the rib and loin are the choicest cuts for roasts or steaks. The leg and rump are less tender, but still provide good roasts. The shoulder chuck, leg roast (front leg), short ribs, and flank are best used for moist cooking in the kitchen or as ground meat.

Game has been cooked over embers for millennia, but much of this was done in a pot of water. Game is generally lean (with the exception of bear and some small game such as opossum or groundhog) and dry cooking on grills and smokers can easily dry it further to the point of being inedible. Use only choice tender cuts from young animals for grill and smoker cooking. Thin cuts of large game, such as steak, are excellent broiled rare to medium, but well done is not recommended. Roasts of large game should be either larded or marinated to add moisture prior to roasting. Fat or oil can be added to game burgers, allowing them to be cooked the same as hamburgers. Wild fowl are usually roasted whole, or only the breast is used. Small game, such as squirrel and rabbit, can be roasted whole or cut into pieces for cooking. Both fowl and small game are best marinated and cooked on a moist smoker. One recipe is included for game that turns out too dry, or too tough. Tough game and leftovers also make excellent stock for use in hearty soups, such as gumbo.

Antlered Game

There are two ways to add moisture to game roasts, larding and marination. Larding is accomplished by using a larding needle to make holes in the meat and then lacing strips of fat into it. The technique is discussed in many cookbooks, especially ones on French cooking. Marination for 2 to 3 days adds fluid and seasoning to the meat. Searing the roast over a hot fire will seal in the added fluid providing a juicy roast. In fact, a well marinated roast will swell with cooking like an inflating balloon. If cooked medium rare to medium, considerable amounts of juice will flow from the meat when carved. Because of its simplicity, marination is recommended for grill or smoker cooking of game roasts. After marination let the meat drain for 15 minutes, then brush with oil, or with a basting sauce that contains oil. This will help to form a seal, especially when the meat is to be seared over direct heat. Many marinades and basting sauces from **Roast Beef** or **Leg of Lamb** can also be used for large cuts of game.

Game steaks should be cooked the same as very lean beef (baby beef and veal). They can be marinated or simply basted, but should not be over cooked. Game steaks cooked more done than medium will be dry.

JERKY

Drying food in the sun was man's first technique for preserving it. This allowed a hunter to preserve the excess meat from a large kill. The English word comes from the Inca word *charqui*. Jerky is now often seasoned and heat dried, commonly with wood smoke for additional flavoring.

Grilled Venison Steak

Use a rib, loin, rump, or leg steak. Rub the meat with a crushed garlic clove and brush with melted margarine or olive oil. Cover the meat with coarse ground black pepper. Pound it with the back of a large spoon to drive the pepper into the meat so it will not fall off during cooking. If you add salt, do so just before cooking. Broil the meat over direct heat as with beef. Use either an open or covered grill. Grilled steaks are good accompanied by table sauces. Serve with the table sauces in this section, or sauces listed under **Broiled Beef** or **Assorted Lamb & Goat**.

Spiced Venison Roast

Serves 4 to 6

Marinate a 3 to 5 pound boneless venison roast trimmed of fat in the marinade below for 3 days, refrigerated. Remove the roast from the marinade and let it drain for 15 minutes. Rub the roast liberally with vegetable oil and cover it with a liberal amount of black pepper. Use fine ground pepper and apply a heavy coating. Cook to no more than medium done (approximately 1 hour) using a meat thermometer. Antlered game should be cooked to the same temperatures as beef. A moderate amount of wood smoke is recommended. This is an excellent choice for rotisserie cooking, but is just as good cooked on a grate.

1 cup dry red wine
1 cup distilled vinegar
1/2 onion, sliced
2 cloves garlic, crushed
3 bay leaves
1/2 tsp ground cloves

Blend ingredients thoroughly.

Paul's Venison Jerky

If you hunt deer, put a few pieces of this jerky in your pocket. It may help when you think you are about to die of hunger. Although making jerky is an old means of preserving meat, be safe and refrigerate it.

Cut lean meat ino strips 1/4 inch thick by 1 inch wide. Marinate in the mixture below for 24 hours. Allow meat to drain for 10 minutes, then pat dry. Smoke meat with moderate to heavy wood smoke over low heat. A very low dry heat is preferred, but a moist smoker will suffice. Be extremely careful to dry the meat without burning it. Depending on heat and moisture, drying takes 3 to 8 hours. Smoking when the outside air is cold will dry the meat more quickly. Jerky can be made in a covered grill by building a very small indirect fire and hanging a folded piece of aluminum foil on a rung of the cooking grate between the fire and meat to block radiant heat. Almost any type of wood smoke can be used.

1/4 cup catsup   Blend ingredients thoroughly.
1/4 cup Worcestershire sauce
1/4 cup soy sauce
1 tsp onion powder
1 tsp garlic powder
1 tsp cayenne
1 tsp black pepper
1 tsp salt

Game Burgers

Serves 4

The fat content of ground game determines how it should be prepared. Many hunters trim and discard the game fat and grind only the lean meat. Others follow this same procedure, but add ground beef or pork fat to it. If fat has not been added, oil should be blended with the meat before the burgers are grilled. The recipe below is for low-fat ground game. Simply blend the ingredients as described, and grill as you would beef hamburgers. If fat has been included, this recipe will have extra oil to produce smoke and a very juicy burger. For the higher fat ground meat virtually any hamburger recipe can be used. Game burgers are also good when made thicker and smaller in diameter, and wrapped with a slice of bacon similar to a filet mignon.

1/4 cup celery, minced	Saute until vegetables are tender.
3 green onions, sliced	
2 cloves garlic, minced	
2 TBS vegetable oil	
1 TBS bacon drippings	
1 TBS dried parsley	Add and saute for 5 minutes,
1/2 tsp dried savory, crumbled	then remove from heat.
1/2 tsp black pepper	
1/4 tsp cayenne	
2 lbs ground game	Add, blend ingredients thoroughly,
1 raw egg yolk	and form into patties.
1 tsp Worcestershire sauce	
1 tsp salt	

Marinades

For any of the marinades below, marinate roasts refrigerated for 2 to 3 days. After marination, let the roast drain for 15 minutes, brush it lightly with vegetable oil, olive oil, or melted margarine. Sear on all sides directly over the fire, then cook on indirect heat until done. Thin cuts, such as steaks can be marinated at room temperature for 1 to 3 hours. Steaks should be brushed with oil or basted with a sauce containing oil. The marinades from **Roasted Beef** can also be used.

Cider Marinade

For those who do not like the sour taste of a marinade with vinegar, try apple cider. Grocery store varieties are good, but those without preservatives (which are more tart) are better. Hard cider is also very good.

Juniper Marinade

Makes 2-3/4 cups

1 cup dry red wine
1/2 cup vinegar
1/2 cup water
1/4 cup vegetable oil
1 medium onion, sliced
1 carrot, sliced
1 stalk celery, sliced
2 cloves garlic, crushed
2 bay leaves
12 dried juniper berries, crushed*
1 TBS dried parsley
1 tsp salt
1 tsp black pepper
1/2 tsp dried thyme
1/2 tsp dried savory

Blend ingredients thoroughly.

*NOTE: Juniper berries are a traditional ingredient in game recipes.

Buttermilk Marinade

Buttermilk has long been used as a game marinade. The lactic acid acts much the same as vinegar (acetic acid), but does not produce a strong flavor. In fact, some people maintain that marination in buttermilk will diminish the "wild taste" of venison. After marination, rinse the meat in cold water and pat dry.

Basting Sauces

Spicy BBQ Sauce

Makes 2-1/2 cups

3 TBS bacon drippings 1 large onion, chopped 2 bay leaves	Saute until tender.
2 tsp chili powder 2 tsp dry mustard 1 tsp black pepper 1 tsp cayenne 1 tsp salt	Add and saute for 1 minute.
1 cup catsup 1 cup dry red wine 1/2 cup distilled vinegar 2 TBS brown sugar	Add, blend thoroughly, and simmer for 30 minutes. Strain through a sieve.

Black Sauce

Makes 1 cup

1/2 cup water 1/2 cup soy sauce 1-1/2 tsp molasses 1/2 tsp onion powder 1/2 tsp ground ginger 1/8 tsp garlic powder	Blend thoroughly, place in a closed bottle, and let stand at room temperature for two weeks, shaking occasionally. Strain through a coffee filter.

NOTE: If used on a roast, the meat should first be rubbed with vegetable oil and seared on all sides before basting.

Table Sauces

Poivrade Sauce

Makes 3 cups

This is a traditional French game sauce. It is robust, flavorful, and goes well with most game or beef.

1 medium onion, chopped **1 carrot, chopped** **1 stalk celery, chopped** **1/4 cup bacon drippings**	Saute over medium heat until vegetables are light brown.
1 bay leaf **1 tsp dried parsley** **1 tsp black pepper**	Add and saute for 3 minutes.
1/4 tsp dried thyme **1/4 cup wine vinegar**	Add and boil for 5 minutes.
3 cups game (or beef) stock	Add, reduce heat, and simmer for 1 hour. Remove from the heat, strain into a new saucepan, and place on moderate heat.
2 TBS flour **2 TBS water**	Combine flour and water, add, and stir while cooking until thickened.

Cumberland Sauce

Makes 1-3/4 cups

This is a traditional English game sauce that goes well with virtually any game recipe, especially steaks and roasts. Grate the zest of **1 lemon** and **1 orange**. Barely cover with water and boil for five minutes. Drain and rinse in cold water, and set the peel aside. Prepare the sauce below.

1 cup Port wine **2 green onions, chopped** **1/4 cup orange juice** **2 TBS lemon juice** **1 TBS brown sugar** **1 tsp Dijon mustard** **1/4 tsp ground ginger** **1/8 tsp ground cloves** **1/8 tsp ground nutmeg** **1/8 tsp cayenne**	Bring to a boil, reduce heat and simmer for 5 minutes.
2 TBS flour **2 TBS water**	Blend the flour and water, add, and simmer while stirring until thickened and smooth.
1/3 cup current jelly	Add, blend, and simmer for 3 minutes.
grated zest (above)	Add, blend thoroughly, and serve.

Small Game & Wild Fowl

Many small game animals and wild fowl are lean and will be dry if not cooked properly. In general they should be cooked much the same as skinned chicken pieces, since they are similar in size and fat content. Marination for 1 to 2 days and basting with a high oil basting sauce is recommended for lean game. Slow cooking on a moist smoker is also recommended.

Small to medium sized game can also be barbecued. Marinate for 1 to 2 days or simmer on low heat for several hours in seasoned water. Brush with vegetable oil and roast with low heat and heavy wood smoke. When the game is done, baste with a thick tomato-based barbecue sauce. Barbecuing has long been used in the south for cooking many medium sized animals that would not otherwise be cooked. Groundhog and nutria are common choices for parboiling in Crab Boil and barbecuing. Even armadillo is sometimes cooked, "possum on the half-shell."

Doves Jasper

Serves 5

Marinate 25 dove breasts for 2 days in the marinade below. This recipe is also good for other dark meat game birds, such as woodcock. Drain the birds for 15 minutes and wrap each breast with a bacon strip. Use toothpicks if necessary to hold the bacon strips in place. Roast on indirect heat in a covered grill or moist smoker with heavy wood smoke. Dove has a strong flavor and hickory wood smoke can be used if desired. Continue to baste with the remaining marinade. When birds are 3/4 done (approximately 20 minutes) move to direct heat for 5 to 10 minutes until the bacon is brown and crisp.

1 cup vegetable oil
1/2 cup lemon juice
2 TBS Worcestershire sauce
2 TBS vinegar
1 TBS black pepper
1 tsp chili powder
1 tsp salt
1/2 tsp garlic powder
1/4 tsp Tabasco

Blend ingredients thoroughly.

Leftovers and Rice

Serves 4

In the event your game is tough or dry, save the meat for this recipe. This is one leftover you can look forward to. It is intended for scraps of large game cooked with heavy wood smoke, but small game and dark meat fowl are also good. A mixture of game leftovers is good, and uncooked game scraps can also be used. Trim all game of fat and gristle. Serve over a bed of boiled rice.

1/4 cup flour   Cook a light brown roux.
4 TBS margarine

1 stalk celery, chopped Add to roux and cook on low heat until
1 medium onion, chopped   vegetables are tender.

1 bell pepper, chopped
3 cups game stock   Add, blend ingredients thoroughly, and
1 cup (or more) game, diced   simmer for 1 to 2 hours.
2 TBS Kitchen Bouquet
1-1/2 tsp salt
3/4 tsp cayenne
3/4 tsp black pepper
3/4 tsp white pepper

RABBITS

Rabbits were first domesticated by monks during the Dark Ages (476-1096 AD), and raised in monasteries to circumvent church food laws pertaining to the eating of meat. At that time rabbits were not classified as meat. Domestic rabbits can be roasted whole on a grate or spit using the recipes for small game, or with many of the beef and poultry basting sauces or marinades.

Game with Wine and Herbs

Serves 6 to 8

Cook 8 squirrels, 2 rabbits, or a comparable amount of other small game in a covered grill on indirect heat with a low fire. Keep the fire low to avoid burning or overcooking. Squirrels will cook in about the same time as skinned chicken pieces (approximately 45 minutes), while rabbits will take longer (approximately 1 hour). Baste frequently with the sauce below to keep the meat from drying out. It contains oil to form a seal to help contain moisture, but the meat will still be drier than when cooked in the oven in a covered roaster.

1/4 cup bacon drippings   Saute until the onion is translucent.
4 large onion slices, chopped
1/2 cup celery, chopped

1 bay leaf   Add and saute for 3 additional minutes.
2 TBS brown sugar
2 tsp dried parsley
1/2 tsp black pepper
1/2 tsp dry mustard
1/4 tsp rubbed sage

1 cup dry white wine   Add, blend ingredients thoroughly, and
1/4 cup vegetable oil   simmer for 1 hour.
2 TBS lemon juice

Spicy Bourbon Game

Serves 6 to 8

Use 8 whole young squirrels, 2 rabbits, or a comparable amount of other small game. Marinate refrigerated for 2 days using the marinade below. Remove the game from the marinade and let it drain for 15 minutes at room temperature. Cook on indirect low heat in a covered grill. Squirrels will cook in about the same time as skinned chicken pieces (approximately 45 minutes), while rabbits will take longer (approximately 1 hour). Baste frequently with the basting sauce below. This sauce has a high oil content to seal in juice, but it also has a high sugar content and will burn if the heat is too high. Baste often to keep the meat from drying out. Each time you baste, stir the basting sauce first because it tends to separate when it sits for a while.

CRAB BOIL MARINADE

1 qt water	Blend ingredients thoroughly.
1 cup vinegar	
2 tsp lemon juice	
1 tsp liquid Crab Boil	

BASTING SAUCE

1/2 cup vegetable oil	Saute until the onion is translucent.
2 cloves garlic, minced	
2 slices onion, chopped	

1/2 cup bourbon whiskey	Remove from heat, add remaining
1/4 cup brown sugar	ingredients, and blend. Let stand for
1/4 cup oriental chili sauce	30 minutes and reblend.
1/4 cup Pickapeppa sauce	
2 tsp lemon juice	
1/2 tsp black pepper	

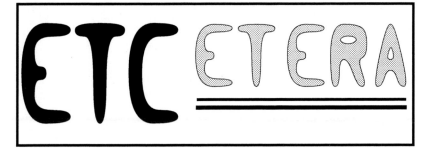

It may seem strange to place appetizers in the last section of a cookbook along with desserts, but many people are not willing to light their grill for these items alone. However, appetizers can often be cooked on the side of a grill while a roast or turkey is cooking, and dessert can still be cooked before the fire goes out. Stocks and soups are not commonly found in outdoor cookbooks, but when they are made from grill and smoker cooked food scraps they transmit the smoke to dishes made from them. Selected vegetables are also excellent when grilled or roasted over coals. Finally, there are recipes that simply do not fit anywhere else in the book.

CANNED FOOD

The French government offered a 12,000 franc prize to any person who could devise a method of preserving food, because Napoleon's solders were sick and dying of malnutrition. Nicolas Appert collected the prize in 1810 by discovering he could seal food in glass jars and heat them to prevent spoilage. Within 2 years the British had perfected the tin lined iron can, or tin can. This was 50 years before Pasteur demonstrated that spoilage was caused by microorganisms. The Mason jar was patented in 1858. This invention allowed fruits and vegetables to be canned at home.

Appetizers

Most kebab or en brochette recipes are good as appetizers. Rather than using large skewers, use small ones of approximately 6 to 10 inches in length. You can also buy disposable wooden ones in most grocery stores. Reduce the size of the meat cubes to approximately 1/2 inch dimension. Another simple variation is to skewer and broil meat using a simple margarine or oil baste, then serve it with a variety of table sauces or dips (barbecue sauce, sweet and sour sauce, etc.).

Rumaki

Drain an **8 oz can of whole water chestnuts**. Marinate them in **soy sauce** for 30 minutes. Cook approximately **12 slices of bacon** until one-half done, not crisp, and drain on paper towels. Cut the bacon strips in half. After the water chestnuts have marinated roll them in **1 TBS sugar**. Wrap each water chestnut in a cut piece of bacon and skewer. These can be skewered individually with tooth picks or several to a small skewer. Roast on moderate indirect heat with mild wood smoke in a covered grill or moist smoker until the bacon is crisp.

Marinated Chicken Wings

Remove the wing tips at the first joint from a package of **chicken wings**. Marinate the remaining portions for 2 days in the marinade below. Drain for 15 minutes after removing from the marinade. Roast the wings on moderate indirect heat in a covered grill or moist smoker until golden brown. Use moderate amounts of wood smoke. Because of the sugar, use care not to burn.

1/2 cup sugar   Blend ingredients thoroughly.
1/2 cup soy sauce
1/2 cup pineapple juice
1 TBS sherry

Roasted Dates

Use seeded **dried dates**. Wrap each date with one-half slice of **bacon** fried or microwaved one-half done and drained on paper towels. Skewer the dates with toothpicks or small skewers to hold the bacon in place. Place the dates on indirect heat in a covered grill or moist smoker. Roast on moderate indirect heat with heavy wood smoke (hickory is good) until the bacon is done.

Benny's Shrimp with Sherry

Marinate medium-sized peeled shrimp in **sherry** for 2 hours, refrigerated. Wrap each shrimp in 1/4 to 1/3 slice of **bacon**, fried or microwaved one-half done (not crisp) and drained. The use of too much bacon will overpower the shrimp. Wrap the bacon around the narrow dimension of the shrimp, and skewer them once through the center of their curved back. Try to overlap the bacon so the skewer will pierce both ends of the strip. Arrange all of the shrimp so they will lay flat on the grill. Broil directly over a moderate fire until the bacon is done (approximately 3 minutes per side).

Yakitori

Take 1/2 pound of **chicken livers** and cut them in half and set aside. Remove the bone, skin, and fat from 2 large **chicken breasts**. Cut the meat into pieces of approximately the same size as the halved chicken livers, and set aside. Cut four large **green onions** into one inch long sections. Marinate the chicken livers, chicken breast meat, and onions refrigerated for 1 to 2 hours in the marinade below. Remove from the marinade and skewer, alternating the onion between pieces of chicken breast and liver. Broil directly over hot coals on a covered or uncovered grill until done. Cook approximately 4 minutes on each side.

1/4 cup soy sauce   Blend ingredients thoroughly.
2 TBS chicken broth (or bouillon)
2 TBS sherry
1-1/2 tsp sugar
1 tsp fresh ginger, grated

Grilled Shrimp with Dipping Sauce

Skewer medium sized **shrimp** with the skewer passing through each shrimp twice, so they will lay flat while cooking. Lightly brush the shrimp with **vegetable** or **olive oil**, and grill approximately 3 minutes per side directly over a hot fire. Remove from the skewers and serve with the dipping sauce below.

1/3 cup catsup   Blend ingredients thoroughly in a blender
2 TBS mayonnaise   or food processor.
1 TBS Creole mustard
1 TBS lemon juice
2 tsp onion, grated
1/2 tsp Tabasco
1/2 tsp Worcestershire sauce
1/4 tsp salt
1/4 tsp garlic, minced

Roasted Chicken Livers

Slice bacon strips in thirds and cook one half done, but not crisp, and drain on a paper towel. Wrap a piece of bacon around each chicken liver and skewer. They can be skewered several to a small skewer, or individually skewered with a tooth pick. Cook on indirect heat in a covered grill with heavy wood smoke. If necessary, after the livers are done, move them over the edge of the fire to brown the bacon. When on direct heat tend them carefully so they do not burn.

Surf and Turf

Take a 1 pound 1/4-inch-thick slice of **sirloin tip**, and trim excess fat. Cut the meat into 3/4 inch squares and lightly salt and pepper. Skewer them on 10 to 12 inch skewers through the thin dimension. Leave small spaces between pieces of meat to allow them to cook quickly. Skewer 1 pound of small to medium shelled **shrimp** in a similar manner. Brush the shrimp lightly with olive oil. Broil the shrimp and meat over a moderately hot fire for 3 minutes on each side, or until done. Remove the shrimp and meat from the skewers to a plate and serve with the dips below, or add one of your own dip recipes. Small cubes of firm-fleshed fish can also be cooked in this manner.

CURRY DIP

1 cup mayonnaise   Blend ingredients thoroughly.
1 tsp lemon juice
1 tsp curry powder
1 tsp chili powder

HORSERADISH DIP

1/2 cup mayonnaise   Blend ingredients thoroughly.
2 TBS prepared horseradish
1 tsp lemon juice
1/2 tsp Tabasco

MUSTARD DIP

1 cup catsup   Blend ingredients thoroughly.
2 TBS honey
1 TBS dry mustard

Sausage with Barbecue Dip

Cut an assortment of **beef** and **pork sausages** in 1/2 to 3/4 inch lengths and skewer, leaving a very small space between each piece of sausage. Roast the sausage on indirect heat with heavy wood smoke until thoroughly done (approximately 30 to 45 minutes) and lightly browned. Remove the sausage from the skewers to a serving platter, where toothpicks can be used to pick it up. Accompany the sausage with **Apricot Baste (Barbecued Pork)** and **Catsup Barbecue Sauce (Chicken, Barbecued Pieces)**, or any other thick barbecue sauces of your choice.

Marinated Blue Crabs

Clean hard crabs by removing their back shell, gills, face, and insides. Crack the crabs in half and marinate them refrigerated for 24 hours in the marinade below. After marination, do not drain but broil them directly over a moderate fire for 5 minutes per side. The legs will be too overcooked to eat, the claws will be edible but overcooked, and the bodies will be delicious. This technique produces a different and flavorful variation that is not as messy to eat as boiled or steamed crab.

2 cups dry white wine
1/2 cup vinegar
1/2 cup olive oil
1 small onion, chopped
1 stalk celery, chopped
1/2 bell pepper, chopped
2 cloves garlic, minced
2 TBS pickled jalapeno, minced
2 TBS lemon juice
1 tsp black pepper
1 tsp salt
1 tsp dried thyme
1 tsp basil
1/2 tsp oregano

Roasted Oysters

This recipe is just like the **Roasted Chicken Livers**, except oysters are used. Slice bacon strips in thirds and cook one-half done, but not crisp, and drain on a paper towel. Wrap a piece of bacon around each oyster and skewer. They can be skewered several to a small skewer, or individually skewered with tooth picks. With large oysters it is sometimes necessary to fold them in half, and then wrap with bacon. Cook on indirect heat in a covered grill with heavy wood smoke until the bacon is done. Before removing from the grill, baste them with **Catsup Barbecue Sauce (Chicken, Barbecued Pieces)** or the tomato-based barbecue sauce of your choice.

Roasted Oysters (Maryland Style)

Oysters on the half shell make an excellent appetizer. However, if you are not adept at shucking them, this is an easy out. Select singles, not clumps, and scrub them with ample water and a stiff brush. When ready for appetizers, lay the oysters directly over a hot fire. When they first open set them off onto a heat-proof platter or cookie sheet. The oysters can now be easily shucked with an oyster knife, or even a paring knife, and served immediately on the half shell. This is not simply a trick to open them, but is an old Maryland recipe. Many volunteer fire departments in "tidewater" still raise money with their oyster roasts.

Beth's Chicken Liver Paté

Smoke **1 pound chicken livers** as in **Roasted Chicken Livers** (this section), and set them aside. Skin, brown, and drain **1 pound Italian sausage** and set it aside. Chop and saute **1 large onion** in **1/4 pound butter** until it is tender. Combine the sauteed livers, onions, and sausage with the additional ingredients listed below and blend all ingredients in a food processor until smooth. Place the mixture in the desired mold (such as a bread pan) and refrigerate for 6 to 12 hours, or until firm. The mold does not need to be greased. Unmold the paté, place it on a board or serving dish, and ice with the frosting below. Sprinkle the top with chopped **fresh parsley**. Refrigerate the completed paté for at least 6 hours. A larger batch can be made and part of it frozen, but do not put frosting on portions that are to be frozen. Defrost frozen paté, frost it, and refrigerate until the frosting is firm (approximately 6 hours).

PATÉ

1 onion (above)	Blend thoroughly in a
1 lb chicken livers (above)	food processor until smooth.
1 lb Italian sausage (above)	
1/4 cup brandy	
1/2 tsp salt	
1/4 tsp nutmeg	
1/4 tsp cayenne	
1/4 tsp black pepper	

1/4 cup whipping cream	Add and blend thoroughly until smooth. If the mixture is too thick, add additional cream and blend.

FROSTING

2 oz Philadelphia-style cream cheese (room temperature)	Blend ingredients thoroughly.
2 TBS butter (room temperature)	

Smoked Fish Deviled Eggs

This recipe uses **Brine Marinated smoked fish** (see **Smoked Seafood**). The recipe is designed for only 6 hard boiled eggs so a minimal amount can be made. Mix the ingredients below and restuff the egg whites the same as in other deviled egg recipes.

6 egg yolks, hard boiled	Mash and blend
3 TBS mayonnaise	ingredients thoroughly.
1/2 tsp American mustard	
1/2 tsp black pepper	
1/4 tsp salt	
1/4 tsp curry powder	
1/2 cup smoked fish, flaked	Add and blend
	ingredients thoroughly.

Smoked Oyster Deviled Eggs

Smoke two dozen small **oysters** by placing them on a piece of aluminum foil in a moist smoker with heavy mild wood smoke. This can be done on the side while cooking other food. After two hours, lightly salt, turn the oysters, and lightly baste them with butter or olive oil. Smoke for an additional hour, or until done. Hard boil one dozen eggs. After the eggs have cooled, remove their shells and cut them in half lengthwise. Remove the yolks and set aside. Place a smoked oyster in each half egg white, cover with the topping below.

1 doz egg yolks, hard boiled	Blend ingredients thoroughly.
1/3 cup mayonnaise	
1 tsp American mustard	
1/2 tsp salt	
1/2 tsp black pepper	
1/8 tsp curry powder	

Vegetables

Vegetables are delicious when cooked on grills or smokers. In general, choose firm vegetables that will not fall apart when cooked. Almost any vegetable that can be handled with tongs or spatula when cooked can be brushed with seasoned oil, and broiled or roasted.

Broiled Zucchini

Serves 4 to 6

Cut the ends off 4 to 6 medium size zucchini and boil in lightly salted water for approximately 10 minutes, or until tender. Split lengthwise, let drain for 10 minutes. Or, split and microwave, two at a time, for 6 minutes rotating once. Marinate in the marinade-baste below for 2 hours at room temperature. Remove zucchini from the marinade, lightly salt and pepper the sliced side. Place in a covered grill directly over hot coals, sliced side down. Cook for three minutes, turn and baste with remaining marinade. Cook approximately five minutes on the other side. Before removing from the grill, lay a thin slice of **Mozzarella cheese** on the top of each zucchini, close the grill lid for one minute to melt the cheese. Remove from the fire and serve.

1/4 cup olive oil   Blend ingredients thoroughly.
2 cloves garlic, minced
1 tsp dried parsley
1/2 tsp dried basil

TOMATOES

Although tomatoes were eaten by the Aztecs and were introduced to Europe in 1596 (from South America), they were feared by many settlers in this hemisphere. The tomato is a member of the nightshade family, which also contains several deadly poisonous plants. The tomato is reported to have been one of Thomas Jefferson's favorite fruits. However, tomatoes were not marketed in this country until 1812 in the French Market of New Orleans. In 1830 Col. Robert Johnson publicly ate a basket full of tomatoes on the steps of the Salem, N.J. courthouse to demonstrate that they were harmless. This event roughly coincides with the beginning of the widespread acceptance of tomatoes as a food in this country. However, many people still feared them as late as the early 20th century.

Stuffed Zucchini

Serves 8

Cut the ends off 4 medium size zucchini and boil in lightly salted water for approximately 10 minutes, or until tender. Split lengthwise, let drain for 10 minutes. Or, split and microwave, two at a time, for 6 minutes rotating once. Scoop out the center portion leaving a one-quarter inch thick shell, and set aside. Prepare the stuffing below and stuff the shells. Place stuffed zucchinis in a covered grill (indirect heat) or moist smoker with moderate, mild wood smoke. Cook until the stuffing begins to brown on top and a smokey flavor is acquired (approximately 20 to 30 minutes).

2 TBS olive oil   Saute until tender, remove from heat.
1-1/2 cups fresh mushrooms, coarsely chopped
2 green onions, sliced
1 TBS dried parsley
1/4 tsp dried thyme

1 cup Monterey Jack cheese, grated   Add and blend
1/4 cup Parmesan cheese, grated   ingredients thoroughly.
1/4 cup bread crumbs
zucchini centers, chopped
1 jar (2 oz) pimento, drained and chopped
2 slices bacon; fried, drained, and crumbled
1/2 tsp salt
1/2 tsp black pepper
1/4 tsp white pepper

Roasted Corn on the Cob

Roasted corn on the cob is an old recipe well suited to the charcoal grill. Prepare the corn by pulling back the husks but not removing them, remove only the silk. It is also useful to leave whatever part of the stalk is still attached. There are now several options. One is to fold the husks back into place and cook, another is to brush with butter or margarine, salt and pepper, then fold the husks back in place and cook. A variety of seasoned salts or oils can also be used. If the husks do not lay down properly, tie a piece of cotton string around the end of each ear. If the husks are dry, sprinkle them with water and let stand for 30 minutes. However, if the corn is fresh this should not be necessary. Roast on indirect heat in a covered grill for approximately one-half hour. When serving simply fold back the husks. The folded husks and stalk provide a handle when eating the corn.

Italian Mixed Vegetables

Serves 6

This is a mix of broiled and roasted vegetables tossed together with olive oil. These can also be served over pasta. Blend the seasoned oil below and set aside. Cut **one peeled eggplant** into 3/4 inch thick slices. Lightly salt and let stand for 30 minutes. Peel and halve **two medium onions**. Wash **two medium bell peppers** and **1/2 pound fresh mushrooms**. After standing for 30 minutes, rinse and pat the eggplant dry, and cut the slices into quarters. Skewer the eggplant and mushrooms (separately), but leave small air spaces between the pieces of eggplant. Brush all of the vegetables lightly with olive oil. Place the onions and eggplant on indirect heat in a covered grill with moderate amounts of mild wood smoke. Place the mushrooms over the edge of the fire (between direct and indirect). Place the whole peppers directly over the fire. Turn the peppers, so the skin chars on all sides. When the peppers feel soft (15 to 20 minutes) remove them from the fire, and remove the skin, seeds, and membranes. Cut the pepper into small squares and put them in a medium sized serving bowl. Lightly baste the eggplant and mushrooms with olive oil and turn. After all the vegetables are done, quarter the onions and break them apart. Cut the mushrooms into smaller pieces. Cut the eggplant slices into cubes. Place the remaining vegetables in the serving bowl, pour the seasoned oil over them, **salt**, grind a liberal amount of **fresh black pepper** over them, sprinkle with **2 TBS Romano cheese**, and toss.

2 TBS olive oil   Blend ingredients thoroughly and let stand
1 clove garlic, minced   for one hour.
1/8 tsp dried oregano
1/8 tsp dried thyme
1/8 tsp dried basil

Grilled Corn

This is a popular dish served by street vendors in Japan. Shuck ears of fresh corn, and remove the silk. Brush the corn liberally with the mixture below. Place the corn directly over a low fire in a covered grill. Light mild wood smoke is recommended. Turn the corn every 3 to 4 minutes to cook evenly on all sides. Total cooking time is approximately 15 to 20 minutes.

4 TBS margarine
1 tsp soy sauce

Blend ingredients thoroughly.

Baked Onions

Peel medium to large onions, and cut a slice off the top and bottom. Thickly spread the top of the onions with **butter** or **margarine** and sprinkle them liberally with **chicken bouillon granules**. Set the onions on indirect heat in a covered grill, or moist smoker. Roast with light to heavy smoke until tender, approximately 30 to 45 minutes on a grill, and 1 to 2 hours on a moist smoker.

Grilled Red Potatoes

Serves 3 to 5

Scrub and boil 6 to 10 small whole red potatoes (with skins) in lightly salted water until barely tender (6 to 10 minutes). Remove, drain, and cut in half. Marinate in the marinade below 3 hours at room temperature. Grill over low direct heat for 10 to 20 minutes. Baste as necessary with the remaining marinade.

1/2 cup vegetable oil
1 tsp onion salt
1/4 tsp dried oregano
1/4 tsp black pepper

Blend ingredients thoroughly, and let stand for 30 minutes.

Smoker Baked Potatoes

Wash and dry medium sized baking potatoes and lightly brush them with **vegetable oil**. Rub the oiled potatoes with your hands to evenly coat them with oil. Place in a moist smoker with medium amounts of wood smoke. Cook until they can be easily pierced with a fork. Cooking time is approximately 1 to 2 hours, depending on size of the potatoes and heat of the fire. Low indirect heat in a covered grill can also be used. This is a good recipe to cook with a roast by simply placing the potatoes around the meat. If you eat the skin of your baked potato try this recipe. The smoke flavored skin is a pleasant change of pace.

Grilled Sliced Potatoes

Serves 4

Cut **4 medium baking potatoes** unto 1/4 inch strips, as would be done for French fries. Microwave the potato strips (2 potatoes at a time) for 8 minutes on a high setting. While the potatoes are still hot, put them in the marinade below for 3 hours at room temperature. When ready to cook, remove the potatoes with tongs, allowing them to drain. Grill the potatoes directly over a hot fire for approximately 3 minutes per side. To prevent the potatoes from falling through the grates, place them perpendicular to the grate rungs. Discard any short pieces, place the potatoes on the grate with tongs, turn and remove them with a spatula.

1/2 cup olive oil   Blend ingredients thoroughly.
2 TBS wine vinegar
1/2 tsp dried thyme
1/2 tsp dried marjoram
1/2 tsp salt
1/2 tsp black pepper
1/2 tsp onion powder
1/4 tsp dried oregano
1/4 tsp garlic powder

Grilled Eggplant

Serves 4

Cut an eggplant (skin on) lengthwise into eight wedges. Sprinkle with salt and let stand for 30 minutes. Rinse in cold water and pat dry. Marinate for 1 to 3 hours at room temperature in the marinade below. Grill with indirect heat in a covered grill until tender (approximately 30 minutes). Baste with remaining marinade as required. Light to moderate mild wood smoke is recommended.

1/2 cup olive oil   Blend ingredients thoroughly.
2 TBS red wine vinegar
1 clove garlic, minced
1/2 tsp salt
1/4 tsp dried oregano

Grilled Green Tomatoes

Slice large green tomatoes into 3/4 inch thick slices. Brush them liberally with olive oil. Sprinkle both sides of the slices with **Foots' Season Salt** (**Roasted Beef**), using approximately 1/4 tsp per side. Ordinary salt and pepper can be substituted. Broil directly over a moderately hot fire until soft (approximately 5 minutes per side). When the slices are turned, sprinkle the cooked side liberally with grated **Parmesan cheese**. These can be cooked directly over the coals while a roast or other barbecue is being cooked on indirect. Wood smoke of almost any variety is recommended.

Roasted Acorn Squash

Cut acorn squash in half lengthwise. Remove seeds and rub the skin side with softened margarine. Fill the cavity with **2 TBS butter or margarine** and **2 TBS maple syrup**. Place on very low direct, or moderate indirect heat, in a covered grill. Cook split side up until tender with moderate to heavy mild wood smoke. Cooking time is approximately 45 minutes.

EGGPLANT

The eggplant was first introduced to Europe by the Turks during the early 16th century. Many people feared to eat it because it is a member of the Nightshade family, which contains several deadly poisonous plants. It was used primarily as an ornamental plant.

To reduce the bitter taste often associated with eggplant, peel, slice, and then sprinkle it with salt. Let it stand for 30 minutes to 1 hour in a colander. Drops of juice extracted from the eggplant will appear on the surface. The eggplant should then be rinsed with cold water and patted dry with paper towels.

Stocks & Soups

Stocks made from grilled or smoked meat and seafood are excellent in many other dishes. The primary reason for including these recipes is to encourage you to make your own stock. **Any recipe that calls for water is better when made with stock.** Stock made from the leftovers of grill or smoker cooked foods will transmit a smoky flavor to the dish in which the stocks are ultimately used. Making stock also utilizes the bones, shells, and scraps associated with food preparation that are normally thrown away. Instead of throwing out freezer burned food, make stock from it. Virtually any meat or vegetable scraps can be used, but specific recipes are presented here to get you started.

Juice and flavor extraction is facilitated by dicing the meat and vegetables, and disjointing or even breaking bones. For a rich dark meat stock, both bones and meat can be browned in the oven before making stock. This process caramelizes the natural sugars and alters the flavor. The addition of large "marrow bones" will produce gelatin. This makes a thick gelatinous product suitable for gravies, but is not desirable for soup. A mixture of raw and cooked bones is not recommended for clear stocks. For clear stocks, remove the scum which forms on the surface during the early stages of cooking. Spices, other than pepper, are not generally recommended. The commonly used vegetables are onions, carrots, celery, and tomatoes. Green peppers and other starchy vegetables are not recommended. The stock recipes in this section use very little salt. Adding these stocks to a recipe are much the same as adding water, in terms of salting.

Cover the ingredients with cold water and simmer covered for 3 to 6 hours. When the stock is done, strain it and let it cool. If you desire clear stock strain it through coffee filters. Refrigerate the cooled stock. As the stock chills, the fat will rise and congeal on the top. If you plan to use the stock soon, leave the fat on the top as a protective cover. If you do not plan to use the stock right away, skim the fat and freeze the stock. This can be done in freezer bags or other containers. If it is being kept for sauces, it is convenient to freeze one cup quantities in small freezer bags. For soups, freeze in quart or gallon containers. Stock can also be concentrated by slowly simmering without a lid until the volume is reduced by approximately one-half, refrigerate and remove fat, or freeze. One technique is to freeze concentrated stock in ice trays and store the cubes in freezer bags.

NOTE: The stock recipes that follow call for very little salt. When using these stocks in other recipes, additional salt will normally be required.

Smoked Poultry Stock

Makes 4 to 6 quarts

1 turkey carcass*, disjointed   Simmer covered for 3 to 6 hours.
water to cover (4 to 6 qts)
2 stalks celery, sliced
1 medium onion, sliced
1 carrot, sliced
1 bay leaf
1 TBS dried parsley
1 tsp dried thyme
1 tsp white pepper
1 tsp salt

*NOTE: A comparable amount of chickens (2 to 3 carcasses) or other fowl can be substituted.

Smoked Fish Stock

Makes 1-1/2 quarts

2 to 3 lbs smoked fish scraps   Combine and simmer covered for
4 cups cold water   3 to 6 hours on low heat.
2 cups dry white wine
2 stalks celery, sliced
1 large onion, sliced
1 carrot, sliced
1 bay leaf
2 TBS dried parsley
1/4 tsp black pepper
1/4 tsp salt

NOTE: For this recipe use brine smoked fish. Fish basted with oil are not recommended. Fresh fish scraps can also be added if you do not have enough smoked ones. Save and freeze scraps from filleting or cleaning fish.

Smoked Brown Stock (Beef, Lamb, or Game)

Makes 2-1/2 quarts

3 to 4 lbs lean meat and bone	Brown in a 450° oven and drain
2 TBS bacon drippings	fat.*
1 medium onion, chopped	
1 carrot, sliced	
1 stalk celery, sliced	
1/2 cup red wine	Add and stir to deglaze the pan.
2-1/2 qts cold water	Add and simmer covered
1 TBS dried parsley	for 3 to 6 hours.
1 tsp salt	
1 bay leaf	
1/2 tsp dried thyme	
1/2 tsp black pepper	

*NOTE: Arrange ingredients in a roasting pan, and place in the center of oven until browned (20 to 30 minutes). Stir occasionally to brown on all sides.

STOCK

Stock is a flavored liquid produced by the slow cooking of meat, poultry, seafood, or vegetables in water. Broth is a term used interchangably with stock, but is most commonly used when discussing soup. Bouillon is the term generally applied to a clear stock that has been strained and has had the fat removed. Bouillon is generally used in table sauces. Bouillon cubes and granules are commercially dehydrated bouillon with a high salt content. Consomme´ is a meat or poultry stock that contains gelatin, and will gell into a solid when cooled. Consomme´ is produced by including marrow bones when cooking stock. It is not generally used in making soup or sauces, other than gravy.

Hunters Soup

Makes 4 quarts

2 quarts Smoked Brown Stock
2 cans (16 oz) tomatoes,
  chopped (including juice)
2 cups lean meat, diced
1 cup dried barley
1 medium onion, chopped
3 carrots, diced
3 ribs celery, diced
3 cloves garlic, minced
1 TBS salt
1 TBS dried parsley
2 tsp Kitchen Bouquet
1-1/2 tsp Worcestershire sauce
1 tsp dry basil
1 tsp black pepper
1/4 tsp oregano

Bring to a boil, reduce heat, and simmer covered for 2 to 3 hours.

NOTE: The homemade stock suggested for this soup is low in salt. Add salt to taste.

Smoked Poultry Minestrone

Makes 5 quarts

3 TBS olive oil	Saute until onion is translucent.
2 cloves garlic, minced	
1 medium onion, chopped	
1 lb. lean ham, diced	

4 quarts Smoked Poultry Stock	Add, bring to a boil, reduce heat,
2 cans (15 oz) tomato sauce	and simmer for 2 to 3 hours.
1 lb great northern beans*	
1 TBS dried parsley	
2-1/2 tsp salt	
1 tsp dried basil	
1 tsp black pepper	
1/2 tsp white pepper	
1/2 tsp dried oregano	

1 pkg. (12 oz) ditali macaroni	Bring soup to a boil, add, keep on low boil for 20 minutes.

***NOTE:** Soak beans in water overnight before cooking. Also, the homemade stock suggested for this soup is low in salt. Add salt to taste.

ROUX

A roux is made by cooking one part oil and one to two parts flour. It should be cooked until it acquires at least a light brown color; otherwise, it will taste like oil and flour. A roux can be cooked fast or slow, but the very slow approach is safer. Constantly stir the mixture as it slowly bubbles over moderate to low heat. If carefully tended it can be cooked until it is black in color, but not burned. Roux forms a delicious basis for gravy type sauces, or for thickening dishes such as soup.

Smoked Fish Chowder

Makes 2 quarts

2 TBS bacon drippings   Saute until onion is translucent.
2 medium onions, chopped
2 cloves garlic, minced

1 TBS flour   Add and slowly cook to a light brown roux.

1 can (16 oz) tomatoes, chopped   Add, bring to a boil, reduce heat
5 cups Smoked Fish Stock   and simmer for 30 minutes.
2 potatoes, diced
1 TBS lemon juice
1 TBS dried parsley
1 bay leaf
1/2 tsp salt
1/4 tsp dried thyme
1/4 tsp ground allspice
1/4 tsp black pepper
1/8 tsp ground clove
1/8 tsp cayenne

1 cup dry white wine   Add and simmer for 10 minutes.
**1/2 to 1 lb brine marinated
    smoked fish, flaked**

NOTE: The homemade stock suggested for this soup is low in salt.
Add salt to taste.

Odds & Ends

Party & Picnic Suggestions

A variety of sandwiches can be prepared on a grill in addition to hamburgers and hot dogs. In addition to cooking meat and putting it in on a bun, a wide variety of sandwiches with cheese fillings can be prepared ahead of time and heated until the bread is toasted and the cheese melted. There also are a number of dishes that are not normally cooked on a grill, but that can be partially prepared ahead of time and their cooking completed on a grill. These are excellent choices to provide variety to picnics and outdoor parties.

Souvalikia

Serves 6

This is a Greek sandwich that uses skewer cooked meat (the meat is always lamb in Greece). Cut **1 pound of lean beef or lamb** into cubes approximately 3/4 inch on a side. Also cut **one medium onion** and **3 semihot banana peppers** (seeds and membranes removed) into similar sized pieces. Marinate the meat and vegetables in the marinade below for 4 hours refrigerated, drain and skewer. It is preferable to use small wooden skewers and prepare individual servings. Cook the small kebabs directly over a moderate fire with light mild wood smoke. Cut loaves of **Greek pita (pocket) bread** in half and place approximately **2 TBS sour cream (or yogurt)** in each half. Remove the cooked food from the skewers and put it into the bread to form a sandwich.

1/4 cup olive oil
1/4 cup lemon juice
1 clove garlic, minced
3/4 tsp dried thyme
1/2 tsp salt
1/2 tsp black pepper
1/4 tsp dried oregano

Blend ingredients thoroughly.

Carmen's Cheese Bread

Cut loaves of French bread, or other small diameter bread or rolls, lengthwise. Spread a liberal amount of the mixture below on the sliced side. Lay a layer of thinly sliced sharp Swiss cheese on the buttered side. Place the loaves on indirect heat of a covered grill, with moderate amounts of mild wood smoke. Tend carefully so the bread does not burn. Cook until the cheese has melted. Slice the bread perpendicular to its long dimension at intervals of 1-1/2 to 2 inches, and serve hot.

1/4 lb butter or margarine, softened
1 tsp Dijon mustard

Cuesadillas

Cuesadillas are similar to tacos, but use a flour tortilla (corn tortillas can be used) and are cooked after the tortilla is folded over a cheese filling. Almost any type of filling that contains grated cheese can be used. Heat a flour tortilla in a lightly oiled skillet to soften. Place a liberal scoop of filling on the tortilla, spread it over one-half, and fold the tortilla in half. Lightly brush the outside of the tortilla with a mixture of equal portions **melted butter (or margarine)** and **vegetable oil**. Set the cuesadillas aside until time to cook, refrigerating if necessary. For cooking, prepare a low direct fire with a light amount of mild wood smoke. Cook directly over the fire until the cheese begins to melt, and the tortilla is lightly browned.

For a basic filling, blend **1 cup grated medium sharp cheddar** or **Monterey Jack cheese** and **1/4 cup chopped onion**. Add any of the ingredients listed below to taste, and mix thoroughly.

pickled jalapenos   **cilantro**
tomatoes   **oregano**
avocado   **chili powder**
black olives   **ground cumin**
salsa

Pizza

In Italy, pizza dough is commonly formed, cooked, and stacked for later use. When a pizza is ordered, a layer of tomato sauce is simply poured over the precooked dough, the desired topping added, and the pizza put in a wood fueled oven to thoroughly heat it. This can also be accomplished on a covered grill with very low direct heat and light mild wood smoke. The smoke provides a unique flavor, not commonly associated with American-style pizza. For ease of handling it is easier to form small pizzas, approximately 8 to 10 inches in diameter. Use your favorite dough recipe, or follow the instructions for a pizza dough mix. Form the individual pizzas and bake them until lightly browned, remove from the oven and cool. Prepare a thin tomato sauce, or use a canned sauce. Before spreading the tomato sauce, lightly brush the cooked pizza dough with olive oil. This will prevent the sauce from soaking into the dough causing it to become soggy.

Any desired topping can be used, however, it is simplest to use a blend of diced vegetables, precooked diced or ground meat, and grated cheese. A mixture of this type can be blended ahead of time and simply sprinkle over the pizza just prior to cooking. Another variation is to eliminate the tomato sauce. Simply brush the cooked dough lightly with olive oil, add the toppings, and cover with grated cheese. Place the pizza on a sheet of aluminum foil and cook until thoroughly warmed and the cheese is melted. A variety of suggested toppings are provided below.

sandwich ham	**Parmesan cheese**
ground beef	**Mozzarella cheese**
pork sausage	**onion**
pepperoni	**mushrooms**
black olives	**fresh garlic**
green olives	**dried thyme**
black pepper	**dried basil**
cayenne	**dried oregano**

MUSTARD

There are several styles of mustard, notably English, French (Dijon-style), Chinese, American, and Creole. French- and English-style mustards are quite similar, have been cooked, and are moderately spicy. Chinese-style mustard is not cooked, making it much hotter than the French or English varieties. American-style mustard is very mild, is colored bright yellow by tumeric, and is the type served with hot dogs. Creole mustard is moderately spicy and contains the husks of the mustard seeds, giving it a brown, speckled appearance.

Grilled Tofu

Tofu is made from bean curd in a manner similar to the making of cheese from milk curd. It is essentially a vegetable cheese that is high in protein, including the "essential amino acids", is low in fat, and has no cholesterol. Tofu does not have flavor but quickly absorbs the flavor of sauces and marinades. Supermarket variety tofu usually comes in approximately 2x3x4 inch blocks sealed in a plastic container. Rinse these briefly in cold water and press carefully to remove excess fluid, then cut into 3/4 inch thick slices. Broil the tofu approximately 3 minutes on each side directly over a moderate fire until golden brown, but take care that it does not burn.

Tofu with Onion Sauce

Serves 2 to 4

Grill 2 to 4 slices of tofu over a medium direct fire in a covered grill until brown (approximately 3 minutes per side). Lay a slice of mild cheese on top of each piece of tofu and put the grill lid back on for 30 seconds. Remove the tofu to heated plates and top with the sauce below.

3 TBS butter or margarine — Saute over very low heat
5 medium yellow onions, sliced — (covered) for 1 to 2 hours,
1/2 tsp salt — stirring every 10 to 15 minutes,
1/4 tsp sugar — until brown.

1 cup beef stock — Add and simmer for 30 minutes.

Tofu Teriyaki

Serves 2 to 4

Marinate 2 to 4 slices of tofu in the marinade below for 1 hour at room temperature. Broil directly over a medium fire in a covered grill until brown (approximately 3 minutes per side). An uncovered grill can be used but a covered grill with mild flavored wood smoke is better.

1/4 cup soy sauce	Blend ingredients thoroughly,
2 cloves garlic, minced	and let stand for 1 hour.
3 TBS dry white wine	
3 TBS brown sugar	
1 TBS sesame oil	
1 tsp fresh ginger, grated	
1/4 tsp dry mustard	

Foil Wrapped Dinners

Foil cooking is a good technique for keeping food moist, but it prevents the food from acquiring the flavor produced by an open fire. The following two recipes simply utilize the heat of the fire, and are included to provide a meal for children while a roast or other large item is cooking for the adults. The foil will reflect the radiant heat and the contents will cook slowly by conduction. This allows them to be placed directly over hot coals without fear of burning, while other food is being cooked on indirect.

To make a foil pouch, tear off 20 to 24 inches of **18 inch wide heavy duty aluminum foil**. Other dimensions can be used, but this size is adequate for the recipes that follow. Fold the foils long dimension in half and press it flat. Place the meat (hamburger or chicken) between the folded halves, and against the fold. Fold the two edges over twice to form a tight seam. You now have a bag with the meat inside. Stand the bag, open end up, and place the remaining ingredients inside. Fold the top over twice as was done with the sides. Take your time and make the folds carefully. The bag must be well sealed or the liquids will run out and spoil the dish.

Cook the foil dinners over hot direct heat for approximately 20 minutes. The bags should swell up like balloons within the first ten minutes. If the bags are well sealed, these dinners can be cooked 30 minutes or more. Remove from the grill carefully with hot pads and serve.

Hobo Dinner

Serves 1 child

If you have ever camped with the Boy Scouts you have undoubtedly eaten a Hobo Dinner. They are delicious and a wide variety of substitutions can be made. See discussion at beginning of section for how to make a foil pouch and cooking instructions.

1/3 lb ground beef patty, salted to taste
1 small potato, diced
1/2 carrot, diced
1/3 cup water
2 TBS onion, diced
2 TBS dry red wine
1/2 tsp Worcestershire sauce
1/2 tsp salt
1/4 tsp black pepper
1/4 tsp dried thyme
1/8 tsp dried oregano

Chicken Hobo Dinner

Serves 1 child

This recipe is simply a chicken variation of the previous recipe. Use a single chicken breast, with skin and bone removed. See discussion at beginning of section for how to make a foil pouch and cooking instructions.

1 chicken breast, boned and skinned
1/4 cup mushrooms, sliced
1/4 cup water
1/4 cup dry white wine
2 TBS onion, diced
1/2 stalk celery, sliced
1/2 tsp salt
1/4 tsp Kitchen Bouquet
1/4 tsp dried thyme
1/4 tsp dried basil
1/8 tsp black pepper

Casseroles

Casseroles are not commonly cooked on grills or smokers, but many can be. They are best when cooked on moist smokers, where the heat is low and they acquire a wood smoke flavor. The best choice for smoker cooking is baked beans of almost any variety. Cooked in an oven proof dish without a lid and moderate to heavy wood smoke, they will acquire a distinctly different flavor than in the oven. Hickory smoke is a good choice for baked beans. Milder flavored wood smoke is recommended for most other dishes. When cooking a casserole along with meat (such as a roast) on a two grate smoker, place the casserole on the top grate. This prevents rendered fat from dripping into the casserole. However, the top grate is hotter and the casserole may have to be removed and kept warm before the meat is done.

Deserts

Grilled Pineapple

Serves 8

Remove the top and peel a fresh pineapple. Cut into circular slices approximately 3/4 inch thick. Brush the slices with the sauce below and let them stand at room temperature for 20 minutes. Grill directly over a hot fire for 2-1/2 minutes per side. Serve as a dessert or as a side dish.

2 tsp lime juice   Blend ingredients thoroughly.
1-1/2 tsp catsup
1/2 tsp Dijon mustard

Peaches and Cream

Lightly sprinkle skinned **fresh peach halves** with sugar, and let them set at room temperature for 2 hours (or longer). Grill the peach halves directly over moderate heat until thoroughly warm (approximately 3 minutes per side). Place a peach half on top of a scope of **vanilla ice cream** and pour 1 jigger of **Amaretto** over the top. Serve immediately.

Banana Kebabs

Serves 4

Peel four moderately ripe bananas, and slice them into 1 inch lengths. They should not be so ripe they fall off the skewer. Skewer each banana, passing the skewer through the sections sideways. Align the sections so the skewers will lie flat. Baste thoroughly with the sauce below and broil on the edge of a moderately hot fire. Cook for approximately 10 minutes turning at least once. Baste the bananas again after cooking, and serve immediately.

1/4 cup brown sugar	Melt margarine and
3 TBS margarine	blend ingredients thoroughly.
1 tsp rum	
1/2 tsp ground cinnamon	
1/4 tsp ground nutmeg	

Baked Bananas

Place 4 well **ripened whole bananas** (skin on) directly over a moderately hot fire. Cook until the outside is charred (approximately 10 minutes), turning at least once. Remove them if the skin begins to split. Place each banana on a dessert plate and split lengthwise, but do not cut completely in half. Pour flaming brandy over the bananas and serve immediately. If you like a sweeter dessert, dissolve 1 **TBS sugar** in each **1/2 cup brandy** while heating it. These can also be topped with various liqueurs (not flamed), such as **Grand Marnier** or **Contreau.**

NOTE: To flame brandy, place it in a pan on a stove burner and heat until it can be ignited with a match. It will ignite before it boils.

Fruit Kebabs

Skewer 1 inch chunks of fresh fruit. A variety such as **banana, cantaloupe, apple, pear, peach, nectarine** and **apricot** are recommended. Prepare the sauce below and brush it liberally over the fruit. Grill directly over a medium to hot fire. Cook until the fruit is warm (approximately 6 minutes, turning once). Remove the skewers from the fire, remove the fruit from the skewers, and pour additional sauce over the fruit. Serve immediately.

1/2 cup dry white wine   Heat until margarine melts and blend
2 TBS orange juice   ingredients thoroughly.
1 TBS margarine
1 tsp brown sugar
1/2 tsp almond extract

Traditional Barbecue

The word barbecue is used to describe a social gathering, a style of cooking, cooking devices, and food. In this section it is used in the traditional sense of the English word, the slow roasting of meat over a smoky fire at large social gatherings. The easiest way to barbecue for a large party, if you do not have a permanent brick or stone barbecue pit, is to borrow or rent a large mobile barbecue grill (the type with a trailer hitch and wheels). However, an old fashioned pit in the ground cannot be matched as the focal point of a party. A pit in the ground is more trouble, but guests enjoy sitting around the pit, talking, and watching the meat cook. Include the guests as part of the cooking process, don't invite them just to eat. Outlined below is a procedure for preparing a traditional barbecue pit suitable to cook quantities of meat adequate to feed 50 people or more.

Excluding restaurants and backyard charcoal cooks, experienced barbecue cooks use wood embers exclusively. The woods of choice are oak, mesquite, or hickory (pecan is also used in the South, but is technically a variety of hickory). The mesquite cooks are from Texas where barbecue means beef brisket. The briskets are usually seasoned only with salt, black pepper, and wood smoke. The hickory cooks are from the southern states, where barbecue means spareribs or pork shoulder. Pork barbecue is commonly seasoned with dry rub or basted with a thin sauce containing vinegar. The oak cooks are from the South or east Texas. Many cooks use 70 to 80% oak mixed with hickory. In addition to beef and pork, which are now commonly cooked throughout the south and west, goat and chicken are also relatively common choices for barbecue.

No matter what kind of meat is used or how it is seasoned, barbecue is cooked very slowly with moderate to heavy wood smoke. The objective is to cook the meat, render the fat, and let it acquire a smoky flavor without allowing it to dry out. Good barbecue is well done, but juicy.

Preparing the Pit

Mark off a four by six foot rectangle and dig a pit to a depth of two feet. If you plan to refill the pit, first cut the sod to a depth of 3 to 4 inches and stack it in a shaded spot. Keep the sod moist, but do not soak it with water or the soil will be washed off of the roots. Take care to try and keep the sides of the pit as close to vertical as possible. Place some of the dirt around the edges of the pit to form a raised edge (3-4 inches after it is compacted). This will prevent water runoff from getting into the pit in the event of rain, prior to or during cooking. Pile the remainder of the dirt six to eight feet away from the pit. This reserves the dirt for refilling the pit and gets it out of the way of guests.

The Cooking Grate

For the cooking grate, place two six foot pieces of 2 inch schedule 40 (or heavier) seamless steel pipe across the four foot dimension of the pit. Place each pipe two feet from the end of the pit, so they divide the pit into thirds. Drive wooden stakes into the ground on each side of the pipes three to six inches from each of their ends. This will keep the pipes securely in place. Lay a 4' x 4' piece of 1" x 3" expanded iron* grating on top of the two pipes to form the cooking grate. Cut six pieces of 16 gauge solid iron wire (do not use galvanized wire) into 12 to 15 inch lengths and bend them into the shape of a "U." Push the wire down through the grate from above so they straddle the pipe and their ends protrude below it. Twist the ends of the wire together tightly with pliers to fasten the grate to the pipe. Put three wires on each pipe. The grate is now fastened securely and ready for cooking. It is also sturdy enough to safely hold several hundred pounds of weight.

*NOTE: Expanded metal, catwalk, and grating are formed by cutting slits in a sheet of steel and streching it to form a grating with diamond shaped openings. There are no standard sizes or terminology, but expanded metal can generally be procured by specifying the length and width pf the diamond shape openings. The thickness and strength of the sheet generally increase with the opening size. The 1" x 3" recommended above will normally be made from a 1/4" thick iron sheet. Because of the lack of standardization, one may not be able to get exactly the desired size. Talk to the salesman of a metal supply company and describe what you want it for. They can generally recommend exactly what you need.

Precautions for Rain

If a barbecue is being planned for a large party, the weather is always a consideration. One has to decide whether to watch the weather with the intent of postponing in the event of rain, or to go ahead "rain or shine." In either case it is advisable to plan the occasion during the driest season of the year, and it is advisable to build a shed roof over the barbecue pit. Four posts (8' x 2" x 4") set one foot into the ground on a square (8' sides) around the pit are adequate

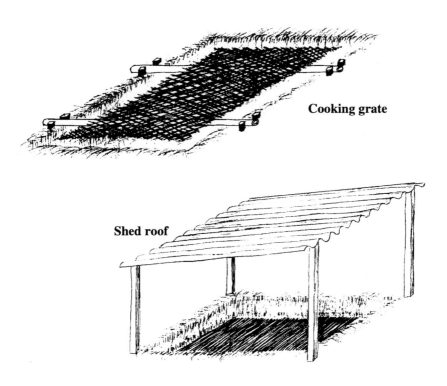

Cooking grate

Shed roof

to support a roof of corrugated fiberglass. This will protect the fire and meat from rain. Setting posts on eight foot spacing will allow nailing sheets of 1/4" plywood on one or more sides in the event of high wind or blowing rain. A 12' x 12' picnic tarpaulin pitched nearby will provide protection for the cooks. Your only remaining problem is where to serve and feed the guests.

Building the Fire

Place a layer of crumpled newspaper on the floor of the pit. Place a loosely spaced layer of dry kindling, or small branches, on top of the paper. Place a second layer of dry kindling on top of and perpendicular to the first. Lay a layer of dry fire wood on top of the kindling, with the logs end to end in parallel rows separated by approximately four inches. Place a second layer of dry firewood on top of and perpendicular to the first. It is advisable to use seasoned wood to produce a bed of coals. Ignite the newspaper at several places around the edges and stand back. Always keep an already connected garden hose handy, as well as a long handled shovel.

This initial fire is too hot for cooking. Its purpose is to heat and dry the ground, and to produce a bed of coals. Once the fire has burned down to coals, it is ready for cooking. Green wood can be used for cooking, it produces more smoke and will ignite once a bed of coals has been established. The distance between the food and the fire is fixed so the heat of the fire must be regulated to prevent burning the meat. If the fire is too hot, spread the coals out with a long handled shovel to reduce the heat. As the coals begin to die down, add logs to continue the fire. Remember, that to ignite fresh wood requires some concentration of coals and the new wood takes time to ignite and start producing heat. The heat of a fire can be regulated by moving the burning logs closer together and farther apart. The objective is to keep the logs burning slowly and producing smoke. Continue checking the meat. If it shows signs of cooking too fast, turn it to prevent burning and spread the logs out to reduce the heat. If the fire appears too cool, move the logs closer together to make them burn faster increasing the heat. Small logs (18" to 24" long) can be easily lifted or rolled with a long handle shovel.

Cooking

Meat can be barbecued directly on the 4' x 4' grate, but if whole animals are to be cooked additional preparation is recommended. Whole animals are difficult to turn. Obtain two 2' x 4' grates of expanded iron grating, similar to the cooking grate, but of smaller opening size (approximately 1" x 3" from 3/16" plate). Since expanded metal comes in 4' x 8' sheets, it will be cheaper and equally satisfactory to have the two smaller grates cut from the same piece as the cooking grate. To prepare a whole animal for cooking, have the butcher butterfly it by splitting it down the backbone from the inside. This allows the animal to be spread out flat. Lay the animal on one of the 2' x 4' grates and lay the other grate on top of the animal. Using the same kind of wire used to hold the cooking grate to its pipe supports, wire the two grates together. Cut lengths of wire (depending upon the size of the animal) that when folded in half can be inserted through the two metal grates and twisted together. Put three wires on the edges of each of the four sides of the grate and twist them enough to hold. After all of the wires are in place, take pliers and twist each of them until the two grates are held tightly together with the butterflied animal between them. The animal can now be lifted and turned as often as desired without fear of it falling apart. To turn, station a cook on each end of the animal (with leather work gloves or padded barbecue mittens) to lift and turn it. For carving, simply cut the wires loose with diagonal cutters (or pliers), remove the upper grate, and start carving. This same technique can also be used for holding several large cuts of meat.

After the barbecue is over the grates should be cleaned and prepared for reuse. Build a fire under them as described in the section Building the Fire. This will burn grease and sauce from them. Let the fire die out and the grates cool. Cut the retaining wires from the cooking grate, brush them with a stiff brush, and spray the grates with non-stick cooking spray, or rub them with vegetable oil. Cover and store them in a dry location. After having been heated the grates will rust easily if not protected.

Barbecue Seasonings

Dry-rubs and thin basting sauces are recommended, because they do not burn easily. Depending upon what is barbecued, the basting sauces or dry-rub recipes from the previous sections can be used. Dry rubs are most easily applied with a large salt shaker. Thin sauces can be applied by sprinkling the meat (milk jug with a perforated lid). Both Thin and Thick Sauces can be mixed in a bucket and applied with a 100% cotton string mop. Small mops are available that are specifically designed for basting. When using Thick Sauces, it is advisable to thin them either with water, a mixture of one half water and one half vinegar, or a mixture of one half water and one half dry white wine or beer. Remember that most Thick Sauces are easily burned, apply them only after the meat is cooked and the fire has died down. Table 10 lists recommended seasonings from the recipe sections that can all be used on large quantities of beef, pork, goat, or poultry.

TABLE 10. Barbecue Seasonings
Listed are recommended seasonings for a traditional pit barbecue. These are all versatile and can be used with a variety of meats (beef, pork, lamb, goat, and poultry).

Seasoning Type	Recipe	Cookbook Section
Dry Rubs	Foots' Seasoning Salt	Roasted Beef
	Mild Dry Rub	Barbecued Pork
	Pepper Dry Rub	Barbecued Pork
	Seasoned Dry Rub	Barbecued Pork
	Sweet Dry Rub	Barbecued Pork
	Cabrito Asado	Assorted Lamb & Goat
	Cabrito Asado II	Assorted Lamb & Goat
Thin Sauces	Oil and Vinegar Baste	Barbecued Chicken
	Brady's Basting Sauce	Barbecued Chicken
	Ken's Barbecue Sauce	Barbecued Chicken
	Beer Ribs	Barbecued Pork
	All Purpose Baste	Barbecued Pork
Thick Sauces	Uncle Harry's Barbecue Sauce	Barbecued Beef
	Catsup Barbecue Sauce	Barbecued Chicken
	Ribs with Brown Sauce	Barbecued Pork
	Molasses Sauce	Barbecued Pork

Vinegar and Oil BBQ

Makes 3-1/2 quarts

1 quart water
1 quart distilled vinegar
1 quart vegetable oil
1/2 cup Tabasco
1/2 cup Worcestershire sauce
1/3 cup salt

Blend ingredients until salt is dissolved.

Carolina Style BBQ

Makes 3 quarts

2 cups vegetable oil **8 onions, sliced**	Saute until tender.
6 cans (12 oz) beer **6 lemons, sliced**	Add, bring almost to a boil, reduce heat and simmer for 30 minutes. Let cool and strain.
1-1/2 cups vinegar **1 cup brown sugar** **3 TBS celery seeds** **2 TBS salt** **1 TBS black pepper** **2 tsp cayenne**	Add, blend thoroughly, and simmer for 30 minutes.

COCHON DE LAIT

Cochon de lait literally translated means suckling-pig, but in south (Cajun) Lousiana it means a 90 to 130 pound hog barbecued whole. Usually, they are butterflied and roasted over pecan wood embers. Seasoning often consists of inserting garlic cloves into slits in the meaty portions and applying a dry rub containing salt, black pepper, and cayenne.

Recipe Index

Appetizers

Beef